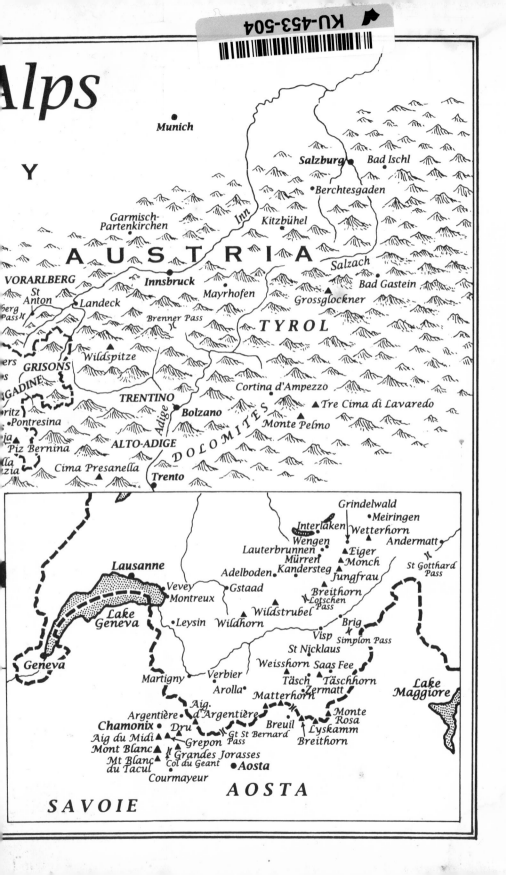

Alps

Munich

Salzburg · Bad Ischl
· Berchtesgaden

Garmisch-
Partenkirchen   Kitzbühel

Y

Inn

A U S T R I A

Salzach

VORARLBERG   Innsbruck   Mayrhofen   Bad Gastein
St
Anton   Landeck   ▲ Grossglockner
berg
Pass   Brenner Pass   T Y R O L

GRISONS   Wildspitze

NGADINE

ritz
·Pontresina   Cortina d'Ampezzo
ia   ▲ Tre Cima di Lavaredo
·Piz Bernina   TRENTINO   · Bolzano
lla   Monte Pelmo ▲
zia   ALTO-ADIGE
Cima Presanella ▲   D O L O M I T E S
· Trento

Adige

Grindelwald
· Meiringen
Interlaken   Wetterhorn
Wengen   ▲ Andermatt
Lauterbrunnen   ▲ Eiger
Lausanne   Mürren ▲ Monch
Kandersteg ▲ Jungfrau   St Gotthard
Adelboden   Pass
Vevey   · Gstaad
Montreux   Breithorn
▲ Lötschen
Lake   · Leysin   Wildhorn   ▲ Wildstrubel   Pass
Geneva   Brig
Visp   Simplon Pass
Geneva   St Nicklaus
Martigny   Verbier   Weisshorn ▲ Saas Fee   Lake
Arolla ·   Täsch ▲ Täschhorn   Maggiore
Aig.   Matterhorn ▲ Zermatt
Argentière · d'Argentière   ▲ Monte
Chamonix · Dru   Breuil   Rosa
Aig du Midi ▲ ▲   Grepon   Gt St Bernard   Lyskamm
Mont Blanc ▲   Pass   Breithorn
Mt Blanc ▲   Grandes Jorasses
du Tacul   Col du Geant   · Aosta
Courmayeur

A O S T A

S A V O I E

How the
English Made
the Alps

How the English Made the Alps

JIM RING

JOHN MURRAY
Albemarle Street, London

First published in 2000
by John Murray (Publishers) Ltd,
50 Albemarle Street, London W1X 4BD

A catalogue record for this book is available from the British Library

ISBN 0–7195–5689 9

Typeset in Garamond MT 12/14 pt
by Servis Filmsetting Limited, Manchester

Printed and bound in Great Britain by
The University Press, Cambridge

For Jessica

Contents

Illustrations   ix
Preface   xi
Map   xiv

'*Anything* but Matterhorn'   1

VENI, VIDI, VICI

Prologue: 'This most mis-shapen scenery'   7
1. Into the Unknown   26
2. The Pleasure Principle   46
3. 'The English did it!'   62

THE ELIXIR OF LIFE

4. The Magician's Wand   83
5. Wider Still and Wider   100
6. Winter Holiday   121

BELLE ÉPOQUE

7. White Leprosy   145
8. The Tables Turn   163
9. Edwardian Summer   183

Contents

DOWNHILL

10.   Après le Déluge   205
11.   The Blizzard   223
12.   The Last Alpine Problem   241

Epilogue: The Rocks Remain   263

Bibliography   269
Index   273

Illustrations

(between pages 144 and 145)

1. Edward Whymper, conqueror of the Matterhorn
2. Tragedy on the Matterhorn, engraving by Gustave Doré
3. Mountaineering, Victorian style
4. 'The Club-Room of Zermatt, in 1864'
5. 'The Chamouni polka'
6. 'Cutting off a fearful corner', cartoon by Sydney Hall
7. Thomas Cook, pioneer of the package tour
8. Grindelwald, before the advent of the railway
9. Leslie Stephen, author, among other things, of one of the wittiest books on mountaineering
10. The Mer de Glace, Chamonix
11. W.A.B. Coolidge, 'the young American who climbs with his aunt and his dog'
12. A.F. Mummery, the first great climber to emerge after the major alpine peaks had been conquered
13. An Edwardian mountaineering party, among them G.W. Young and George Mallory
14. Four generations of the Lunn family
15. The Arnold Lunn medal, awarded by the Kandahar Ski Club
16. Zermatt, once 'a crowded assemblage of dark, dirty-looking wooden houses'
17. The Oberland village of Mürren

18. A lady competitor on the Cresta Run, 1908
19. Horse-play in St Moritz, 1938
20. Leni Riefenstahl and camera crew on the summit of Mont Blanc, 1929
21. The Cambridge University ski team, 1938
22. Hitler at the Winter Olympics, 1936
23. The Alps at War, 1945
24. George Mallory and E.F. Norton on Everest, 1922

The author and publishers would like to thank the following for permission to reproduce photographs: Plates 1, 4, 5, 8, 9, 11, 12, 13, 14 and 24, Alpine Club Collection; 2, 3, 6, 7, 10, 18, 19, 20, 21, 22 and 23, Hulton Getty; 15, 16 and 17, Ski Club of Great Britain.

Preface

If this book's subject is self-explanatory, the title perhaps is not. I have chosen to use the term English rather than British, though I am conscious, as Michael Flanders once remarked, that you have to be careful in these matters. 'If we've done something good, it's another triumph for Great Britain. If not, it's "England lose again."'

Of course the Welsh, Irish and Scots were very much part of these islands' invasion of the Alps. During the period on which this book focuses, however, it was the custom – in the words of a Scot – 'to let the part – the larger part – speak for the whole'. Those countries which received them – France, Italy, Austria, Germany, and above all Switzerland – all talked of the English, and the presence of the English in the Alps was precisely so described. To use the term British would thus have been an anachronism. Moreover, again as a Scot put it, the alternative 'lacks both bouquet and aftertaste. One can love or hate England but not so easily Britain. It was England and not Britain that the Germans prayed God to strafe.'

Its title aside, the book's publication owes a great debt to its editor, Gail Pirkis, whose enthusiasm has guided it from conception to birth. It is, too, the consequence of the indulgence of my wife, who not only typed it but also put up with the writer's, and the book's, incessant demands. At a time when my leisure might reasonably have been spent with a growing family, she countenanced the visits to the Alps that the subject required, and even enjoyed the Hotel Monte Rosa at Zermatt and the Kulm at St Moritz.

The Alpine Club and the Ski Club of Great Britain provide the chief archives for alpine studies in England. Both institutions have been generous in their hospitality. I would particularly like to thank Margaret Ecclestone, the Alpine Club's librarian, for her unfailing patience and guidance. In the Alps themselves, the local archivists have been invariably helpful. I am greatly indebted to Timothy Nelson at Davos and Corina Huber at St Moritz.

A number of people took the trouble to read and comment on the book at various stages in its development. These were my mother Stella Ring, my stepmother Sheila Ring, my father Peter Ring, my brother Christopher Ring and my mother-in-law Jane Faire. Ian Jackson and Clive Jenkins looked at the book from the perspectives of skier and historian respectively. Of professional readers, Howard Davies has winkled out numerous inconsistencies and solecisms, the alpinist Lindsay Griffin similarly. Other faults are my own.

My thanks finally go to Alan Page, partly for his company's work on the cover, but principally for moral support.

In the steamy, stuffy Midlands, 'neath an English summer sky,
When the holidays are nearing with the closing of July,
And experienced Alpine stagers and impetuous recruits
Are renewing with the season their continual disputes –
Those inveterate disputes
On the newest Alpine routes –
And inspecting the condition of their mountaineering boots:

You may stifle your reflections, you may banish them afar,
You may try to draw a solace from the thought of 'Nächstes Jahr' –
But your heart is with those climbers, and you'll feverishly yearn
To be crossing of the Channel with your luggage labelled 'Bern',
Leaving England far astern
With a ticket through to Bern,
And regarding your profession with a lordly unconcern! . . .

A.D. Godley, 'Switzerland', *Climbers' Club Journal*, 1899

The

GERMA

FRANCE

Rhine

Lake
Constanc

Basel

Zürich

SWITZERLAND

Aare

Lucerne

Rhine

Neuchâtel

Bern

Mt Pilatus

Brunnen

Chur

Aro

Mt Rigi

Lake
Neuchâtel

Lausanne

BERNESE ALPS

Lake
Geneva

Geneva

Lake
Maggiore

Lake
Como

Chamonix

Mt Blanc

Aosta

AOSTA

Milan

Rhône

Isère

SAVOIE

Ticino

DAUPHINÉ

Grenoble

Meije

Turin

Pte des Ecrins

Mt Aiguille

Pelvoux

ITALY

Monte Viso

kms 0   200
mls 0   125

Genoa

MC

'Anything but Matterhorn'

It was only on descending from the summit – until an hour before, one of the last of the major alpine peaks to be conquered – that the tragedy struck.

Towering over the village of Zermatt at the head of the St Nicholas valley in Canton Valais, the 14,780-foot Matterhorn not only looked unscalable, but was also reputed to be inhabited by demons who would resist all human approaches. As the leader of the expedition, Edward Whymper, wrote later, 'There seemed to be a *cordon* drawn around it, up to which one might go, but no farther.' Such was its reputation that, even in the golden age of mountaineering in the late 1850s, few had been tempted to make an assault. In 1860, on his first visit to the Alps, Whymper recorded that the mountain was virtually untouched. In the following seasons he himself made a number of attempts on it, despite the discouragement of his guides, who would mutter in their pidgin English: '*Anything* but Matterhorn, dear sir! *Anything* but Matterhorn.'

His attempts, however, greatly interested a local guide from the southern, Piedmontese side of the massif. This was Jean-Antoine Carrel, whose life's aim became – according to Whymper – 'the ascent from the side of Italy for the honour of his valley'. When Whymper returned to the mountain in the summer of 1865 and asked Carrel to join him, the guide regretfully told him he was previously engaged. He concealed the fact that he was just about to take his own expedition on to the peak. Whymper, equally eager to claim

1

the ascent for himself and for England, was left entirely without party or guide. He was, as he put it, 'a general without an army'.

In his haste to beat Carrel's expedition in its attempt on the mountain's southern face, Whymper put together an ad hoc party. It comprised himself, two local guides called Taugwalder – father and son – the Chamonix guide Michel Croz, and two talented and experienced climbers, Lord Francis Douglas and the Reverend Charles Hudson. There was also a young novice, Roger Hadow. On Thursday 13 July, two days behind Carrel, the party set out from Zermatt at 5.30 a.m. on a brilliant day. By mid-morning they were on the eastern face of the mountain itself, and by noon had found – at 11,000 feet – a sensible place to bivouac. Following a successful reconnoitre, the attempt on the summit was set for the following day. So far the route had been easier than expected, and the party was in good heart, although Whymper was naturally tormented by anxiety at Carrel's possible progress.

They began at dawn next morning and climbed without much difficulty, seldom roping themselves together. By mid-morning they had reached, at about 14,000 feet, the foot of the escarpment which, seen from the valley below, looked almost perpendicular. Here they turned on to the northern face. As the slope soon steepened to some forty degrees, with relatively little to hold or grasp, it became sensible for the experienced – Croz, Whymper and Hudson – to take the lead. Here Hadow began to struggle, needing continual assistance from the elder Taugwalder. Alarms, too, were constantly raised that there were already men – Italian men – on the summit. Soon, though, the slope eased, and only an awkward corner blocked the summit itself. Croz and Whymper, desperate lest they be beaten at the last, unroped themselves and dashed for the summit. 'At 1.40 p.m.,' wrote Whymper, 'the world was at our feet and the Matterhorn was conquered! Hurrah! Not a footstep could be seen.' Moments later they spotted Carrel's vanquished party, 'mere dots on the ridge, an immense distance below'.

The weather still held: there was little wind, and it was so clear that they could see all the great alpine peaks around them, from the Dent Blanche to the Monte Rosa, and a hundred miles to the south-west the Viso, the Pelvoux and, in the west, 'gorgeous in the full sunlight rose the monarch of all – Mont Blanc'. Eight thousand feet below them were 'forests black and gloomy, and meadows bright and lively; bounding water-falls and tranquil lakes; fertile lands and savage wastes; sunny plains and frigid plateaux. There were the most rugged forms and the most graceful outlines – both perpendicular cliffs and gentle, undulating slopes; rocky mountains and snowy mountains, sombre and solemn or glittering and white, with walls, turrets, pinnacles, pyramids, domes, cones and spires! There was every combination that the world can give, and every contrast that the heart could desire.'

The party lingered on the summit for just under an hour before beginning the descent. Croz, the most sure-footed, went first. He was followed by Hadow, the least. Then came the Reverend Hudson, Lord Francis and the elder of the Taugwalders, the latter linked by a rather old rope. Whymper himself and the younger of the Taugwalders brought up the rear, at first roped together separately as a pair. Then, at about 3 p.m., Lord Francis asked Whymper to attach himself to the elder of the Taugwalders, as he doubted the latter's ability to hold his ground should a slip occur. In this way the whole party was roped together to tackle the most difficult part of the descent. They took care. Only one man was allowed to move at a time, and only when he had gained a firm footing was the next allowed to follow. Hadow, unfamiliar with the procedure and exhausted by the morning's climb, was again in trouble, his nailed boots sliding on the rocks, his eyes drawn irresistibly down the precipitous slope to the fields far below. Again and again, Croz had to turn, lay aside his alpenstock, and take hold of Hadow's feet, putting them, one by one, into the correct positions.

Whymper, his view at the rear of the party obscured by a rock, never knew exactly what happened in the instants that followed. He surmised that, having secured Hadow, Croz was turning round to go down a few steps when Hadow slipped, fell against the guide, and sent them both plunging down the slope. Hudson and Douglas were only just behind them and were at once dragged in their wake. Whymper and the elder Taugwalder, alerted by a cry from Croz, braced themselves to take the strain on the rope. Together they held fast. But the rope between Taugwalder and Lord Francis broke, leaving the latter and the three below him sliding downwards on their backs, then over the precipice and down to the Matterhorngletscher four thousand feet below.

When Whymper at last reached Zermatt thirty-six hours later, he was met by the innkeeper Seiler, who followed him in silence to his room. 'What is the matter?' asked Seiler. 'The Taugwalders and I have returned,' Whymper replied. Seiler, so Whymper wrote, 'did not need more'.

News of the tragedy swept across Europe and horrified the reading public. 'Is it life? Is it duty? Is it common sense? Is it allowable? Is it not wrong?' thundered *The Times.* And underlying those questions was the larger question of what drew these Englishmen to the Alps. What was it that possessed these men to throw themselves with such courage, not to say recklessness, at these mountain ranges far from home?

It is the curious story – sometimes tragic, sometimes comic, almost invariably dramatic – of the English in the Alps that this book sets out to tell.

Veni, Vidi, Vici

'The Col de la Faucille, on that day, opened to me in distinct vision the Holy Land of my future work and true home in this world.'

John Ruskin, *Praeterita* (1885–1900)

Prologue

'This most mis-shapen scenery'

'Before the turning-point of the eighteenth century, a civilized being might, if he pleased, regard the Alps with unmitigated horror.'
Leslie Stephen, *The Playground of Europe* (1871)

It was a measure of their power over the human mind that by the time of the Matterhorn tragedy men – English and otherwise – were fully prepared to risk their lives in search of a closer acquaintance with the Alps. Yet the attraction was a relatively recent one, and the English had done much to generate it.

The Alps came into existence a hundred million years ago as a result of the collision of two of the plates that form the earth's crust; in the process the two colliding land masses thrust hundreds of miles of rock thousands of feet towards the heavens. Through time, and the natural processes of erosion, these mountains were gradually worn down to little more than low hills. Then, about a quarter of a million years ago, further movement of the tectonic plates and profound glaciation produced something approaching the Alps as we see them today – a great crescent that runs for eight hundred miles from the southern coast of France through Italy, Switzerland and southern Germany to the borders of Austria, where a northern spur thrusts towards Vienna, a southern towards Zagreb. Dividing Europe's northern plains from the Mediterranean basin, they constitute a watershed from which flow four of Europe's largest rivers: the Rhône, feeding the Mediterranean itself; the Po, flowing east through

Italy into the Adriatic; the Rhine, running to the North Sea; and the Danube, making its way to the Black Sea. Along with the Rockies, the Andes and the Himalaya, the Alps are one of the world's great mountain ranges.

They are also something more. Visually, the Alps provide a far greater contrast than is usual in mountain ranges. The low snow-line caused by their northerly latitude, and the depth of the heavily glaciated valleys, permit the conjunction of green meadows and blinding snow. This contrast is reflected in a remarkable variety of flora and fauna, adapted to the varying altitude. The other great ranges typically present a more uniform and relatively barren impression of rock and snow, at their higher altitude unrelieved by brighter colours and hues; unrelieved, too, by such riches of plant and animal life. The geology of the Alps is also unusually complex, and provides an unprecedented mixture of mountain structure, from the gothic towers of the Chamonix Aiguilles to the soft fantastical forms of the Italian Dolomites. Then there are the glaciers, unusual in the Alps for their profusion. These serpentine masses of ice flowing slowly down the mountain valleys, riven by deep crevasses, lend a strange, primeval quality to the scene. At lower altitudes the glaciers give way to springs, streams, waterfalls, rivers and lakes – the lakes more numerous than elsewhere. Those of Geneva, Constance, Neuchâtel, Lucerne, Zürich, Maggiore, Como and Garda are the greatest. The more northerly are austere. By contrast *Murray's Handbook*, the first popular guidebook to the region, described those on the Italian side of the chain as a byword for delicate beauty: 'Their character is soft and smiling; blessed with a southern climate, their thickets are groves of orange, olive, myrtle and pomegranate; and their habitations villas and palaces.'

If elsewhere in the world mountains have remained remote wildernesses, the Alps everywhere exhibit the hand of man. The valleys have been tilled, the high pastures grazed from prehistoric times; fine medieval cities such as Grenoble, Geneva, Bern, Zürich, Innsbruck, Salzburg, Vienna, Turin and Milan have grown up in the mountains' shadow; the great highways over, the railways under the Alps remain – to Murray – 'the most surprising monuments of human skill and enterprise, which surmount what would appear, at first sight, to be intended by Nature to be insurmountable'. Conversely, the Alps too have shaped man. The cultural and political disposition of Europe has been dictated by their presence. Distinct northern and Mediterranean cultures – distinct in poetry, prose, architecture, music, painting – are the inevitable consequence of the divisions created by the chain; the establishment and extent of nations and empires have been largely determined by their form; the very neutrality of Switzerland, the political embodiment of the Alps, is a consequence of her location at what is at once the centre, but at least until the 1850s the largely inaccessible citadel of Europe.

The Alps are not simply the Alps. They are a unique visual, cultural, geological and natural phenomenon, indissolubly wed to European history.

Strange to say, however, as recently as the 1700s the Alps were generally abhorred. The monk John de Bremble, one of the earliest English alpine travellers, was so horrified by his experience on the Great St Bernard pass that he prayed, 'Lord restore me to my brethren, that I may tell them not to come to this place of torment.' The seventeenth-century diarist John Evelyn was distressed by 'horrid and fearful crags and tracts'. Bishop Berkeley on a journey across the Alps in 1714 complained that 'Every object that here presents itself is excessively miserable.' What was it that so disenchanted those whose descendants would rhapsodize over the Alps?

Traditionally, such terrain held little appeal. The awesome presence of mountains made them the natural inspiration of cult and myth. To some they held a special power by virtue of being the first land to emerge from the primeval waters. To others they were stairways to heaven, the clouds that surrounded them providing life-giving rain. Conversely, those that were volcanic might be seen as doors to an underworld of fire and brimstone. Inevitably they were thought to be the habitations of gods, demons, witches and trolls; places to be feared and avoided at all costs.

Though the lower valleys had long been inhabited, the Alps were no exception to this rule. It needed little imagination to attribute to supernatural causes their violently unpredictable weather systems, terrible avalanches and mysterious, creeping glaciers. As late as 1723 Johann Jacob Scheuchzer, a distinguished Zürich scholar and Fellow of the Royal Society, devoted a chapter of a learned book to the detailed description of alpine dragons, one of which he claimed to have seen. Even maps of a later date included indications of such creatures.

Dragons or not, from man's early days it had been necessary to force a passage through the Alps and to broach the barrier that divided Europe. Whether for the purposes of pilgrimage, trade or war, routes through the chain which combined modest height with relative ease of ascent and descent were gradually located, and rough footpaths or bridle-paths established. The Romans significantly improved these tracks to promote communications within their empire, thereby permitting the crossing of the chain by Hannibal, his army and his elephants in 218 BC. Thereafter, with the exception of the establishment of the high alpine hospices in the Middle Ages, little was done to improve the passes until the coming of Napoleon at the end of the eighteenth century, and the invention of dynamite soon after.

Any passage of the Alps in the eighteenth century was thus an ordeal to all but those few who were untouched alike by fears of the supernatural, cold or heights. According to Murray, astride his mule or packhorse, the traveller would endure tracks

steeper than any staircase, sometimes with ledges of rock two or three feet high, instead of steps. Sometimes they are covered with broken fragments, between which the beasts must pick their way, at the risk of breaking their legs; at others, they traverse a narrow ledge of the mountain, with an abyss on one side and a wall of rock on the other; and here the mule invariably walks on the very verge of the precipice – a habit derived from the animal's being accustomed to carry large packages of merchandise, which, if allowed to strike against the rock on one side, would destroy the mule's balance, and jostle him overboard.

Even in the summer, 'the air is often icy cold, and exercise and quick motion are necessary to keep up the circulation of the blood'. With snow falling on the passes in the second week of October, and frequently lasting until mid-June, it was often necessary for travellers to combat snow and ice as well as the heights. Of the Great St Bernard pass the *Handbook* declared: 'the hospice is rarely four months clear of deep snow. Around the building, it averages 7 or 8 feet and the drifts sometimes rest against it, and accumulate to the height of 40 feet. The severest cold recorded was 29° below zero; and has often been observed at 18° or 20° below.'

There was more, though, to compound the traveller's physical and mental discomfort. In an age that was beginning to demand its creature comforts, those obliged to cross the Alps found little to their taste. As late as 1814, an Englishwoman at Simplon recorded that

> After vain attempts to demolish the remains of some venerable cow, we feasted on a dish of fritters, so delicate and tempting in appearance that they would have graced the table of an Alderman. We of course congratulated ourselves upon having found such young and tender chickens upon the top of Mount Simplon, when suddenly my Father exclaimed, 'Clara, you have been eating frogs!'

Of the inns, that on the Col di Tendi between Turin and the frontier fortress of Ventimiglia was typical – 'a crazy hovel, containing scarcely one whole window, and no sitting-room, except that which serves in common for the postilions, gentlemen, poultry and hogs'.

As to the alpine peoples to be encountered on such journeys, opinions varied. At best they were robust peasants whose isolated life was felt to breed an admirable degree of independence. In Switzerland this was illustrated both by the tale of William Tell and – in William Wordsworth's words – the 'several battles in which the Swiss in very small numbers have gained over their oppressor, the House of Austria'. Similarly, the peasants of the Dauphiné, Piedmont and the Tyrol were renowned for their independence. The poverty common among these peoples, however, was remarked upon by all. It was inevitable in a pastoral region of thin soil and steep slopes, where life was typically sustained by the herding of beasts to the high summer pastures when the snow retreated, and their return to the valleys in the autumn. Equally distressing was the incidence of disease. As *Murray's Handbook* recorded in 1843,

> It is a remarkable fact that, amidst some of the most magnificent scenery of the globe, where Nature seems to have put forth all her powers in exciting emotions of wonder and elevation in the mind, man appears, from a mysterious visitation of disease, in his most degraded and pitiable condition. Such, however, is the fact. It is in the grandest and most beautiful valleys of the Alps that the maladies of goitre and cretinism prevail.

Goitre, the swelling of the thyroid gland in the neck, was commonplace, though little more than unsightly. Cretinism was far more serious in that it affected the mind, rendering the sufferer incapable of rational thought or action, and thus 'a creature who may almost be said to rank a step below a human being'. Both were the consequence of an iodine deficiency.

Other aspects of the region were hardly more congenial. Its topography formed such convenient borders that it was for long divided up into a bewildering variety of principalities, dukedoms and independencies. This posed a considerable handicap to the convenience, and not infrequently the safety, of the traveller. At the gates of Geneva, Bern, Innsbruck and Turin passports were demanded; there were four major languages – French, German, Italian and Romansch – to master, several minor ones, and countless local dialects. In Switzerland alone 'almost every canton has a coinage of its own, and those coins that are current in one canton will not pass to the next'. Similarly, each had its own customs and excise. Travel between the countries was uncoordinated, so that passengers might have to wait for hours for the arrival of the next coach to their destination, 'sometimes being set down in a remote spot to pass the interval as they may, and this not infrequently in the middle of the night'. With Protestant and Catholic living cheek by jowl through much of the area, religious squabbles were endemic. And though some of the Swiss cantons were amongst the earliest republican democracies, more often government was in the hands of aristocratic oligarchies as illiberal and repressive as any in Europe.

The final objection of the eighteenth-century observer to the Alps was in a sense the oddest. They were ugly. This perspective was bound up with the feelings of the age towards nature as a whole. The classical tradition embodied in the Renaissance might have made something of the beauty of the human form, but it thought little of natural beauty, either of land or seascape. As Kenneth Clark put it: 'The average layman would not have thought it wrong to enjoy nature; he would simply have said that nature is not enjoyable. The fields meant nothing but work, the sea meant storms and piracy.' As to the mountains, they were structures that – like others – were to be judged by classical notions of beauty. These called for qualities such as purity, order and proportion – standards against which the Alps were unlikely to measure up well. On the contrary, to the eighteenth-century eye the very appearance of the Alps was unsympathetic – disordered, chaotic and uncouth. Bishop Berkeley thought every object miserable, the Bishop of Geneva, François de Sales, talked of those 'cursed mountains', the essayist Joseph Addison of 'this most mis-shapen scenery'.

A region essentially supernatural, a hazardous and uncomfortable journey, inhabitants stricken with poverty and disease, all the institutions and arrangements of civilized life missing or awry, deplorable scenery – it was scarcely surprising that, far from being an attraction, the Alps were seen as an ordeal; scarcely odd that visitors were few; scarcely peculiar that Leslie Stephen, the pioneering mountaineer, biographer, and father of the novelist Virginia Woolf and painter Vanessa Bell, could write: 'Before the turning-point of the eighteenth century, a civilized being might, if he pleased, regard the Alps with unmitigated horror.'

Yet within a generation that view began to change, partly because of increasing intimacy with the mountains, partly as a consequence of the Enlightenment.

The work of the great thinkers of the seventeenth and eighteenth centuries created an intellectual climate that swept away some
of the credulity surrounding man's relationship with both the
natural and the supernatural world, and introduced revolutionary
ideas about God, reason and nature that encouraged men to regard
the world around them with fresh and critical eyes. In this turmoil
of thought on the state, the monarchy, social inequalities, religion
itself, there emerged two ideas particularly germane to the Alps. In
contrast to the spurious sophistication and artificiality of urban
society, the notion of the 'noble savage' began to celebrate the
virtues of the simple life in close association with nature. At the
same time came a revival of the biblical notion of nature as a
manifestation of God's work. Though initially of limited circulation, by the second quarter of the eighteenth century these ideas
had begun to take hold in popular form in the poetry of those such
as the Swiss natural scientist Albrecht von Haller and the
Englishman Thomas Gray.

Haller was a distinguished anatomist and physician. A native of
Bern, he had the most impressive of the alpine chains, the Bernese
Oberland, on his doorstep. He took the then unusual step of going
to see the mountains for himself, mainly for the purposes of investigating their geology and botany. From a series of expeditions came
a cycle of poems, published in 1729 as *Die Alpen*. These were a
celebration less of natural beauty than of the purity of the peasant
life:

> Blessed is he who with self-raised oxen can plough the soil of
> his own fields; who is clothed in pure wool, adorned with
> wreaths of leaves, and enjoys unseasoned meal made of sweet
> milk; who can sleep carefree on soft grass, refreshed by Zephyr's
> breeze and cool waterfalls; who has never been awoken on high
> seas by rough waves, nor by the sound of trumpets at troubled
> times; who is satisfied with his lot and never wants to improve
> it! Luck is much too poor to improve his well-being.

Today such sentiments may seem idealistic, the underlying attitude
over-simple. Yet they struck a chord with the public: eleven editions

of the book were printed in Haller's own lifetime, and the work was translated into all the major European languages.

Gray, born in 1716, had rather further to travel to find the source of his own inspiration. The poet was one of the increasing numbers of Englishmen who encountered the Alps as part of a 'grand tour'. Undertaken as the culmination of a wealthy Englishman's education, these journeys became popular in early Georgian times for the purpose of providing an introduction to foreign languages and an appreciation of Continental – principally classical – art and culture. Typically the 'grand tourists' took their own carriage and retinue, pursuing a westerly route through France and across the Alps to Italy before returning via Germany and the Low Countries. In 1739 Gray, not himself prosperous, set out on just such a tour with Horace Walpole, the climax of which proved to be a visit to the valley of the Grande Chartreuse. Here, just north of Grenoble in the Dauphiné, the Carthusian St Bruno had in the eleventh century established a remote monastery. Gray thought the scene breathtaking:

> It was six miles to the top; the road runs winding up it, commonly not six feet broad; on one hand is the rock, with woods of pine trees hanging overhead; on the other, a monstrous precipice, almost perpendicular, at the bottom of which rolls a torrent, that sometimes funnelling among the fragments of stone that have fallen from on high, and sometimes precipitating itself down vast descents with a noise like thunder, which is made still greater by the echo from the mountains on either side, concurs to form one of the most solemn, the most romantic, and the most astonishing scenes I ever beheld.

For Gray there was nothing mis-shapen, nothing hideous, nothing horrific about the Alps. There was rather majesty, grandeur and a profound spiritual excitement. The mountain scenery represented God's work in its most dramatic and poignant form: 'Not a precipice, not a torrent, not a cliff, but is pregnant with religion and piety.'

Writers like Gray and Von Haller opened the chapter of a book that was – at least for the English – to be firmly closed by the Seven Years' War. Yet when the war concluded in 1763, the English returned to the Continent in such unprecedented numbers that a contemporary wrote, 'Where one Englishman travelled in the reign of the first two Georges, ten now go on a grand tour. Indeed at such a pitch is the spirit of travelling that there is scarce a citizen of large fortune but takes a flying view of France, Italy and Germany.'

Gray may have pointed the way for such people but the main stimulus came from two much more significant developments, the agricultural and the industrial revolutions. The former, through the enclosure system and the rotation of crops, greatly increased the country's food production and in turn its population; the latter led to greatly improved means of transport that enabled people to travel for the first time with comparative ease. These developments also created a new class who, in the tradition of the nouveaux riches, were keen to display their wealth. In the last quarter of the eighteenth century Continental travel became one of the most fashionable ways of doing so, and gave rise to the belief that the English were the first tourists. In Europe as a whole, the English had a virtual monopoly on tourism, and it was said that their requirements largely set the style for the most hospitable coaching inns. Of Switzerland herself, Johann Wäber, a Swiss artist who accompanied James Cook on his last voyage, recorded that, in a typical inn, fourteen out of every twenty guests would be English.

Given the means, a further incentive to travel was provided by Jean-Jacques Rousseau and the naturalist Horace de Saussure. Rousseau is familiar to us as a social critic at the centre of the Enlightenment. His masterpiece, *Du Contrat Social*, would become the bible of the French Revolution, his slogan 'Liberté, Égalité, Fraternité' its rallying cry. It was his novel, however, *La Nouvelle*

Héloïse, published in 1760, that was chiefly responsible for focusing changing perspectives on the Alps. Rousseau's thesis was that evil stems less from something intrinsic in man than from human structures and society. As he remarked elsewhere, 'Men are not made to be crowded together in ant-hills . . . the more they congregate the more they corrupt one another.' In the novel this idea is conveyed in the form of a love affair. His simple peasant heroine Julie, in her alpine surroundings on the shores of Lake Geneva, is the embodiment of natural beauty and goodness. His hero Saint-Preux, separated from Julie, finds consolation in the beauty of the mountains. The tale struck a powerful chord among Rousseau's readers, not least the English. Indeed, his enduring impact was such that Leslie Stephen would declare, 'If Rousseau were tried for the crime of setting up mountains as objects of human worship, he would be convicted by an impartial jury.'

Despite the novel, Rousseau's knowledge of the mountains and its peoples was limited. Perhaps like his successor as a prophet of mountain beauty, John Ruskin, he thought the Alps were 'better seen from below'. Some of Rousseau's more adventurous contemporaries, though, were beginning to think that there might really be positive virtues in climbing. Hitherto the mythology of mountains had discouraged such adventures, despite several famous ascents in the Middle Ages. In practical terms a society in which the vast majority lived at little more than subsistence level had little appetite for such esoteric pursuits. Moreover, it was understood that the atmosphere thinned with altitude, and it was thought hard if not impossible for men to survive on high mountain peaks. The new thinking, however, in stimulating the quest for scientific knowledge, had done much to diminish the force of this mythology. It also explains the career of a figure far less familiar than Rousseau, Horace-Bénédict de Saussure.

De Saussure was born in 1740 to a Huguenot family of wealth and distinction, exiled in Geneva. A prodigy, he was appointed Professor of Natural Philosophy at the Geneva Academy at the age of twenty-one, and he was to devote his life to the scientific study of the Alps. Very little was then known of their flora, fauna, geological structure, physical history, meteorology or glaciology. The young naturalist fell under the spell of what was thought to be the highest peak in the Old World, the 15,782-foot Mont Blanc – popularly known as 'the Monarch'. This massif, in what was then the Duchy of Savoy, was within relatively easy reach of Geneva. Some English contemporaries of Gray, William Windham, a rich young man completing his education in Geneva, and the oriental traveller Richard Pococke, established it as a subject of scientific interest. Together they had investigated the glacier – the Mer de Glace – at the mountain's foot above the little village of Chamonix on 19 June 1741. De Saussure followed the trail of this party in 1760. So enthusiastic was he at what he saw that he offered a substantial reward to the man who should first reach the summit.

The people of Chamonix were doubtful about the idea. Like most alpine peasants they climbed only so far as they needed for their various purposes of herding beasts, pursuing chamois, hunting mountain crystal, or smuggling. Moreover, their sporadic attempts on the mountain over the years that followed were discouraging, the adventurers suffering everything from altitude sickness to frostbite and snow blindness. Eventually, though, two men seized the chance. Jacques Balmat and Dr Michel-Gabriel Paccard were both local men who shared a fascination with the mountain. Their independent attempts having failed, in the summer of 1786 they agreed to try together. In the early part of the season the weather was poor, only lifting as August approached. Having provisioned themselves with food, brandy and a barometer, on 7 August the pair set out. They climbed at first with relative ease up to the rock buttress of Montagne de la Côte. Here they slept until dawn. They then passed with some difficulty over the icy chaos of the glacier split by the ridge of La Côte, and surmounted the Grands Mulets, the conical rocks at the head of the Glacier des Bossons. Then, after almost twelve exhausting hours of climbing, battling against winds which threatened to pluck them from the mountain face, they gained the Grand

Plateau, the highest of the three huge steps between the Grands Mulets and the Rochers Rouges. This put them within three thousand feet of the summit. Husbanding their strength, the two then trudged up the increasingly steep slope, each taking turns to cut steps in front of them with a sharpened alpenstock. By 5.00 p.m. they had surmounted a precipitous ledge of snow and were within reach of the summit. At last, at half-past six on 8 August 1786, the pair together reached the highest place in their world. 'The Monarch', in Balmat's words, 'lay at the proud foot of a conqueror.'

The following summer de Saussure himself and a party of eighteen repeated their success, equipped with what amounted to a mobile laboratory. He found the experience a revelation. 'What I really saw as never before, was the skeleton of all those great peaks whose connection and real structure I had so often wanted to comprehend. I hardly believed my eyes. It was as though I was dreaming when I saw below me the Midi, the Argentière, and the Géant, peaks whose very bases I had found it difficult and dangerous to reach.' The climbing of mountains as a legitimate scientific pursuit was established, and when de Saussure's account of his various expeditions was published in 1779 as *Voyages dans les Alpes*, a second pioneering alpine tract appeared to complement Rousseau's.

The Alps were no longer simply an overawing phenomenon. At least for 'citizens of large fortune' they were beginning to be objects of curiosity in their own right. Edward Gibbon, then living in Lausanne, was less enthusiastic. 'I shall add, as a misfortune rather than a merit, that the situation and beauty of the Pays de Vaud, the long habit of the English . . . and the fashion of viewing mountains and glaciers have opened us up on all sides to the incursions of foreigners.'

If the English by force of numbers had played a significant role in alpine development, they had done less by force of argument. This began to change in the summer of 1790 with a tour of the Alps made by a young poet inspired by his upbringing amongst the Cumbrian lakes and mountains.

William Wordsworth's first visit to the Alps comprised an ambitious journey of three thousand miles, two thousand of them on foot. Although the habit of walking for pleasure in the mountains was by this time established amongst the Swiss, they were the exception to the rule; pedestrian travel was the mode of the poor. 'We were early risers in 1790,' recalled Wordsworth's companion Robert Jones, 'and generally walked twelve or fifteen miles before breakfast, and after feasting on the morning landscape afterwards feasted on our *déjeuner* whatever the house might afford.' They followed the course of the Rhône, visited the 'wondrous vale of Chamouni', and eventually crossed the Simplon pass into Italy. The highlight of their tour proved to be the Grande Chartreuse that had so inspired Gray fifty years previously. Wordsworth's sister Dorothy wrote, 'I do not think that any one spot made so great an impression on his mind . . . in his young days he used to talk of it so much to me.'

The result of the trip, a long poem entitled 'Descriptive Sketches Taken During a Pedestrian Tour Among the Alps', indicated a changing mood towards nature in general and the Alps in particular. Whereas Bishop Berkeley had found the alpine scenery miserable, Wordsworth saw it as profoundly therapeutic. He remarked on the way in which a walking tour enabled the pedestrian to experience the country – 'lonely farms and secret villages' – and its people at first hand. Like Von Haller and Rousseau, he saw particular virtue in the peasants' primitive state. Above all he celebrated what he saw as the communion with nature to be experienced by the traveller, in words which were certain to inspire the more literate and leisured with a desire to visit the Alps.

> He holds with God himself communion high
> There where the peal of swelling torrents fills
> The sky-roofed temple of eternal hills;
> Or, when upon the mountain's silent brow
> Reclined, he sees, above him and below,
> Bright stars of ice and azure fields of snow.

Any enthusiasm for alpine travel that the publication of the 'Sketches' themselves might have generated was, however, dispelled by the outbreak of the French Revolution, and the subsequent declaration of war by France on Great Britain in 1793. When, in 1798, Napoleon seized the greater part of what is now modern Switzerland, creating the 'Helvetic Republic', the country became a symbol of freedom suppressed. In 'Thoughts of a Briton on the subjugation of Switzerland' Wordsworth associated the yearning for liberty of the alpine peoples with that of the English:

> Two Voices are there; one is of the sea,
> One of the mountains; each a mighty Voice:
> In both from age to age thou did'st rejoice,
> They were thy chosen music, Liberty!

At last, in 1815, Waterloo saw the defeat of Napoleon and the brokered peace of the Congress of Vienna. An agreement of particular significance for alpine development was the guarantee by the great powers, Great Britain, France, Prussia, Austria and Russia, of the future neutrality of Switzerland. With the Alps once again easily accessible the floodgates opened. Soon, Wordsworth himself joined the stream of travellers heading for the Continent. His prose journal of this tour, *Memorials of a Tour of the Continent*, published in 1822, was to confirm him as one of the leading European interpreters of the Alps. By the time of his death he could take much of the credit for transforming English attitudes to nature, and by extension to the Alps.

Like Wordsworth, two other Romantic writers took advantage of the end of the Napoleonic wars to explore the Alps, and by their example they would do more than anyone to popularize the mountains. They were George Gordon Byron and Percy Bysshe Shelley.

Both a development of, and a reaction to, the ideas of the Enlightenment, Romanticism shared the same enthusiasm for nature and a disposition to see the natural world as a manifestation of the divine. More importantly, however, the movement rejected its predecessors' taste for perfection, order and proportion, finding beauty in altogether more rugged natural forms. At the same time, drawing inspiration from the new-found centrality of the individual in creation, it stressed those qualities of imagination and self-expression that the age of 'reason' had tended to suppress. The result was a climate of aesthetic opinion that was likely to find the Alps not simply sympathetic, but the very best expression of its new ideas of beauty. It was one which would revel in the charismatic personalities of Shelley and Byron.

Shelley's reputation was in the ascendant when he accompanied his mistress, Mary Godwin, and her half sister Claire Clairmont, to Geneva in the summer of 1816. The trio settled there for the season. Byron, who had taken the Villa Diodati at Cologny on the southern side of the lake, resumed the affair he was conducting with Claire. The two poets, however, had not previously met. Taking to one another, they spent a week sailing around the shores of Lake Geneva and making a literary pilgrimage to the sites of *La Nouvelle Héloïse* which their writings would make famous. The following year saw the publication of Shelley's *The History of a Six Weeks' Tour*, which culminated in the poet's lyric, 'Mont Blanc'.

Although Shelley shared Wordsworth's love of the Alps, his feelings for the great mountains were very different. Enthusiastic as he was about nature, the sceptic in Shelley was less inclined to portray the alpine scene as a manifestation of the hand of God. Nor did he romanticize the alpine peasant. Yet his response to the Alps was as direct, immediate and vividly conveyed as that of any of his contemporaries, and expresses both the philosophy of Romanticism and the wonder of such scenes to an English eye familiar with a more subdued countryside. It is Shelley's letters rather than his poetry that best bring out this quality, particularly his first sight of the Alps:

From Servoz three leagues remain to Chamouni – Mont Blanc was before us – the Alps, with their innumerable glaciers on high all around, closing in the complicated windings of the single vale – forests inexpressibly beautiful, but majestic in their beauty – intermingled beech and pine, and oak, over-shadowed our road, or receded, whilst lawns of such verdure as I have never seen before, occupied these openings, and gradually became darker in their recesses. Mont Blanc was before us, but it was covered with cloud; its base, furrowed with dreadful gaps, was seen above. Pinnacles of snow intol-erably bright, part of the chain connected with Mont Blanc, shone through the clouds at intervals on high. I never knew – I never imagined – what mountains were before. The immen-sity of these aerial summits excited, when they suddenly burst upon sight, a sentiment of ecstatic wonder, not unallied to madness.

At the time of their meeting, the publication of the first two cantos of Byron's poetic travelogue *Childe Harold's Pilgrimage* had already earned him a European reputation. The alpine travels of that summer then led to the publication of the third canto of the poem. This epic, the verse drama *Manfred*, the poem *The Prisoner of Chillon* and his contemporary journals established Byron as the most famous poet of the Alps. His work was more strictly topograph-ical than Wordsworth's or Shelley's, dramatizing and giving meaning to places readers themselves might visit, often in vivid and sensuous terms. It provided a commentary on Rousseau as the alpine prophet, and on the setting of what was by then the widely read *Nouvelle Héloïse*. Above all – particularly in *Childe Harold* – Byron used the travelogue as a means of portraying a complex and contradictory character, sustained by the varying qualities of nature:

> Where rose the mountains, there to him were friends;
> Where roll'd the ocean, thereon was his home;
> Where a blue sky, and glowing clime, extends,
> He had the passion and the power to roam;
> The desert, forest, cavern, breaker's foam,
> Were unto him companionship; they spake

A mutual language, clearer than the tome
Of his land's tongue, which he would oft forsake
For Nature's pages glass'd by sunbeams on the lake.

Together with Wordsworth, the two younger Romantic poets completed the transformation of the Alps' reputation. In part, this was a
consequence of the quality of their writing, which painted the Alps
in newly glamorous colours and caused the scenes they depicted to
be associated forever with the poets in the minds of English travellers. And the poets' personalities were a prime source of this appeal.
The Romantic movement set a premium on self-expression, and it
was what Byron and Shelley said and did – together with the manner
and prematurity of their deaths – that set them apart from their fore-
runners, Gray and Wordsworth, and from their great Continental
counterparts Goethe, Schiller and Alexandre Dumas, who had all
celebrated the Alps in their writings. They were public figures in the
modern sense of the term, their foibles and liaisons discussed in the
same way as those of such personalities today. English visitors in
Geneva – agreeably scandalized – observed the poets' activities
through telescopes.

By the 1830s, the Alps – or rather, the way in which they were viewed
– had changed radically. In Gray's youth a century before, a 'civilized
being' might well regard them with unmitigated horror. Now, as
Leslie Stephen put it, 'even a solid archdeacon, with a firm belief in
the British constitution, and Church and State, was compelled to
admire, under penalty of general reprobation'.

This change was the work not only of poets, but of several practical developments. A regular cross-Channel steamer service had
been introduced in 1820, and similar vessels – often of English
design, engine and crew – appeared on the larger alpine lakes. Under
Napoleon, the roads in France, Switzerland and Italy, and particularly
through the Alps themselves, had greatly improved, and with the

increase in traffic many of the alpine inns had been smartened up. More importantly, the Alps were no longer seen simply as a barrier to northern peoples in their quest for the pleasures and riches of the south. According to Rousseau they were of moral effect; according to de Saussure, worthy of scientific interest; according to Wordsworth, spiritual presences; according to Byron and Shelley, sources of inspiration and enlightenment.

It was now a mark of taste, respectability and wealth to go and pay homage to their splendours. The summers of the 1830s saw visits from Alexandre Dumas, Michael Faraday, Franz Liszt, Henry Longfellow, Charles Sainte-Beuve, even the young Florence Nightingale. Like other visitors, they probably clasped *Murray's Handbook* on their travels, for the guidebook's success was itself indicative of the growing popularity of the region. By the time of the accession of Queen Victoria in 1837, the Alps had become fashion-able enough for her future husband Prince Albert to be sent on an alpine tour. Indeed, it was as a token of his affection that the young German presented Victoria with an album of views from the tour, bringing her from Geneva a scrap of Voltaire's handwriting and, from the slopes of Switzerland's celebrated Mount Rigi high above Lucerne, a pressed alpenrose. In 1840, the year of the royal marriage, Dr Arnold of Rugby remarked with only a degree of exaggeration that 'Switzerland is to England, what Cumberland and Westmorland are to Lancashire and Yorkshire, the general summer touring place.'

The Alps had been transformed, and the great love affair of the English with the mountains had begun.

Chapter One

Into the Unknown

'I was urged toward Mont Pelvoux by those mysterious impulses which cause men to peer into the unknown.'

Edward Whymper, *Scrambles Amongst the Alps* (1871)

If the fashion of the Alps had been established by the time Queen Victoria came to the throne, the number of visitors nonetheless remained small by modern standards. In the years up to the great European revolutions of 1848 this began to change, more and more of the English being inspired to visit the alpine paradise. Although much of this may again be credited to poets and painters, artists and the arts, as inspirers and begetters they were now joined by the mountaineers. In their adventures approaching and above the snow-line, these were men who – in their own words – were stepping into the unknown.

Horace de Saussure had established the principle of scaling the great peaks when in 1787, with his eighteen-man party, he had followed in the tracks of Balmat and Paccard and ascended Mont Blanc, the Alps' highest mountain. Yet his monument, *Voyages dans les Alpes*, had the disadvantage for the English of being written in French. Moreover, pioneer as he was, others were slow to follow. Even though Chamonix by the late 1830s was established as a fashionable resort, the ascent of the mountain itself was attempted by few. To the south-west, the Dauphiné, to become one of the great alpine mountaineering centres, remained virtually undiscovered.

Zermatt and the peaks that towered above the adjoining valleys had begun to attract visitors, but they did little more than stare at the forbidding Matterhorn. Further north, in the Bernese Oberland, the 13,642-foot Jungfrau had been conquered by the Meyer brothers of Aarau in 1812, but the adjoining Eiger and Mönch still repelled all advances. Untested, too, was the 13,284-foot Piz Bernina, the highest of the great Bernina group in Canton Grisons. This was the only peak east of the St Gotthard pass above what was regarded as the ledger mark of four thousand metres, equivalent to 13,120 feet. The mountains in the Tyrol were scarcely better known. Only the highest – the 12,812-foot Ortle and the 12,461-foot Gross Glockner – had been climbed. South across the Brenner pass, the Dolomites were virtually untouched.

This was hardly surprising, for those who ventured into the high Alps were still embracing an experience almost as remote and alien as space today. *Murray's Handbook* identified five principal threats – the yielding of snow bridges covering crevasses, or of snow cornices overhanging precipices; the risk of slipping on slopes of ice, rock or even steep turf; the fall of ice or rocks from above; the slipping beneath the feet of a steep snowfield, which might bury the traveller; the sudden approach of bad weather. To these dangers were to be added the risk of mountain sickness and frostbite, both of which could prove fatal. There were moreover no reliable maps; weather forecasts were non-existent; the sophistication of climbing equipment extended to nailed boots, wooden ladders, hemp ropes, Norfolk jackets and unwieldy alpenstocks. Mountain shelters were primitive, mountain rescue teams virtually unknown. It needed curiosity and courage of a very high order to climb.

The English having been the most numerous amongst the early tourists in the Alps, it was to be expected that they would be prominent amongst the first mountaineers. Colonel Mark Beaufroy of the Coldstream Guards was to climb Mont Blanc in 1787, within a week of de Saussure's ascent, becoming the first Englishman to conquer a high peak. But thereafter the French revolution and the Napoleonic wars called a halt to mountaineering enterprise, both English and Continental. A few of the major peaks were conquered by climbers local to them, but little concerted effort was made to tackle them until, in 1839, there came to the Alps the father of English mountaineering, James David Forbes.

Forbes was born in 1809 to the seventh baronet of Pitsligo, and Williamina Beeches, an early love of Sir Walter Scott. Of delicate constitution, as an adult thin and pale, he was taught elocution by Mrs Siddons, and at sixteen was sent to Edinburgh University to study law. Soon, though, he discovered that his real talent was for the sciences. By 1832, at the age of twenty-three, he had been elected to the Royal Society, and a year later was appointed to the chair of natural philosophy at Edinburgh. One of the great scientific questions of the day was the nature of glaciers, what caused them to form, how and why they moved. It was this that took the young professor to the Alps. He had first visited Chamonix and the Mer de Glace in 1826. He returned in 1833, the year he took his chair, and in 1837 he was in the Tyrol.

In 1839 and 1841 came two far more ambitious journeys often described as writing the first paragraph of the story of British mountaineering. The first was a complete tour around the 12,602-foot Monte Viso, the highest peak in the Queyras region where France encroaches into Italy. This involved the crossing of a series of high and difficult passes, including the 9,679-foot Col de la Traversette, the 8,704-foot Col de Viso, and the 9,269-foot Col de Vallante. The second trip was an exploration of the Veneon valley in the Dauphiné. Forbes had visited the valley briefly in 1839. Now, setting out from Grenoble, he went via the 7,169-foot Sept Laux to the village of Bourg d'Oisans, then through the Veneon itself to La Bérarde. Then he undertook the first passage of the 10,289-foot Col du Says, and the first by a foreign traveller of the 10,063-foot Col du Sella. With both journeys involving lengthy periods of travel above the 8,000-foot snow-line, these were amongst the earliest sustained trips at such altitudes.

Following the second of these trips, on 9 August 1841, Forbes encountered Louis Agassiz, a young naturalist from Neuchâtel in north-western Switzerland. So interested was Agassiz in his subject that he had spent two summers in the Bernese Oberland camped in the most primitive conditions beside the Unteraar glacier. At first little more than a cave with a rug over the entrance, his observation post was ironically dubbed the 'Hôtel des Neuchâtelois', a sordid den in fine weather, a hell-hole in a storm. Here the professor came visiting, the pair happily speculating for hours on end on the curiosities of the formation, structure and movement of glaciers. However, when Forbes's considered views on glaciers were published in 1843, establishing him – in the words of a biographer – as 'the Copernicus or Kepler of this science', Agassiz began to believe that Forbes had acquired rather more information than he had imparted. As the twentieth-century alpinist Arnold Lunn was later to put it, this 'forged the first link in a daisy chain of alpine quarrels, for [Professor] Tyndall quarrelled with Forbes, after which the torch of strife passed from the scientific mountaineers to the unscientific, Tyndall quarrelling with Whymper, Whymper with Coolidge, and Coolidge, the Lord of the Battles, with almost every contemporary mountaineer who put pen to paper, and many who did not'. Lunn, born in 1888, father of English skiing, Christian controversialist, prolific writer, knighted for his services to Anglo-Swiss relations, will have much else to say in this story.

Forbes, though, was both scientist and mountaineer. Following his stay at the Unteraar hotel, in the company of Agassiz on 28 August he embarked on his first major climb, tackling the 13,642-foot Jungfrau – one of the three heroic peaks that dominate the Bernese Oberland. The spectacle of this great trio, and their attendant glaciers, had drawn visitors to the village of Grindelwald since the time of Haller. Masquerading under the names of the maiden, monk (Mönch) and ogre (Eiger), together they form one of the most arresting spectacles in the alpine chain. With the adjoining peaks, they comprise a wall of some nine miles thrown across the Lauterbrunnen valley, rising to close to 13,000 feet. Two great glaciers, the Unteraar and the Oberaar, cascade down from the fortress, and the Eiger's bitter grey north face rises abruptly from the saddle of the Kleine Scheidegg to contrast sharply with the pristine white of the maiden and the monk.

According to Murray, Grindelwald itself then consisted of picturesque wooden cottages and a couple of inns, the Eagle and the Bear. Its inhabitants occupied themselves with the rearing of cattle, a few of the peasants doubling as guides. The womenfolk picked up a little money singing at the inns, and the village children were mostly beggars, 'occupations arising from the influx of strangers into the valley, which has exercised an injurious influence on its morals and ancient simplicity of manners'.

Here, high on the slopes of the Jungfrau, Forbes's party was suddenly engulfed by cloud so dense that they could see only a few yards around them. Even the stoic Forbes felt that their position, 'hanging . . . on a slope of unbroken slippery ice, steep as a cathedral roof, or those high pitched Dutch houses . . . with precipices at the bottom of the slope, of an unknown and dizzy depth', was 'rather frightful'; and the cold was such that he could feel his toes freezing, 'and had some trouble to restore animation by shaking and striking them' – dangerous on such a slope. After two hours scrambling up the incline they were within a few feet of what appeared to be the summit itself, but it proved to be false. The real peak, a stone's throw further, was a few feet higher. Joining the twin summits was a ridge of snow some thirty feet long, 'resembling an excessively steep house roof'. To reach their goal, it was necessary for Forbes's guides to make on one slope of the ridge 'a series of footsteps with the toes inwards'. By means of these the party, one by one, 'advanced sideways, securing ourselves by the alpenstock planted on the opposite slope, until we reached the apex'. This method, the professor conceded, was 'awkward', but there was 'no real danger, the footing being good'.

Forbes's ascent of the peak was the first made by a foreign climber, and only the fourth in all. The following year, 1842, he would break new ground by opening up the so-called high level route – the magnificent track that threads its way through some of the Alps' highest peaks between Chamonix and Zermatt – and then conquer the 11,594-foot Zermatt Stockhorn. He thus became the first British mountaineer to make the first ascent of a major alpine peak.

The fruit of these adventures was his book, *Travels Through the Alps of Savoy and other parts of the Pennine Chain, with observations on the Phenomena of Glaciers.* Published in 1843, this gathered together the experience of his travels above the snow-line. Hitherto, travellers had been voyaging into the unknown. Now they had to hand the first book in the English language to detail the realities and practicalities of high alpine travel. In the words of the Victorian alpine scholar W.A.B. Coolidge: 'The list of Forbes's climbs is really superb for the time, and entitles him to be considered as the earliest English mountaineer, who regularly undertook high ascents for a series of years . . . Forbes had discovered by quiet observation how one could travel among the peaks in relative safety.'

As its title suggests, Forbes's book was an amalgam of travelogue and scientific textbook. It nevertheless attracted attention outside the tiny coterie of English mountaineers, and served as a stimulus to general alpine tourism in the mid-1840s, more especially when the book was reissued without its scientific sections. Yet the numbers visiting the Alps were still small, and it would require a more spectacular form of publicity for the attraction to catch fire. In short, a prophet was required – if possible, two. This was not a role the professor envisaged for himself. Nor does it seem likely that he recognized the sage-to-be in the tall, slightly stooping, sandy-haired young man of twenty-five whom he met in 1844 at the Simplon pass. John Ruskin, though, was to prove such a man.

It was the habit of Ruskin's prosperous parents to undertake annual excursions with their only child; these normally entailed visits to the romantic scenery then popular, particularly Wales, the Scottish Highlands and the English Lakes. Not until Ruskin was sixteen did the family first visit the Alps, a carriage tour of some six months taking them to France, Switzerland and Italy. Duly primed with de Saussure, Wordsworth and Byron, Ruskin came to the mountains with great expectations. These were amply fulfilled, for he found 'the Alps and their people were alike beautiful in their snow and their humanity'. Indeed, an experience on the Col de la Faucille, the pass that provided travellers from Dijon with their first proper view of the Alps, was to set the pattern for the whole of his life. Here, in 1835, in the course of the second of what became virtually annual summer trips to the Alps, Ruskin wrote that 'The Col de la Faucille, on that day, opened to me in distinct vision the Holy Land of my future work and true home in this world.' By the time of his meeting with Professor Forbes he had launched himself on the world with the publication in 1843, by 'A Graduate of Oxford', of *Modern Painters*. Published in a series of volumes over sixteen years, this would forge his reputation. His obituarist, the alpinist Douglas Freshfield, wrote: 'He saw and understood mountains, and taught our generation to understand them in a way no one – even of those who had been under their shadow – had ever understood them before . . . no writer has added so much to our appreciation of Alpine scenery.'

Ruskin's own famous description of mountains as the 'cathedrals of the earth' would have to await the fourth volume of his masterpiece twelve years hence. In the second half of the 1840s it was less his own artistry that popularized the Alps than his championing of the work of a genius in quite another form, that of paint.

For Ruskin's contemporaries the principal means by which they obtained ideas of places they had not themselves visited was topographical painting, a medium second only in importance to writing in developing the vogue for the Alps. Despite the grandeur of the scenery described by the Romantic poets, it was some time before painters began to rise to the challenge of capturing their complex forms in paint. Certainly mountains as a subject in their own right had already been depicted by French, Swiss and Tyrolese topographical artists of the eighteenth century. A number of talented English water-colourists had also been at work in the Alps since the 1780s. Nevertheless, as late as 1824, Louis XVIII's librarian commented:

> It is certainly a very remarkable fact that in the presence of such grand scenes of nature, in a country which, at every step, offers a vegetation so rich and powerful, ground features so varied and striking, unheard of riches of water peaceful or foaming, rocks naked or forest-clad, in a word, all the forms of nature and, so to say, all the climates of the earth, side by side or intermingled, it is remarkable that the talent of artists has so rarely risen to the levels of such a model . . . This is what struck me at the last exhibition held in Berne . . . what I looked for in vain in this gallery of Swiss views was Switzerland.

An exception was J.M.W. Turner, the greatest landscape painter of the nineteenth century, who in the 1840s was making the final sketches of the scenes that had inspired some of his best work.

Turner was something of an oddity. Born in 1775 to a Covent Garden barber, his education was limited. He was thought to have the manners of a seaman, and he spent the final years of his life living in Chelsea under the assumed name of Booth. He was also somewhat grasping in character. Ruskin recorded his bargaining with Mr Griffith of Norwood, one of his agents, over what are perhaps the best of his Swiss water-colours – *The Pass of Splugen, Mont Rigi in the Morning, Mont Rigi in the Evening* and *Lake Lucerne from above Brunnen.*

> Says Mr Turner to Mr Griffith: 'What do you think you can get for such things as these?'
> Says Mr Griffith to Mr Turner: 'Well, perhaps commission included, eighty guineas each.'
> Says Mr Turner to Mr Griffith: 'Ain't they worth more?'
> Says Mr Griffith to Mr Turner: after looking curiously into the execution which, you will please note, is rather what some people might call hazy, 'They're a little different to your usual

style' – (Turner silent, Griffith does not push the point) – 'but – but – yes, they are *worth* more, but I could not *get* more.'

So the bargain was made.

The association between Ruskin and Turner began with the former's defence of Turner in 1836, in the course of a squabble with *Blackwood's Edinburgh Magazine*. Turner had submitted *Juliet and her Nurse*, *Rome from Mount Aventine* and *Mercury and Argus* to the Royal Academy. *Blackwood's* attack on these pictures roused Ruskin, himself later a superb alpine painter, to the 'height of black anger'. His riposte was sent to Turner. The painter guardedly welcomed the seventeen-year-old's intervention, on the grounds that he himself had little time for such matters. He did not anticipate that the controversy would inspire *Modern Painters*. This, as its subtitle suggested, was no more nor less than a tract on the superiority of modern painters, Turner in particular, 'to all the Ancient Masters'. This was argued on the grounds of the extreme accuracy of the artist's rendition of nature, a point of view that inspired the writer to colour his pages with passages inspired by his own response to landscape.

Given Ruskin's enthusiasm for the Alps, it was perhaps inevitable that Turner's own alpine subjects should have been treated with particular sympathy in the book. One of the best passages, in the words of Ruskin's first biographer W.G. Collingwood, was 'his word-picture of a night on the Rigi, with all its wonderful successive effects of gathering thunder, sunset in tempest, serene starlight, and the magic glories of Alpine sunrise . . . ingeniously embroidered with a running commentary on a series of drawings by Turner'. Ruskin simultaneously celebrated the Alps and Turner's interpretation of their beauties. The result was both a revaluation of the Alps themselves and of Turner's alpine subjects. There had been many of the latter both in water-colour and oil. Now paintings like the *Fall of the Rhine at Schaffhausen* – described by one critic as 'madness' – *The Passage of Mount St Gotthard*, *The Devil's Bridge*, *Hannibal Crossing the Alps*, and various views of Lake Geneva and the Rigi began to be seen as the masterpieces they were, capturing the intrinsic drama of many of the locations – and often their sublimity – with an expressive handling of colour that was virtually unprecedented. In Turner, as a modern

critic has written, 'The Alps stood as it were discovered. Turner had
. . . revealed not simply what they looked like, but also what they
could mean.'

Alongside these aesthetic qualities that for many gave the Alps their
abiding value and appeal, another mountaineer of practical bent was
required to carry on the work of Forbes, whose failing health gradually restricted his alpine adventures. This was a post to be filled with
distinction for many years by John Ball.

Born in 1818, Ball was the son of a leading Dublin judge. From an
early age he showed a talent for observing every facet of nature, one
of his childhood pastimes being to measure the height of hills by
using a mountain barometer. Introduced to the Alps at the age of
seven, he had his first glimpse of the range from the Col de la Faucille
– a sight, as with Ruskin, that proved the formative influence of his
life.

> We reached the top of the Col . . . just before sunset. The sky
> was almost cloudless. We all got out [of the coach]. I managed
> to get a little apart from the others, and remained fixed for
> almost half an hour. The light gradually stole upwards from the
> lake over the nearer mountains, and then over the Savoy Alps,
> and finally the peak of Mont Blanc above remained illuminated.
> One little cloud only hung just over the peak. As the peak also
> became dim the cloud remained like a glory over its head. For
> long years the scene recurred constantly to my mind, whether
> asleep or awake, and perhaps nothing has had so great an
> influence on my entire life.

Brought up a Catholic, he was educated at Oscott College, near
Birmingham. In 1835 he went up to Christ's College, Cambridge,
where he studied natural sciences, notably under Darwin's mentor

John Stevens Herslow. In his final examinations in 1839 he passed out twenty-seventh wrangler, his Catholicism preventing him from taking a degree. He then set out on a series of scientific journeys that would take him all over Europe. One trip took him to Sicily, where his studies were mainly botanical. Then, in 1845, he arrived in Zermatt partly to pursue his botanical interests, partly to study glaciers.

De Saussure had visited the tiny village at the head of the St Nicholas valley in 1789. George Cade, the first English visitor, arrived in 1800, and the curé delighted in telling him of the terrors brought by the invading French in 1799. Ball himself found little more than 'a crowded assemblage of dank, dirty-looking wooden houses', and was obliged to throw himself on the hospitality of the curé. Murray was more complimentary. The *Handbook* described Zermatt as an 'elevated and retired village, with more cleanness and comfort among its inhabitants than is to be found in many places of greater pretensions. This has perhaps been effected by the influx of strangers, for many mineralogists, botanists, and entomologists come here to collect rich harvests in the neighbourhood.' Installed in the village which, despite its privations, provided easy access to the great Valaisian glaciers, Ball equipped himself for scientific observations. He did so in a manner typical of his day, and suggestive of its challenges:

> To my knapsack is strapped a stout piece of rope about thirty feet long, with a Scotch plaid and umbrella; the last – though often scoffed at, is an article that hot sunshine, even more than rain, has taught me to appreciate. A couple of thermometers, a pocket clinometer, and a Kater's compass with prismatic eye-piece may be carried in suitable pockets, along with a notebook and a sketch-book, having a fold for writing-paper etc; a good opera-glass, which I find more readily available than a telescope; a strong knife, measuring tape, a veil, and spectacles, leather cup, spare cord and matches. A flask with cold tea, to be diluted with water or snow, a tin box for plants, a geological hammer of a form available for occasional use as an ice-axe, with a strap to keep all tight, and to prevent anything swinging loosely in awkward places, complete the accoutrement.

Ball's tour marked the beginning of a career remarkable and diverse, ranging as it did from the post of Poor Law commissioner during the Irish famine to that of Under-Secretary of State for the Colonies under Lord Palmerston – all this alongside purely scientific studies, geographical, physical and historical, which were described by the botanist and traveller Sir Joseph Hooker as 'deserving of a corner of the same shelf with the works of Humboldt, Darwin, Bates and Wallace'.

Ball's great work, however, was *The Alpine Guide*, published between 1863 and 1868. Although guides to the Alps had existed for more than a generation, neither of the standard works of the 1840s – Murray and his German counterpart Baedeker – had pretensions to provide detailed, reliable and up-to-date information for climbers and mountaineers. There had been Forbes's pioneering book, together with accounts of specific climbs, like Charles Fellows's *Narrative of an Ascent to the Summit of Mont Blanc*. Though these were useful for repeating such adventures, they were no help on the thousands of other routes and climbs that might tempt the adventurous.

Ball's stated object was 'not to conduct his readers along certain beaten tracks, but to put them in a position to choose for themselves such routes as may best suit their individual tastes and powers, to give advice as to what is best worth notice, and to show what is open to the prudently adventurous'. The guide was far less anecdotal than Forbes or Fellows. Rather, it was a remarkably comprehensive survey of challenging walks, scrambles and climbs all over the Alps, from the Col di Tendi in the west to Semmering in the east. In its preparation, Ball estimated that he had crossed the main alpine chain forty-eight times by thirty-two different passes, besides traversing nearly one hundred of the lateral passes. Coolidge said of him that 'Few men, if any, have ever known the whole of the Alps better than he did, while none did while he was in his prime.'

Like Forbes, Ball was essentially a scientific traveller rather than a great climber, yet he undertook some remarkable ascents. Amongst these was his discovery of the route between Zermatt and Gressonay, south across the mountains in Piedmont, then under Sardinian rule. This was at a time when – as Ball himself recorded – even among the Zermatt locals, knowledge of the passes communicating between the

valley of St Nicholas and the adjoining valleys was 'vague and unsatisfactory to a degree that would surprise those who do not know how
amazingly our knowledge of this part of the Alps has increased since
1845'.

Anxious both to dispel this ignorance and to make a number of
scientific observations, Ball made a careful survey of the possible
routes. He selected one that would take him between the eastern end
of the 12,461-foot Breithorn and two smaller peaks of equal height
called because of their proximity and similar profile 'the Twins', now
better known as Castor and Pollux. The difficulty was that he was
uncertain whether, in the first place, ascent was possible or, in the
second, whether – the summit of the pass having been reached –
descent was possible on the other side; and even if both proved practicable, whether he could avoid being benighted and having to take
shelter – as he proposed – in a crevasse. Still, like Forbes himself and
in due course Edward Whymper, he was 'drawn by those mysterious
impulses which cause men to peer into the unknown'.

Having found a companion in the form of a local guide called
Mathias Tangwald, on 16 August 1845, Ball prepared to depart. First,
though, he had to be wished well by the locals, for the whole village
had turned out to see him off. 'A quite unusual depth of excitement
was apparent,' Ball wrote:

> but it was only just before I started that I learned the real cause
> of the interest that had been shown in the success of my
> project. It was not any abstract interest in geographical science
> nor a desire to enter into a closer relationship with the German
> population of Gressonay, nor yet the notion that Tourists might
> be attracted to the valley by a new and interesting pass: the prac-
> tical mind of Zermatt had detected in the new route a grand
> opportunity for carrying on free trade with Piedmont unin-
> terrupted by the douaniers of His Sardinian Majesty.

The pair finally set off at 3.00 a.m. the following morning, Mathias
being urged by their landlady of the 'necessity for caution and pru-
dence, with both of which excellent qualities Nature had largely
endowed my companion'. At first they proceeded without difficulty,

pausing at 5.00 to study the route over the Schwarz glacier, and easily traversing its lower part. Their problems began when they reached the higher elevations, where a good deal of fresh snow had fallen. On a snow bridge over a crevasse Ball at once plunged up to his waist, and was fortunate to fall no further: 'It was the first time that such an accident had occurred to me, but as I wished to keep Mathias in good spirits, I treated it as a mere matter of course.' The guide, though, was much perturbed, and proposed that the attempt should be abandoned, 'a request which was to be repeated very often in the course of the day'.

Roping themselves together, the two proceeded until confronted by a great mass of ice cliffs, some of which were one hundred feet high. Here the only way forward was to pass along the face of the cliff, the slope of which was 'formidably steep, certainly not less than 60 degrees'. To do so safely Ball led the way, making clear imprints in the snow, and progressing until the rope linking him to the guide would stretch no further. Then he would secure his position by means of his alpenstock, gradually drawing in the rope as the guide followed: 'I was most afraid of his being unnerved, if his eye were to wander down the dizzy slope into the yawning crevasses of the glacier that lay far beneath us, and I ordered him to keep his eyes constantly fixed upon the spot where he was to place his foot.' Eventually, at 1.15 p.m., they reached the summit of the ridge. There, at 12,800 feet, they lunched, although Mathias showed little appetite, having in the course of the ascent had 'recourse to wine and seem[ing] to be rather the worse for it'.

At 2.00 p.m. the descent began; unfortunately, the immediate route was far from clear, and cloud prevented them seeing the more distant route down in the valley below. Obliged again to traverse a glacier riven with wider and more numerous crevasses, they made only slow progress, and evening was drawing on. But at last, after thirteen hours on snow and ice, they reached firm ground. A local herdsman then directed them to the nearest village. This proved to be San Giacomo d'Ayas, some way from where they had imagined themselves to be, and still well up the valley from Gressonay. There, after a further weary walk, they found lodging, and Ball whipped up 'a good size omelette' from the butter and eggs in the larder.

'Mathias, however, was regularly knocked up. It was not, he declared, from fatigue, but from mortal anxiety, *grosser Angst*, that he was now in a sort of collapse, unable to eat or extend himself in any way.'

It was a remarkable day's work. In the course of it the pair had conquered what became known as the Schwarz Thor pass. At 12,777 feet, this was the highest then crossed in the Alps.

Despite the achievement, Ball's portrait of his guide is unflattering enough for the very word to seem a misnomer. To some extent his view was shared by Whymper, to whom guides represented 'pointers out of paths and great consumers of meat and drink, but little more'. Others complained that their disinclination to wash meant that they could be followed by the nose as much as by the eye. Whymper, however, was later to recant. For in truth, as in due course he recognized, from the earliest days of modern mountaineering guides played a major part in their employers' adventures.

Local people living around the more prominent peaks were seldom tempted to any form of exploration for the sake of exploration without external encouragement. They took their herds up to the high pastures in the spring, hunted crystal, marmot, fox and chamois, and indulged themselves in the smuggling that the excise arrangements between the tiny alpine countries fostered. In no other sense and for no other purpose were they mountaineers. After all, there was no incentive; if anything, the reverse. The mountains were still a looming, and dangerous, presence to them. But as mountaineering became established as a scientific pursuit, opportunities – financial opportunities – presented themselves for those with local knowledge of particular areas, and the role of guide came into being.

In the early days guiding was largely an ad hoc arrangement, but in 1821 the Compagnie des Guides de Chamonix, the first such organization in the Alps, was founded. Individual guides were grouped under a chief guide, restricted by certain regulations, entitled to certain pay. These men were indeed pointers-out of paths – a valuable function for the stranger in the absence of anything pretending to be an accurate map. They also acted as porters, a similarly important role for a class of climber unfamiliar with manual work of any nature – be it the carrying of rucksacks or the cutting of steps in ice – and who would in any case think such work beneath him. Finally they were companions insofar as the class barriers of the day permitted. The Edwardian climber Geoffrey Winthrop Young called them a 'peasant aristocracy . . . a status familiar to Englishmen, that of the huntsman or gamekeeper, with a dash of tiger-hunter thrown in'.

Both nominally and largely in practice assistants, on occasion they acted as hindrances to exploration rather than aids. As Ball implies, and as Claire Éliane Engel points out in her standard history of alpine mountaineering, 'Devising new climbs required imagination and foresight. Hardly any route was ever discovered by local peasants when not prompted or led by their patrons, and they usually did much to prevent the latter from having their own way.' Yet the greatest of the guides played an invaluable part in the feats of mountaineering that were soon taking place. W.A.B. Coolidge identified the qualities of an outstanding guide as

> the gift for path-finding; the physical strength to undergo hard bodily labour, such as long-continued step-cutting; the power of deciding, without hesitation, what is to be done in what exact state of weather or snow; the faculty of preserving his presence of mind if and when a crisis arises; the strength of will, regardless of any possible consequences in the future to his professional reputation, though only among silly people, to decide on retirement if he deems it desirable.

These were very necessary qualities in the upland world. If it was rarely the guides' own ambition that prompted them to venture into the unknown, without them the Alps would not have been won.

In 1847 Ruskin was discouraged from returning to the Alps by Turner. The painter was professedly concerned for the young man's safety, for war was in the air.

The Congress of Vienna had seen the grouping of the Swiss cantons into a federation. Almost from its inception this arrangement had been compromised by military and political struggles between the cantons, culminating in 1845 with the formation of an alliance of the seven Catholic cantons. Opposed by the federal government and the remaining, predominantly Protestant cantons, a civil war for the preservation of the federation was brewing. In these circumstances Turner was sensibly cautious, although Ruskin suspected that in reality he disapproved of Ruskin's intention to revisit the scenes of some of the painter's alpine masterpieces with a view to ascertaining their 'truth to nature'.

As it turned out, Ruskin's summer tour was completed before hostilities broke out in November 1847. As signatories at Vienna, the great powers of Austria-Hungary, Prussia and France wished to intervene in the struggle. Escalation was prevented by the successes of the Federalist forces, the resistance to the plan by England, and – in 1848 – the outbreak of revolutions in Italy, France and several of the states and principalities that were to become Germany. In France the abdication of Louis Philippe saw the establishment of the Second Republic, and in Germany the first national assembly of all the constituent Teutonic states. Switzerland, however, progressed further, and in doing so created the basis of political and economic stability in the heart of the Alps that would prove the foundation of its tourism. A new constitution guaranteed republican government in all the cantons and – as in England – equality of all before the law, liberty of conscience, speech, press and public meeting. Bern was established as the federal capital, and uniform systems of coinage and postage would follow. With this came the abolition of the customs barriers between the cantons that a few years previously had so interested the citizens of Zermatt.

If this made alpine adventure more practicable, conditions in England herself were rendering escape to the clear skies, clean air and scenery of the mountains desirable. By 1847 England was on the verge of becoming the first country in the world where the majority of the population would be living in cities rather than the country-side, and be employed in occupations predominantly industrial rather than agricultural. Whether the exodus was ultimately beneficial was doubted. The very notion of cities in which millions of people might live was novel, and the management of such essentials as water, coal, sewerage and refuse disposal was primitive in the extreme. Sheffield was described as 'a putrid bog or morass'; the English population as a whole was being 'poisoned by its own excrement'. Disease as a consequence was rife. The cholera epidemic of 1832 killed 50,000, and would return in 1848–9 and 1853–4. Influenza, measles, scarlet fever and diphtheria were endemic. This was the claustrophobic urban cesspit that Charles Dickens described in the opening passage of *Bleak House*:

London. Michaelmas term lately over, and the Lord Chancellor sitting in Lincoln's Inn Hall. Implacable November weather. As much mud in the streets, as if the waters had but newly retired from the face of the earth, and would not be wonderful to meet a Megalosaurus, forty feet long or so, waddling like an elephantine lizard up Holborn Hill. Smoke lowering down from chimney-pots, making a soft black drizzle, with flakes of soot in it as big as full-grown snow flakes – gone into mourning, one might imagine, for the death of the sun. Dogs, undistinguishable in mire. Horses, scarcely better; splashed to their very blinkers. Foot passengers, jostling one another's umbrellas, in a general infection of ill temper, and losing their foot-hold at street corners, where tens of thousands of other foot passengers have been slipping and sliding since the day broke (if the day ever broke), adding new deposits to the crust upon crust of mud, sticking at those points tenaciously to the pavements, and accumulating at compound interest.

It was not surprising, therefore, that Dickens was dazzled by Switzerland. On crossing the St Gotthard in 1845, on his return from Italy, he wrote: 'The whole descent between Andermatt and Altdorf, William Tell's town . . . is the highest sublimation of all you can imagine in the way of Swiss scenery. O God! What a beautiful country it is!' The following year he would return to Lausanne, and there write *Dombey and Son* and *The Battle of Life*. Similarly inspired, a namesake of Professor Forbes, the Queen's physician John Forbes, was to publish a popular account of an alpine tour, which took in the Rigi, Grindelwald and Zermatt. He remarked:

> It may be stated, without any risk of mistake, that there are very few residents in large towns, particularly in our large manufac- turing towns and in London, whom such a tour as is described in the following pages will not benefit in a very marked degree. It will enable a large proportion of such persons to lay in a fresh stock of health sufficient to last through the year, in spite of all the exhausting influences of confined air, sedentary occupa- tions, and that over-tasking of the mind to which so many of them are exposed, and which is a fruitful source of so many dis- eases . . . – A Course of Travelling of this sort – to speak med- ically – carried out in the fine season, in one of the healthiest localities in Europe, in pure and bracing air, amid some of the most attractive and impressive scenes in nature, in cheerful company, with a mind freed from the toils and care of business or the equally oppressive pursuits, or rather non-pursuits of mere fashionable life, will do all that the best medicines can do in such cases, and much that they can never accomplish.

By 1848 the number of English travellers in the Alps had increased and the class of travellers broadened. Hitherto, travel had indeed been largely restricted to 'those of large fortune'. Now, however, the grand tour was waning and – thanks to two prophets and two practi- tioners – the Alps were slowly becoming the domain of the English upper-middle classes. What could be better, more appropriate or more just? If the mountaineers themselves were still largely peering into the unknown, then at least they were doing so in congenial company. As the Queen's physician complacently remarked, the Hôtel de Londres et d'Angleterre at Chamonix was 'a splendid establishment [where] we joined the table d'hôte at dinner, and partook of an excellent dinner in the company of thirteen other persons – all English'.

Chapter Two
The Pleasure Principle

'The Alps themselves, which your own poets used to love so reverently, you look upon as soaped poles in a bear-garden, which you set
yourselves to climb and slide down again, with "shrieks of delight".'
John Ruskin, *Sesame and Lilies* (1869)

In 1851, the year of the Great Exhibition that symbolized England's
pre-eminence as the first industrialized nation, a new and most surprising figure stepped on to the alpine stage. With none of the high
seriousness of Ruskin, he was still further removed from the
scientific muse that inspired Professor Forbes and John Ball. Albert
Smith was nothing less than an alpine impresario, who made it his
aim to introduce the mountains to the middle classes.

Born in 1816 to a Surrey surgeon, Albert Richard Smith was
marked out at first to follow his father's profession. He was educated
at Merchant Taylors' school, and studied medicine at the Middlesex
Hospital and in Paris. But from his earliest days he had been an
enthusiast of mountain literature, his favourite a work that recounted
the story of Mont Blanc, *The Peasants of Chamouni*. While in Paris he
took the opportunity to visit the scenes that had so stimulated his
imagination as a child and conceived the ambition to climb the
mountain. He was only prevented from doing so by the very considerable expense involved in such an expedition.

Returning to England and joining his father's practice in the
Surrey village of Chertsey, Smith soon gave rein to the more creative

aspects of his personality. Beginning in 1840 with a series of articles in the *Medical Times* entitled 'The Confessions of Jasper Buddle, a Dissecting Room Porter', he became a contributor to the magazine *Punch*, then turned his hand to the humorous novel, his tales featuring frequent allusions to Mont Blanc. Next he became involved in the popular theatre, staging highly successful productions of pantomimes such as *Aladdin* and *Whittington and his Cat*. He reintroduced the alpine theme in 1848 with the monthly shilling serial *Christopher Tadpole*, which took Smith's ineffectual hero up Mont Blanc. Both its tone and intended audience are suggested by the dangers Tadpole faced on the ascent, listed by Smith as: 'fog freezing so hard you can't get through it; tumbling into great holes in the glacier, never getting out again for four and twenty hours and then coming up in the middle of the lake of Geneva; getting butted by wild chamois, and pecked at by eagles; rolling down into Italy like a football, never once stopping except you pitch into a crevasse'. In 1849 Smith travelled to Constantinople, capital of the Ottoman empire. Out of this came, first, *A Month at Constantinople*, an account of his visit, followed by a popular entertainment, written and produced by the traveller himself. Called *The Overland Mail*, this illustrated travelogue proved hugely popular with its London audience and, spurred on by its success, he was at last in the position to climb Mont Blanc.

Here was neither a scientific traveller nor a man in pursuit of revelation, but a journalist after copy, and in a sense Smith's assault in August 1851 was a match for his own mock-heroic literary talents. De Saussure's expedition had itself been on a large scale, but Smith excelled him. Although climbing parties at this period generally provisioned themselves generously, few went as far as Smith, whose inventory included sixty bottles of ordinary wine, six bottles of Bordeaux, ten bottles of Bourgogne, fifteen bottles of St Jean, eleven large and thirty-five small fowls, four parcels of prunes and a bottle of raspberry syrup. This in turn dictated a retinue of porters, guides and hangers-on who together, Smith claimed, amounted to 'the largest caravan that had ever gone off together'. Most of this was obtainable in Chamonix itself, where Smith based himself. Ten years previously, *Murray's Handbook* had described this as 'a large and important community, which displays almost the bustle of an

English watering-place in the most retired, heretofore, of the alpine valleys'.

As to the climb itself, the thirty-five year old was sufficiently strongly built. He lacked, though, the physical condition to make it an effortless triumph. Despite being suitably equipped with 'a pair of high gaiters . . . a fine pair of scarlet garters to tie them up with . . . a green veil . . . and a pair of blue spectacles', he had neglected to prepare his own body. He had come from 'my desk to the railway, from railway to diligence, and from that to the charabanc'. The result was that he overdid it in the early hours of the adventure, and could not sleep when the party bivouacked for the first night on the mountain.

The following morning, setting out for the summit proved no easier. Confronted by what he melodramatically described as 'an almost perpendicular wall of ice' – the Mur de la Côte – he told his guides he would go no further. They might leave him there, if they pleased. Eventually, after much persuasion, he was induced to continue. In the course of the last two hours up to the peak, overcome with cold and fatigue, the impresario fell into a sort of stupor, 'fast asleep with my eyes open'. When at length, on 12 August 1851, the triumph was at hand, 'The ardent wish of years was gratified; but I was so completely exhausted that, without looking around me, I fell down in the snow, and was asleep in an instant.' Yet conquer 'the Monarch' he did, and he soon revived sufficiently to celebrate with the fine wines and fowls which his porters had laboured to carry up the mountain.

This was merely the beginning. Back in London, Smith hired the Egyptian Hall in Piccadilly – the Earl's Court of its day – and created an illustrated entertainment dramatizing the ascent and the romance of alpine life. It became one of the most popular entertainments of its kind. His properties included a cardboard chalet, a pair of chamoix, several St Bernard dogs, maids in Bernese costumes and 'a trough where water-lilies of zinc floated in a manner which was considered realistic'. The show ran for nine years, with fresh exaggerations added every year. In 1854, Smith was invited to Osborne to tell his story to the Prince of Wales. Two years later, he was called to Windsor, accompanied by the girls and the dogs; one of the dogs was subsequently presented to Dickens. The whole performance spawned a range of merchandise that might have been the envy of Twentieth Century-Fox. There were popular melodies like 'The Mont Blanc Quadrille' and 'Les Échos du Mont Blanc', sketches of the ascent painted on fans, and a sort of alpine version of snakes and ladders, 'The Game of Mont Blanc'.

It is easy to decry Smith, and people were not slow to do so. Ruskin, in Chamonix at the time of Smith's noisy and triumphant return to the village, regarded Smith as a desecrator. He wrote sourly to a correspondent, 'There has been a cockney ascent of Mont Blanc, of which you will doubtless soon hear.' Likewise, when Smith in his account of the ascent admitted that he had made no scientific observations on the grounds that de Saussure sixty years previously had already done 'every thing that was wanted by the world of that kind', he was bitterly attacked in the press, which espoused the conventional view that the dangers of mountaineering were only justifiable on grounds of scientific interest. Despite this, the popularity of Smith's entertainment gainsaid the traditional view; it effectively introduced the alpine experience to a far wider audience than had hitherto known of it, and for the first time created an appetite for mountain travel and exploration outside a relatively narrow social and intellectual élite.

The success of Smith's entertainment was attributable to several factors: romanticism, its creator's taste for melodrama, the claustrophobia of a newly urban society. The alpinist Douglas Freshfield was also right when he pointed out that Smith's timing was brilliant. For he appeared just at the moment when railways had brought the Alps within reach of the Englishman's holiday.

The railways proper had begun with the use of steam locomotives on the Liverpool to Manchester line in 1831. By 1838 there were 490 miles of railway line in operation in Great Britain; by 1851, an astonishing

6,621. The Continent was by comparison slow to take up the new invention. Only Belgium created more or less simultaneously a system of comparable density to that of Great Britain. France produced no railways worthy of the name until 1837, and then they were built mainly by Englishmen. The various principalities and kingdoms that comprised Germany began construction only in 1839.

Gradually, however, the Continental network grew, and by the time of Smith's ascent the railways had brought the Alps within the Englishman's reach; or rather, as Freshfield wrote, within reach of his long vacation. For vacation implies employment, and the essential quality of the railway was that for the first time it placed Continental travel within reach of those obliged to work for their living. Not only did it enable them to travel long distances relatively cheaply, it was also fast enough for them to make such journeys within the short space of time available as holiday. As a social development, this was of immense importance. Hitherto, anyone obliged to earn a living found it extremely difficult to do much beyond their own vicinity. For the first time the railway made it possible for large numbers of people to venture abroad.

Yet the development of the railways in the Alps themselves, Switzerland in particular, remained problematic. The political fragmentation of the region was an obvious barrier to a coherent railway system. Murray noted in this context the 'extraordinary and incredible jealousies between not only the different cantons, but the different communes or parishes'. Equally important was the topography of the Alps. The gradient even of their foothills was too steep for the power of the early locomotives, and indeed for a system that relied on gravity alone to maintain adhesion between the engine and coaches and the track itself. The victory of the Swiss Federalist forces in 1847 and the subsequent foundation of the national parliament, the Bund, put an end to the country's political fragmentation, and in 1850 the Bund conferred on itself the right to appropriate land in the interests of a national railway system. The next step was to call in consulting engineers.

Here the Swiss turned to the English. A group led by George Stephenson's son Robert – then Britain's leading railway engineer –

visited Switzerland and toured the country extensively with a view to creating a satisfactory national (as opposed to piecemeal) system. Stephenson recommended an arrangement based on the 'railway cross'. This would comprise one main line running from lakes Geneva to Constance, another from Basel to Lucerne, the 'cross' occurring at the town of Olten, roughly half-way between Zürich and Basel. There would also be a series of branch and feeder lines. As far as possible it was intended that the lines would run alongside rivers in the valley beds, minimizing tunnel and bridge construction. The passage of the Alps themselves was considered impractical on both financial and technical grounds.

This scheme was logical enough in its way, but was compromised from the first by the fact that the surveyors in their journeying attracted camp followers in the form of 'soothsayers' – investors who speculated on where the lines would go and attempted to influence the engineering decisions. The network as designed also excluded a number of significant cities and towns, not least Geneva. In the end, the new federal government abandoned its plans for a coherent and integrated national system in favour of allowing the individual cantons to make their own arrangements, albeit with vague federal supervision.

In practice, thanks to private enterprise, many of the lines envisaged by Stephenson were constructed. The years from 1852 saw the arrival of a number of English financiers, contractors, engineers and consultants who worked throughout the nascent system, often employing English workmen who came over specially for the job. Amongst these engineers were Charles Vignolles, who built the first line in western Switzerland, and Thomas Brassey, who constructed the Hauenstein tunnel north of Olten – at that time the longest bore in Europe. The creation of what would in due course coalesce into one of Europe's most comprehensive national railway systems had begun, even if the problem of running lines over and under the Alps was for the moment unsolved.

By this time the inhabitants of the Alps – or rather of the tourist spots – had been familiar with the English for nearly a century. They had had plenty of opportunity to observe their visitors, adapt themselves to their ways, and make them as far as possible welcome.

In 1819 the civil engineer Sir John Rennie had recorded that

> On our way, being at Meyringen [in the Bernese Oberland] and short of ready cash, we proposed either to return direct to Geneva, or to change one of Herries' circular notes; but on offering one of these notes to the landlord, he at once said that there was no occasion for it, as we were Englishmen and that was enough. Having produced a large bag of five-franc pieces, he told us to help ourselves, and was with difficulty persuaded to take one of Herries' notes in exchange.

This was charming, but there was doubtless a certain self-interest involved too. According to Thomas Martyn's *Sketch of a Tour through Swisserland*, published in 1787, when it came to overcharging, alpine innkeepers had long regarded the English as fair game, and fleecing them was a traditional sport. Besides, the English could easily afford it; they were ten times as rich as anyone else. Noblemen or otherwise, they were usually referred to as 'milords'.

With prosperity came insularity, for which the nation was also notorious. The eighteenth-century writer and literary hostess Lady Mary Wortley Montagu complained of the Englishman's 'inviolable fidelity to the language their nurses taught them'. George Sand observed that 'Albion's islanders [have] with them a peculiar fluid which I shall call the British fluid, enveloped in which they travel, as inaccessible to the atmosphere as is a mouse in the centre of a pneumatic machine.' They pleased themselves. A future Lieutenant Governor of the state of Victoria, Charles Joseph Latrobe, wrote in 1839:

> I have seen a party of English arrive at a mountain cabaret [hut or chalet] at nightfall, when the host and his family have been thinking of their beds; they order dinner, and insist upon having flesh, fish or fowl, foreign wines and liqueurs, just as

though they were in the Star and Garter at Richmond; abuse the master and the domestics, dine at eight or nine, and sit over cheese till well past midnight. Mine host can put up with a good deal of extra trouble, with no small quantity of abuse, and will stay up all night with considerable temper because he knows he can make them pay for it in hard money.

The results of this insistence by the English that their surroundings adapt to their own expectations rather than vice versa, and their ability to pay for it, were various. As the English public schools still taught the classical languages largely at the expense of the modern, anyone dealing with English tourists – voituriers, innkeepers, shopkeepers, waiters – was obliged to pick up a smattering of English. John Forbes, the Queen's physician, wrote that 'At the inns, the waiters all understand French as well as German, and in every inn of note there are always one or two waiters who understand and speak English very fairly.' The inns were at the same time adapted to the requirements of their best customers. Murray would note that 'Switzerland is well provided with inns, and those of the large towns yield, in extent and good management, to few hotels in either France or Germany.' Both writers also remarked upon the provision, at the principal hotels and many more middling ones, of a late table d'hôte dinner at four or five o'clock, 'expressly for the English', whose habit was to dine rather later than was the Continental custom. Forbes, though, noted in Grindelwald that, satisfactory though the roast beef table d'hôte proved, 'the wine was less approved of by our party who partook of it; but I observed that it was cordially taken by some of the other guests less fastidious than Englishmen'.

Beyond the general run of hotels there were also a number of establishments that focused with such dedication on meeting the needs of English alpinists that they became venerable institutions in their owners' lifetimes. Often doubling as both proprietor and manager, these owners took an interest in the idiosyncrasies of their wealthy English customers that went well beyond the merely commercial. Admiring the Englishmen's climbing ambitions, they tailored the premises and their services precisely to their guests' requirements. English mustard, English currency exchange, afternoon tea, water-closets, winter opening, skating rinks – for these people, nothing was too much. The result, even as early as 1838, was that – as Murray recorded – many of the innkeepers were wealthy men, wielding considerable power and influence. Some, too, were in the process of founding great hotel dynasties, members of which still run these hotels today.

The principal ones were established in the earliest alpine resorts. In Chamonix there was the Hôtel de Londres et d'Angleterre. *Murray's Handbook* of 1842 remarks that this 'has never forfeited the reputation of being one of the best inns in the Alps; where Victor Tairrez and his excellent wife are so practised in their acquaintance with, and their provision for, the wants of travellers, especially English, that more *comfort* will be found here than in almost any other inn out of England'. Soon the Couttets' pension would supplant them as the mountaineers' hotel, Murray going so far as to describe it as 'excellent in all respects'. In Grindelwald Murray recommended the Bear or the Eagle. Both were run by 'Messrs. Boss, most obliging and courteous of landlords, who speak English, and may be safely consulted by travellers as to guides, etc. English notes and cheques changed.' Zermatt had the Seilers, whose first auberge was the Monte Rosa. Whymper took this as the backdrop to his most famous engraving, 'The Club-Room of Zermatt in 1864'. Of Seiler and his influence he wrote: 'No one who knows the facts will dispute that the capacity and tact with which Alexandre Seiler directed his affairs, the geniality with which he received his patrons, and the kindliness which he and his esteemed wife extended to all who were in difficulties, had much to do with the development of the place.'

Alongside this covert colonization, the early years of the 1850s saw conquest of a rather more energetic and aggressive nature. Up until this time activity on the peaks themselves had been conducted primarily as a scientific exercise in pursuit of glaciological, botanical or geological knowledge. This certainly did not preclude pleasure, as John Ball himself enquired rhetorically:

> What enjoyment is to be compared to an early walk over these great glaciers of the Alps, amid the deep silence of Nature, surrounded by some of her sublimest objects, the morning air infusing vigour and elasticity into every nerve and muscle, the eye unwearied, the skin cool, and the whole frame tingling with joyous anticipation of the adventures that the day may bring forth?

Pleasure, however, the lure of adventure and the rewards of conquest were for the present – at least ostensibly – regarded as by-products of the more high-minded pursuit of scientific knowledge. Mountaineering was not a sport.

There was of course nothing particularly English about sport, which is as old as man himself. It was in England, however, where increasing numbers of men were occupied in sedentary urban employment, that more organized forms of sport were first developed. A means of dispelling energy and providing an acceptable expression of competitive instincts, sport was also believed to be morally and socially formative. As the Hon. Edward Lyttelton, man of letters and politician, expressed it:

> A boy is disciplined by athletics in two ways: by being forced to put the welfare of the common cause before selfish interests, to obey implicitly the word of command and act in concert with the heterogeneous elements of the companies he belongs to; and, secondly, should it so turn out, he is disciplined by being raised to a post of command where he feels the gravity of responsible office and the difficulty of making prompt decisions and securing obedience.

Whether or not Waterloo had been won on the playing-fields of Eton, the mid-nineteenth century saw the foundation of the principal national sporting associations, ranging from the Football Association to the Rugby Union and the Amateur Athletics

Association. The phenomenon of organized sport was one in which the English led the world, the mountaineer and writer R.L.G. Irving later speculating that 'comparative peace gave Englishmen the opportunity to turn their competitive instincts to sport, while the peoples of Europe were struggling with each other to alter political boundaries or political regimes.' In the Alps the movement was reflected in Alfred Wills's ascent of the Wetterhorn. Despite legitimate earlier claimants, this was the first climb to which predominantly sporting motives were attributed at the time.

Wills was typical of the cadre of English mountaineers who were to conquer the major alpine peaks. Born in 1828 to the Birmingham JP, William Wills, and educated locally, he was then sent to University College, London. In 1846 he took an exhibition in both classics and mathematics. He followed these in 1851 with a scholarship in law, a field he was to make his profession. By 1851 he had been called to the bar, taking silk in 1872. By 1884 he was a High Court judge, distinguished not least by the fact that his predecessor had died in the arms of a prostitute in a brothel. In 1895 he presided over the trial of Oscar Wilde, sentencing him at the Old Bailey on 25 May to two years' hard labour. He was one of the great and good of Victorian England, who in their spare time took it into their heads to conquer the Alps.

Wills's honeymoon took him on a tour of the Bernese Oberland in the summer of 1854. This was still primitive. As Latrobe wrote:

> The traveller in the Oberland is sadly subjected to the persecution of beggars – some under the pretext of offering him strawberries, flowers or crystals, others with no excuse but their poverty, not infrequently united to goitre and cretinism, as an additional recommendation to the compassion of strangers. Every cottage sends forth its ragged crowds of dishevelled and unshod children; behind every rock is an ambuscade of native minstrels who, drawn up in a line, assail the passer-by with the discordant strains of their shrill voices.

It was at Interlaken, the settlement that forms the gate to the Oberland, that Wills thought to improve the shining hour by attempting the soaring 12,142-foot Wetterhorn. This was the 'peak of tempests' whose three great spires tower over Grindelwald. Removing himself to the village, Wills hired two outstanding guides. The innkeeper, however, was discouraging. '"Try to return alive," he told Wills. "But –" he broke off, and shook his head gravely.'

Wills's party of five set out at half-past one in the afternoon of 16 September 1854. Taking a path up beside the Upper Grindelwald glacier, by early evening they had reached a cave, crudely formed by three rocks, in which they were to spend the night. There was no other possible shelter, and the men were obliged to sleep together like a litter of puppies. They rose before dawn, and Wills stripped and bathed in a nearby torrent. Setting out, they climbed steadily until they reached the brink of the precipice overlooking the village, hitherto hidden from view. It was 9 o'clock, and they breakfasted, a meal ruined for Wills by the garlic that tainted their mutton. They then abandoned all their belongings with the exception of brandy and alpenstocks, and set out for the summit.

The party roped together as their path steepened abruptly, and the guides cut steps in the snow. Gradually the snow thinned, and at 10 o'clock they approached some rocks about 600 feet from the summit. Above them rose a glacier, surmounted by a cornice of ice. They worked their way slowly up the glacier, an hour later reaching the cornice. Since this might easily collapse under the party's weight, the only course was to 'cut boldly into the ice, and endeavour to hew deep enough to get a sloping passage on to the dome beyond'. One of the guides set to work and soon penetrated the icy parapet. Then a breach was made, and the party – one by one – crept over what proved to be the main ridge of the mountain. Wills describes the moment:

> The instant before, I had been face to face with a blank wall of ice. One step, and the eye took in a boundless expanse of crag and glacier, peak and precipice, mountain and valley, lake and plain. The whole world seemed to lie at my feet. The next moment I was almost appalled by the awfulness of our position. The side we had come up was steep; but it was a gentle slope, compared with that which now fell away from where I stood. A

few yards of glittering ice at our feet, and then, nothing between us and the green slopes of Grindelwald, nine thousand feet beneath. I am not ashamed to own that I experienced, as this sublime and wonderful prospect burst upon my view, a profound and almost irrepressible emotion – an emotion which, if I may judge by the low ejaculations of surprise, followed by a long pause of breathless silence, as each in turn stepped into the opening, was felt by others as well as myself. Balmat [his guide] told me repeatedly, afterwards, that it was the most awful and startling moment he had known in the course of his long mountain experience. We felt as in the immediate presence of Him who had reared this tremendous pinnacle, and beneath the 'majestical roof' of whose deep blue Heaven we stood, poised, as it seemed, half-way between earth and sky.

The ascent was thought at the time to be the first (it was in fact the fourth), and Wills was met on his return by the whole of the village, the landlord even telegraphing the happy news to Bern.

For Wills this proved the beginning of a whole series of adventures in the Alps. These included retracing Professor Forbes's steps on the high level route from Arolla to Zermatt, the exploration of a number of high glaciers, and the ascent both of Mont Blanc and the Matterhorn's great neighbour, the 15,203-foot Monte Rosa. He then bought a chalet in the remote Sixt valley north of Chamonix, which he called 'The Eagle's Nest'. In 1855 – as the Crimean War was at its height – he published *Wanderings Among the High Alps*. Forbes had presented mountain climbing under the guise of scientific exploration, John Ball as a practicable procedure. Now, for the first time, climbing was presented as an end in itself, an opportunity for adventure, a physical, intellectual and emotional challenge, almost a way of life. It was the ascent of the Wetterhorn that first attracted the attention of those other than devoted alpinists, whilst the book itself enjoyed a circulation much wider than its academic predecessors.

The following year saw the success of Wills's work capped by the publication of perhaps the single most influential work in alpine development. This was the fourth volume of Ruskin's *Modern Painters*, 'Of Mountain Beauty'.

Since the publication of the first part of this meandering masterpiece – the author in the preparation of the third and fourth volumes remarked that he had had to make various remarks on 'German Metaphysics, on Poetry, Political Economy, Cookery, Music, Geology, Dress, Agriculture, Horticulture, and Navigation' – its creator's reputation had mushroomed. The first volume of the work had been published under the name of 'A Graduate of Oxford', lest his youth should do a disservice to the maturity of his views. Soon, however, with *The Seven Lamps of Architecture* and the *Stones of Venice*, Ruskin shed the cloak of anonymity and emerged as one of the principal literary figures of his day. Then came his defence of the Pre-Raphaelites, and a series of highly controversial lectures in Edinburgh on the Gothic Revival. By 1855 he had become the country's leading authority on painting. Yet despite the breadth of his intellectual interests and the pressures of his architectural studies, Ruskin was rarely far from the Alps in his imagination, and he maintained an intense interest in the physical, spiritual and aesthetic qualities of the great range. The result in 1856 was a volume that represented, as Arnold Lunn was later to put it, 'the first . . . rational apologetic of the mountain cult'. Hitherto, most obviously in the works of Wordsworth, Byron and Shelley, mountain beauty was celebrated by the poets as they dramatized their aesthetic responses to their surroundings. Now, in four hundred closely worded pages, Ruskin set out to analyse and rationalize the sublimity of the peaks.

Whatever we may think of his arguments, the book had a profound impact on his own generation. Ruskin was a conscious follower of Wordsworth in his apprehension of the spiritual quality of mountains. As he wrote: 'It will need no prolonged thought to convince us that in the hills the purposes of their Maker have indeed been accomplished in such measure as, through the sin and folly of men, He ever permits them to be accomplished.' At the same time Ruskin paved the way for later writers by pointing to the chief source of beauty in the Alps:

The best image which the world can give us of Paradise is in the
stage of the meadows, orchards, and cornfields of the sides of
a great Alp with its purple rocks and eternal snows above; this
excellence not being in any wise referable to feeling or individual preferences, but demonstrable by calm enumeration of the
number of lovely colours or rocks, the varied grouping of the
trees, and quantity of noble incidents in stream, crag, or cloud,
presented to the eye at any given moment.

Yet Ruskin's own poetic prose is as memorable and persuasive as his
attempts at demonstration, and it was its force that moved his contemporary readers. 'Mountains', he wrote in a passage often quoted
and anthologized, 'seem to have been built for the human race, as at
once their schools and cathedrals, full of treasures of illuminated
manuscript for the scholar, kindly in simple lessons for the worker,
quiet in pale cloister for the thinker, glorious in holiness for the wor-
shipper . . . these great cathedrals of the earth, with their gates of
rock, pavements of cloud, choirs of stream and stone, altars of
snow, and vaults of purple traversed by the continual stars.' Ruskin
in this volume of *Modern Painters* taught his generation to appreciate
the sublime in Nature – 'storms and sun rises, and the forests and
snows of the Alps'. It was not that such things were then unknown
to others. It was rather that Ruskin, in the words of his first biographer, 'impressively united the merely poetical sentiments of their
grandeur with something of a scientific curiosity as to their details
and conditions; he has brought us to linger among the mountains,
and to love them'. Leslie Stephen, too, remarked on this extraordinary talent:

His power of seeing the phenomenon vividly was as remarkable as his power, not always shared by scientific writers, of
making descriptions interesting . . . Many people had tried their
hand upon alpine descriptions since Saussure; but Ruskin's
chapters seemed to have the freshness of a new revelation. The
fourth volume of *Modern Painters* infected me and other early
members of the Alpine Club with an enthusiasm for which, I
hope, we are still grateful.

There is a certain irony in the fact that Ruskin closes the chapters which he would ultimately regard as the most valuable of his writings with a passage deploring the results of that very admiration he had done so much to encourage. Chamonix, he declared, was rapidly becoming 'a kind of Cremorne Gardens' – a fashionable Chelsea riverside promenade. The proposed railway round the head of Lake Geneva would ruin 'the one spot in Europe whose character and influence on the human mind are special'. The majority of those attracted – in ever-growing numbers – to the Alps would be those 'whose objects in travelling will be, first, to get as fast as possible from place to place, and, secondly, at every place where they arrive, to obtain the kind of accommodation and amusement to which they are accustomed in Paris, London, Brighton or Baden'.

The Alps, in short, were being vulgarized. And not only were they attracting those insensitive to 'certain truths and dignities to which we owe the founding of the Benedictine and Carthusian monasteries in the thin Alpine air', they were also appealing to those Englishmen – like Alfred Wills – 'in the habit of regarding mountains chiefly as places for gymnastic exercise'. The Alps, Ruskin later complained, 'which your own poets used to love so reverently, you look upon as soaped poles in a bear-garden, which you set yourselves to climb and slide down again, with "shrieks of delight"'. Once a sanctuary, they were becoming a playground, a term that Leslie Stephen would promote. It was appalling.

Chapter Three
'The English did it!'

'When we look at the chronicle of the "Golden Age" today, we have to admit it – the English did it!'

Herbert Maeder, *The Lure of the Mountains* (1971)

In 1857 an association was founded in London that would soon possess an influence and importance entirely out of proportion to its size. Its formation heralded the beginning of systematic mountaineering, the dominance of English climbers in the mountain playground, and the arrival of the sport's golden age. The following eight years were to see the conquest of the vast majority of the great alpine peaks, most of them by existing or future members of what was known simply as 'The Alpine Club'. It was an epoch that was to culminate in the ascent by Edward Whymper of the most striking and reputedly the most inaccessible of them all, the Matterhorn.

With the growth of modern sport and the formation of sporting associations in England, it was inevitable that, as mountaineering began to prosper in the late 1840s and early '50s, the idea of an alpine club would recommend itself to those Englishmen interested in the pursuit. Here men might meet their fellow enthusiasts, compare notes, discuss adventures, plan future expeditions and – in a high-minded age – contribute towards the advance of knowledge.

The club was the brainchild of William Matthews, the eldest of six sons of a prosperous Worcestershire land-agent, two of whom were also distinguished mountaineers. Born in 1828, Matthews was one of a generation of Cambridge men to further the cause of English alpinism. He first mooted the idea to the Reverend H.L.A. Hort, a fellow climber, in February 1857. It was more firmly seeded on the first ascent later that year of the 14,019-foot Finsteraarhorn, the highest peak in the Oberland. This Matthews conquered in the company of another leading mountaineer of the day, Thomas Stuart Kennedy. When Kennedy dined with the Matthews family that November, the matter was settled. The club's *raison d'être* was more fully discussed and a list of prospective members was drawn up. Membership, it was decided, should be by qualification approved by committee. It would take the form of completing some of the more difficult ascents, but contributions to alpine literature, science or art would also be acceptable. Meetings would be held in London, at first at suitable hotels or inns.

The inaugural meeting of the Alpine Club took place on 22 December 1857 – the year of the Indian Mutiny – at Ashley's Hotel in Covent Garden. With a nucleus comprising mountaineers such as Alfred Wills, Kennedy and Matthews, Professor Forbes and the redoubtable John Ball, within two years the club had a membership of one hundred and fifty. Matthew Arnold and Ruskin were early to join. So, too, was the publisher John Murray, son of Byron's publisher, who had written as well as published the original *Handbook*. According to the club, he owed his election to the fact that his 'Handbook on Switzerland had at that time contributed so much to our knowledge of the Alps that he was admitted as almost the sole authority on the subject'. Predominantly graduates of Oxford and Cambridge, most members also belonged to those professions that demanded primarily intellectual qualities: university dons, civil servants, lawyers, clergymen and diplomats. Many were leaders in their fields. They were an odd collection to find at the top of a French, Swiss or Tyrolese mountain, but perhaps these moving forces of the Victorian age were more in need of an antidote to the dynamic entrepreneurial world they had created than others.

The conquest of the Finsteraarhorn was one of several ascents that came early in the golden age of mountaineering, but for sheer insouciance Kennedy and Matthews's triumph was capped by Charles Barrington's ascent of the nearby Eiger.

Barrington was an all-round sportsman who had won the Irish Grand National on his horse *Sir Robert Peel*. He was not, however, a practised cragsman, and indeed in the summer of 1858 was on his first visit to Switzerland. Drawn to what had become the established climbing centre of Grindelwald, he set himself up at the Bear hotel – soon to become one of the temples of the Alpine Club – and surveyed the scene. His first thought was the Jungfrau. This was the peak that Forbes had climbed sixteen years previously, and which had given him a fright just short of the summit. Barrington, though, found it an easy climb, and was unimpressed. Remarking on this to two compatriots he met on returning to the Bear, he was advised to try the Eiger or the Matterhorn. Reluctant to undertake the trek south to the St Nicholas valley, Barrington chose the Jungfrau's neighbour, the 13,025-foot Eiger. Although this was slightly lower than the Jungfrau, its name was as forbidding as its tremendous north face. At the time, too, it was unclimbed. Amongst the locals its reputation was such that Barrington – his decision made – was abused by the families of his two guides for risking their lives.

The following evening Barrington's party set out and walked over the hill to the hotel at Wengern Alp, more or less at the Eiger's base. Here, according to Murray, in full view of the great peaks Byron had composed *Manfred*. Barrington's plan was to tackle the north-west face whose cliffs, in appearance precipitous, are in fact climbable. By 3.30 a.m. the next morning the party was on the slopes, duly equipped with a flag to claim the mountain's summit. Soon they ran into difficulties, confronted with an exceedingly steep, rocky incline. The guides declared the route impossible. Barrington wrote to his brother:

> So I went off about 300 or 400 yards over some smooth rocks to the part which was almost perpendicular. I then waved the flag for them to come on, and after five minutes they followed

and came up to me. They said it was impossible; I said: 'I will try.' So, with the rope coiled over my shoulders, I scrambled up, sticking like a cat to the rocks, which cut my fingers, and at last got up say fifty or sixty feet. I lowered the rope and the guides followed with its assistance.

Thereafter the going was rather easier, the guides more co-operative. By noon Barrington was proudly planting a flag on the Eiger's summit, and by early evening he had returned to the Wengern Alp hotel. There, everyone turned out to welcome them. 'The hotel proprietor had a large gun fired off, and I seemed for the evening to be a "lion". Thus ended', Barrington wrote, 'my first and only visit to Switzerland.'

If Barrington was something of a maverick, one of his fellow visitors at Grindelwald was at first glance a more conventional figure. Leslie Stephen was the grandson of the slavery abolitionist James Stephen. Born in London in 1832, he was given a strict Christian upbringing within the confines of what was known as the 'Clapham sect', his mother being the daughter of the leading south London evangelist John Venn. In 1840 the family moved to Brighton for the sake of the boy's health. Two years later, he was sent to Eton. Making poor progress, in 1848 he was removed to King's College, London. Eventually, in Michaelmas term 1850, he entered Trinity Hall, Cambridge, taking a scholarship in mathematics at the end of the year. In 1864 he was ordained, and became a Fellow of his college.

Stephen's fine, enquiring mind was matched by remarkable athletic prowess. A tall, lanky figure, at Cambridge he rowed with distinction, and ran sufficiently well to win the 1860 university mile in a time of 5 minutes 4 seconds. In 1855 a tour of the Bavarian Tyrol had introduced him to the Alps. Two years later, he made his first ascent of a major peak. By 1859 he was tackling the Blümlisalp cluster of peaks, amongst the most rugged in the Oberland. Here he conquered the rocky 12,900-foot Bietschhorn, not entirely helped by his guide:

I was rather out of training, and was conscious of a strong disposition in my legs to adopt independent lines of action, which could not be too severely reprehended. I felt rather nervous on commencing the snow arête [sharp ridge], and made a stumble nearly at the first step. Old Appener, emitting a fiendish chuckle, instantly gripped my coat-tails – with the benevolent intention, as I am willing to believe, of helping me, and not of steadying himself. If so, his design was better than his execution. He did not progress very rapidly, and whenever I made a longer step than usual, the effect of the manoeuvre was to jerk me suddenly into a sitting position on the ice. I denounced the absurdity of his actions, both in German and dumb-show, but as I only elicited more chuckles and a firmer grip on my coat-tails, I finally abandoned myself to my fate, and was truly thankful when, at the end of the arête, my equilibrium ceased to be affected by the chances of tumbling down a precipice on either side, or being lugged over backwards by a superannuated and inarticulate native.

Stephen was among the vanguard of recreational mountaineers: for him it was the adventure and challenge of mountaineering that constituted its real appeal. He once said simply of the Jungfrau Joch that it was 'a joch [pass] which cannot be climbed, so we have to do it'.

By contrast, Professor John Tyndall was little less than a throwback to Horace de Saussure, Louis Agassiz and Professor Forbes. Born in County Carlow in 1820, Tyndall came from a family that claimed descent from William Tyndale the martyr. His school gave a sufficient grounding in mathematics for him to be taken on as assistant on the Ordnance Survey of Ireland. This proved a useful background for progressing to one of the leading jobs of the age, that of railway engineer. His bent for the sciences, though, was such that by the age of thirty-three he was installed as professor of natural philosophy at the Royal Institution.

Chance then took Tyndall to the slate mines of North Wales, to examine the scientific problem of the cleavage of slate. A lecture he gave on the subject was attended by Professor T.H. Huxley, soon to become a great advocate of Darwinism. The biologist suggested that the crystalline structure of slate that Tyndall described might explain the nature of glacier ice outlined by Professor Forbes in *Travels Through the Alps*. Conferring together, Tyndall and Huxley agreed in

1857 to visit the Alps to investigate the matter. There was born Tyndall's remarkable passion for the heights, and a distinguished career as both alpinist and mountain writer. *The Glaciers of the Alps,* published in 1860, was to become the standard work on glaciology. This was also the year in which Tyndall made one of the first attempts on the Matterhorn, and the summer of which saw the first visit to the Alps – and to that mountain – of Edward Whymper himself.

Given the composition of the Alpine Club and the existing publications on alpine adventure by a number of its members, it was not surprising that the idea of a club publication began to be discussed. The club's first president, John Ball, thought it might add to the sense of community and common purpose within the association, forward its aims of bringing to a wider public outside its membership the fascination of alpine travel, and contribute to its coffers – a 'permanent place of meeting' had yet to be acquired. The idea was to produce an anthology of alpine adventure by a series of different hands, to be distinguished by the quality of the writing, the excitement of the tale – 'an account of some desperate excursion' – and the need 'rather to condense than extend' the narratives. It was also supposed that the collective resources of the club would provide the volume with 'a degree of excellence in the illustrations . . . that could not easily be attained if several writers had separately given their productions to the public'.

The result was a series to be known as *Peaks, Passes and Glaciers,* the first volume of which was published in 1859. If anything it exceeded expectations. With its woodcuts, maps and coloured plates, it was certainly well produced; it brought together the records of the extraordinary successes of its members, and it did so in a manner which was typically understated, yet effectively communicated the thrill of the alpine pioneers and the extraordinary country they were discovering. With contributions from amongst others Ball himself, the Reverend J.F. Hardy, E.S. Kennedy and John Tyndall, it comprised a roll-call of the leading alpinists of the day. Some of the tales were intensely dramatic. Here is Kennedy's 'A Night Adventure on the Britenstock', the 10,089-foot pyramid close to the St Gotthard pass:

At length, after a descent of two hours, during the whole of which our energies, both mental and bodily, were taxed to the utmost, we appeared to be not more than 600 feet above the upper part of the glacier where it was separated from the rocks by the usual bergschrund [a deep crevasse at the head of a glacier]. Many of my readers have, doubtless, crossed the Strahleck, and remember the famed descent of the Wall at the head of the Finsteraar glacier on that glorious pass. Let them imagine that Wall, variously estimated as it is at from 500 to 800 feet in height, about five times magnified in height, and greatly increased in difficulty, and they will have an idea of this face of the Britenstock. We were at this moment apparently in the position of the traveller at the top of the Strahleck Wall, but with this essential difference, that we had already made a descent of some 2,000 feet, and that the position beneath us was quite impracticable. It had been our intention to reach the glacier below us, and then to cross it diagonally in a north-westerly direction, so as to reach the lower extremity of the western lateral moraine. From the spot where we were standing, however, the wall of rock appeared to go sheer down to the ice; there was no mode of descent that we could possibly discover, and on neither hand could we discern foothold even for a chamois. I saw that there was nothing to be done where we were, and that it was impossible to remain much longer clinging to the slippery ledges of these precipitous rocks.

To the writer Donald Robertson it was 'a volume so fascinating, so inspiring a gospel of adventure and full, free life, that the call summoned to the hills an army of seekers after the promised gold'. The series stood alongside the individual works of de Saussure, Professor Forbes, Ball himself and Ruskin, as a set text of the Alps.

At the same time as English mountaineers were making names for themselves on the great alpine peaks, so too was beginning to develop an entirely different phenomenon. Far from serving the needs of the very fittest, far from utilizing the mountains as places for gymnastic exercise, this was the creation of the Alps to serve the needs of the sick. It was to influence the development of the whole region.

The natural springs in which the Alps abound had been prized since Roman times for their therapeutic qualities. They were supposed to cure ailments of the body and mind of almost every variety, from arthritis and heart disease to depression, infertility and gout. By the time of the Renaissance their popularity was such that – according to *Murray's Handbook* – no fewer than fifty treatises were published during the sixteenth century dealing with twenty-one different bathing resorts. St Moritz was already amongst the most famous, so too Leukerbad, Brieg, Masino, Pfafers and Tarasp; the reputation of Baden was such that 'Zürich ladies are said to have insisted on a covenant in their marriage settlements, that they should be taken there once a year'. Beyond the Swiss redoubt were resorts in the Dauphiné like Aix les Bains and Grenoble, Bad Gastein and Bad Ischl in the Tyrol, and Meran on the south side of the Brenner.

The development of the Alps from the 1760s onwards had seen these places flourish. This was particularly so in the Grisons, the easternmost canton of Switzerland, where – remarked the pioneer English tuberculosis practitioner Dr J. Burney Yeo – 'every third village is a "Kurort" and has its "Kurhaus", its "Kurliste", its "Kurzart", its "Kurmusik", and finally its "Kuristen", as those are termed who come to be cured'. Then, with the publication in 1861 of Mrs Henry Freshfield's account of a summer tour of the Grisons, it became necessary to book accommodation in places like St Moritz a year in advance.

Alongside this tradition, something altogether more novel was taking place. In an age in which the occurrence and transmission of disease was still little understood, doctors had noted certain medical phenomena from which they drew practical conclusions. The fact that scrofula rarely attacked fishermen led to the pioneering English sea-bathing infirmaries at the end of the eighteenth century. Similarly, in 1826, a Warwickshire doctor called George Boddington had noted that the prognosis for tuberculosis sufferers was much improved by exercise and fresh air. Although Boddington's ideas were more enthusiastically received in Germany than in England, the virtues of the outdoor life began to filter through the English medical profession. By the late 1840s, John Forbes was trumpeting the benefits of the Alps' clean air, fine weather and magnificent scenery as an antidote to the dirt and claustrophobia of England's fast-growing manufacturing cities. Then, in the following decade, the idea of the 'alpine' or 'air' cure was more properly established by the German-Swiss physician Alexander Spengler.

Spengler had first visited Davos, not far from St Moritz, in the summer of 1853, and described it as an 'unheard of and roadless collection of crude wooden chalets'. In this it differed little from the majority of other alpine villages at the time. Ten years previously, *Murray's Handbook* had found little to say about the village other than that 'The Rathaus was formerly decorated with more than thirty wolves' heads slain in the neighbourhood – a proof of the preva-lence of these animals.' In other respects, however, its inhabitants were blessed, for they appeared to be immune to a disease that was elsewhere commonplace and frequently fatal – tuberculosis. Not only were the villagers free from the complaint, but those who had contracted it elsewhere and then spent some time in Davos were quite often – almost miraculously – cured.

In due course Spengler concluded that the villagers' immunity was attributable to Davos's climate. Davos was one of a series of villages in the Grisons protected by some of the intervening mountain ranges from moist air coming up from Italy. In the normal 'season' between June and September, this created a climate which was remarkably warm and dry. Spengler accordingly began to advocate the alpine cure for diseases of the lung, tuberculosis in particular. Like many medical reformers – Boddington included – he was at first ridiculed, and it was another ten years before his perseverance began to have any impact on the bastions of medical opinion. When, in 1862, he published a full account of his findings in the German medical periodical *Deutsche Klinik*, a number of other practitioners took up the cudgels on his behalf, not least among them the English.

Tuberculosis was a common affliction throughout the British Isles. Like many infectious diseases, its spread was effectively promoted by the concentration of people in towns, and exacerbated there by the damp climate and the concentration of smoke from factories and homes alike. In the middle of the century it accounted for one death in six, whilst the duration of its symptoms amongst survivors spawned the all too apt description of tuberculosis as 'the most pauperizing of all diseases'. Spengler's work thus came to attract much attention in England.

The first sufferers from English shores were sent to Davos in the early 1860s, where they joined a couple of hundred Gemans, Austrians and Dutch. Soon an English doctor would remark of Davos that there 'meat when hung up does not putrefy, but is thus dried and best for use . . . nor do lungs rot in the living man'. In the Grisons, Sils-Maria, Pontresina and Arosa would in due course follow Davos and become what were known as 'cure-stations'. Further west in the Valais, Leysin and Montana would similarly become celebrated. Gradually, as the decade advanced, groups of English visitors began to appear in the Swiss mountain villages in increasing numbers. Their arrival marked the advent of a new chapter in the Alps.

Following the success of the first volume of *Peaks, Passes and Glaciers* in 1859, there was an immediate call for a sequel. With the enthusiasm for mountaineering at its height, there was plenty of material to fill it. Professor Tyndall had mastered one of the highest peaks of the Alps, the 14,780-foot Weisshorn, within striking distance of Zermatt and one of the most beautiful mountains in the Alps. J.C. Davies had climbed the nearby 14,757-foot Täschhorn, Thomas Stuart Kennedy had taken on and beaten the 14,295-foot Dent Blanche, a few miles west. D.C. McDonald and F.C. Grove had conquered the 13,684-foot Dent d'Hérens, to the west of the Matterhorn. Leslie Stephen had conquered the 12,021-foot Blümlisalphorn in the Bernese Oberland, the nearby 13,375-foot Great Schreckhorn, the 13,848-foot Zinal Rothorn close to Zermatt, and the 12,067-foot Monte della Disgrazia, one of the principal peaks in the Bregaglia mountains just across the border from the Bernina Alps in Canton Grisons. Potential contributors to the publication were accordingly approached, amongst them Tyndall for his account of the conquest of the Weisshorn, and Stephen for the Rothorn.

Stephen, though still only in his early thirties, had become a highly accomplished writer, and editor of the *Cornhill Magazine*, and was later to found the *Dictionary of National Biography*. He took the opportunity to deliver his piece at the winter meeting of the Alpine Club. Tyndall – the standard-bearer of scientific exploration of the Alps – happened to attend. There was much there to entertain Stephen's listeners: at M. Épinay's inn at Zinal, the accommodation was so limited that his companions were obliged to sleep in 'two cupboards opening out of the coffee-room, whilst I occupied a bed, which was the most conspicuous object of furniture in the coffee-room itself'; on the mountain the keen wind penetrated Stephen's coat 'as though it had been made of gossamer, pierced my skin, whistled merrily through my ribs, and, after chilling the internal organs, passed out the other side with unabated vigour'; one of the guides made so desperate an assault on a steep cliff that to support him 'in a few moments I was [myself] scrambling desperately upwards, forgetting in a moment the promptings of self-esteem which would generally induce me to refuse assistance and to preserve a workmanlike attitude'.

One cannot imagine that Tyndall enjoyed such levity, though perhaps he was, temporarily, mollified by Stephen's allusion to his passing the time in Zinal by turning 'a table of heights expressed in metres into feet, and thereby . . . richly contributing to the fund of amusement provided for scientific visitors who may have a taste for correcting arithmetical blunders'.

Having then described the final ascent, Stephen turned to its results:

'And what philosophical observations did you make?' will be the enquiry of one of those fanatics who, by a reasoning process to me utterly inscrutable, have somehow irrevocably associated alpine travelling with science. To them I answer, that the temperature was approximately (I had no thermometer) 212° (Fahrenheit) below freezing point. As for ozone, if any existed in the atmosphere, it was a greater fool than I take it for. As we had, unluckily, no barometer, I am unable to give the usual information as to the extent of our deviation from the correct altitude; but the Federal map fixes the height at 13,855 feet.

For Tyndall, by this time one of the best-known scientists of his day, this was too much. Taking it as a personal insult, he stormed out of the meeting, refused to have his account of the Weisshorn adventure published alongside Stephen's work in *Peaks, Passes and Glaciers*, and resigned from the club. The introduction to the original collection had suggested that 'the community of taste and feeling amongst those who in the life of the High Alps have shared the same enjoyments, the same labours, and the same dangers, constitutes a bond of sympathy stronger than many of those by which men are drawn into association'. If this was so, then Stephen and Tyndall's quarrel was nevertheless indicative of the schism within the club between those who climbed primarily for the challenge, and those who mountaineered for some higher scientific purpose. It was also suggestive of the ability of the new sport to engender great passions. If the squabble between Forbes and Agassiz had been a foretaste, this was the first falling out to result in a major alpine quarrel. A controversy that undoubtedly helped to publicize the Alps, it was by no means the last.

Like all the great mountaineers of the age, Professor Tyndall had been drawn to the Matterhorn by its majestic presence and its reputation for inaccessibility. He had paid his first visit there in 1860, forming part of a large party which was obliged to turn back two thousand feet from the summit. Returning the following year, the Professor was discouraged by his guide's reconnoitre. 'Herr, I have examined the mountain carefully', he was told, 'and find it more difficult and dangerous than I imagined . . .' Tyndall decided to abandon the quest. Yet in 1862 he was back, and secured the services of the Italian guide Jean-Antoine Carrel, Whymper's 'cock of the Val Tournanche'. From the village of Breuil on the southern side of the massif, Tyndall, Carrel and two other guides began their ascent on 25 July. Observing their progress with passionate interest and concern was Edward Whymper.

Whymper, born in 1840, was the son of a distinguished wood engraver, Josiah Whymper. Inheriting his father's talents both as a water-colour artist and engraver, following a private education he joined the family firm. This proved to be the entrée to the world in which he would make his name. The publisher William Longman, who was to succeed John Ball as president of the Alpine Club, had taken on the responsibility of publishing the second series of *Peaks, Passes and Glaciers* (the volume over which Tyndall and Leslie Stephen fell out). He needed someone to prepare illustrations of the Dauphiné mountains for this purpose. Whymper accepted Longman's commission, and travelled to the region in the summer of 1860 to make the initial sketches.

As it turned out, the young engraver was captivated less by the mountains' splendour than by the challenge of climbing. In the course of only three or four years he established a formidable reputation, with a series of virgin peaks and passes to his credit. This included two of the highest peaks in the Dauphiné, the 13,458-foot Barre des Écrins, and the 12,900-foot Mont Pelvoux. Yet he was drawn unfailingly and unceasingly to the Matterhorn, was very nearly killed when climbing alone on the mountain in 1862, and only succeeded – in the prelude to the tragedy – at his eighth attempt. Of Tyndall's assault he wrote: 'Everything seemed to favour it, and they set out on a fine morning in high spirits, leaving me tormented with envy and all uncharitableness. If they succeeded, they carried off the prize for which I had long been struggling; and if they failed there was no time to make another ascent.'

Happily for Whymper, Tyndall failed. He took a route which led him to the lower end of the summit ridge, and found himself unable to pass the deep notch between the lower and the higher end. On his return, Tyndall told Whymper that he had reached 'within a stone's throw of the summit', and admonished him 'to have nothing more to do with the mountain'. By this Whymper understood him to mean that he would not himself try again. The younger man took heart.

Whymper was back again the following year more fully equipped for his task, with luggage 'highly suggestive of housebreaking'. It included 'two ladders, each twelve feet long . . . and several coils of rope and numerous tools of suspicious appearance'. These caused him a good deal of trouble with the customs at Calais. The douaniers assumed there was something irregular about his possessions, the purpose of which he was obliged to explain in some detail. Eventually escaping from Calais rather the poorer for the experience, he reached Breuil and contacted Carrel with a view to him acting as his guide. An attempt was planned, but postponed because of poor weather. The party then commenced a tour of the mountain which took them in relatively easy stages around to Zermatt, returning after an absence of six days to Breuil. The area of the Val Tournanche, which constituted the southern approach to the Matterhorn, was, Whymper noted, much behind the times: 'The paths are as bad as, or worse than, they were in the time of de Saussure, and their inns are much inferior to those on the Swiss side. If it were otherwise there would be nothing to prevent the valley becoming one of the most popular and frequented of all the valleys in the Alps; but as it is, tourists who enter it seem to think only about how soon they can get out of it.'

The reconnoitre confirmed to Whymper the merits of continuing his campaign from Breuil. Accordingly, when the weather brightened he tried again. Soon, though, the party encountered loose newly fallen snow covering the older, harder beds. For Carrel, this almost spelled disaster:

He stepped on some snow which seemed firm and raised his axe to deliver a swinging blow, but just as it was at its highest the crust of the slope upon which he stood broke away and poured down in serpentine streams, leaving long bare strips, which glittered in the sun, for they were glassy ice. Carrel, with admirable readiness, flung himself back on to the rock off which he stepped, and was at once secured. He simply remarked, 'It is time we were tied up', and after he had tied up he went to work again as if nothing had happened.

It was a portent. Soon the party was caught in a terrible thunderstorm which brought with it snow lasting some twenty-six hours. When it finally stopped they recommenced their ascent, but after two hours they had managed only three hundred feet. Then the snow started again. Obliged to return to London by the end of the week, Whymper had to abandoned the attempt. Yet, defeated and disconsolate though he was, here – in his own words – was 'a gambler who loses each throw, only the more eager to have another try, to see if luck would change'. He returned to England 'ready to devise fresh combinations and to form new plans'.

With many of the peaks around the traditional climbing centres of Chamonix, Grindelwald and Zermatt now conquered, Whymper spent much of the season of 1864 in the Dauphiné, pursuing a campaign of almost unbroken success that included his first ascent of the Barre des Écrins. When he finally reached Zermatt he again found himself recalled to London, and was unable to return until the following year.

The programme he then set himself was, he later conceded, ambitious. 'It included all the great peaks which had not then been ascended.' Nevertheless, he conquered the 14,295-foot Dent Blanche in the Val d'Hérens, the highest 13,727-foot spire of the Grandes Jorasses above Chamonix, the neighbouring 13,523-foot Aiguille Verte and the 12,727-foot Ruinette. There remained the Matterhorn, the attempt on which brought him to Zermatt on 19 June. Here he established himself at Alexandre Seiler's Monte Rosa hotel, which by then rivalled Grindelwald's Bear as the Alpine Club's summer home.

His decision to establish his base at Zermatt indicated that he had abandoned the traditional south-western approach from Breuil, in favour of an assault on the eastern face. From Zermatt this looks extremely steep. In fact it is deceptive, its angle – as Whymper gradually came to appreciate – being no more than forty degrees. He also thought that the face might be less susceptible to the storms that he had frequently encountered on his way up from Breuil. His guides, however, were less convinced that the route was practicable, and Whymper therefore ascended the 11,393-foot Théodulhorn to prospect another route. This appeared to be feasible, and the party set out from Breuil early on 21 June 1865. After some four hours they found a place to rest adjoining a gully, and began unpacking food when – virtually without warning – they were caught in an avalanche:

> rocks, boulders and stones, big and little, dart round the corner eight hundred feet or so above us, fly with fearful fury against the opposite cliffs, rebound from them against the walls on our side, and descend . . . the men looked wildly around for protection, and, dropping the food, dashed under cover in all directions. The precious mutton was pitched on one side, the wine-bag was let fall, and its contents gushed out from the unclosed neck, while all four cowered under defending rocks . . .

It was an unfortunate, unsettling beginning, and by lunchtime there was a further check. They had intended to take the most direct path to the Hornligrat, the base of the Matterhorn's north-east ridge. There they would sleep before making the assault on the eastern face, but the route they had decided to use had been rendered impassable by the shrinking of a glacier. They were confronted instead by a short, steep wall of rock, which seemed unclimbable. Then, as the weather worsened, the men went into a huddle. They had had enough. 'Why don't you try to go up a mountain that *can* be ascended?' asked one. Another, Michel Croz, remarked that if they lingered on the Matterhorn he would be unable to accompany Whymper to the Mont Blanc chain, which the climber also had in his sights for the year. So Whymper acceded to the requests of his men, and the party retreated.

'I cannot but regret that the counsels of the guides prevailed,' commented Whymper famously six years later. 'If Croz had not uttered his well-intentioned words he might still have been living. He parted from us at Chamonix at the appointed time, but by a strange chance we met again at Zermatt three weeks later; and two days afterwards he perished before my eyes on the very mountain from which we turned away, at his advice.'

Up until the events of 14 July 1865, the Matterhorn had been – in Whymper's words – the last great alpine peak which remained unscaled. Its conquest in a sense signalled the end of the sport's golden age, when the great peaks had fallen to a group of mainly English amateurs. Yet it was the tragedy of the descent rather than the conquest of the peak that marked the end of the epoch. Hitherto, the adventures of the great climbers had been followed by the public as if they were sporting heroes. Here, though, was quite another tale. It was that of a nobleman, a clergyman and a young fellow just out of school with his whole life before him – not to mention a distinguished guide – risking and losing their lives in a suicidally dangerous activity for the sake of little more than personal glory. To a serious-minded age this amounted to scandal. The *Edinburgh Review* asked: 'Has a man a right to expose his life, and the lives of others, for an object of no earthly value, either to himself or his fellow creatures? If life is lost in the adventure, how little does the moral guilt differ from that of suicide or murder?'

The story was headline news throughout Europe, the Queen herself noting in her diary, 'four [*sic*] poor Englishmen including a brother of Lord Queensberry have lost their lives in Switzerland, descending over a dangerous place from the Matterhorn and falling over a precipice.' Letters followed to the press expressive of astonishment, alarm, condemnation and – occasionally – defence. Charles Dickens himself berated the Alpine Club as the 'society for the scaling of such heights as the Schreckhorn, the Eiger, and the Matterhorn [which] contributed about as much to the advancement of science as would a club of young gentlemen who should undertake to bestride all the weathercocks of all the cathedral spires of the United Kingdom'. In modern terms it was a public relations disaster. W.A.B. Coolidge was later to write: 'There was a sort of palsy fell on the good cause, particularly among English climbers. Few in number, all knowing each other personally, shunning the public as far as possible, they went about under a sort of dark shade, looked on with a scarcely disguised contempt by the world of ordinary travellers.'

The sport's age of innocence was over. Its enthusiasts could no longer reckon to indulge themselves without being called to more or less public account. Later, Arnold Lunn would take the robust view that the Alpine Club's efforts to promote mountaineering had been positively aided by the Matterhorn accident, 'which did much to popularize the amusement, and which only needed the advertisement of a little hostile criticism'. At the time, though, it certainly seemed as if – in thoroughly unhappy circumstances – the Alps had come of age.

The Elixir of Life

'The Alps . . . the elixir of life, a revelation, a religion . . .'
Frederic Harrison, *My Alpine Jubilee* (1907)

Chapter Four

The Magician's Wand

'When Queen Victoria came to the throne . . . a return trip by diligence to Switzerland via the Rhine had cost £36 and taken sixty-six days. It can now be accomplished in two weeks for £9. Since Thomas Cook's first excursion train it is as if a magician's wand had been passed over the face of the globe.'

The Excursionist, June 1897

In the course of the trip that was to culminate in his ascent of the Zinal Rothorn Leslie Stephen reflected on how remote was the immediate locale of that great peak. In a glade close to the village of Gruben in the Valais, taking the opportunity to admire the 14,780-foot Weisshorn, often regarded as the most beautiful peak in the Alps, he remarked, 'Nowhere have I seen a more delicate combination of mountain massiveness, with soaring and delicately carved pinnacles pushed to the verge of extravagance.'

The perspective was an unusual one, for the normal view of the peak from the Riffel above Zermatt was among the best known in the Alps. The Riffel, however, was crowded; here in the Turtman valley, no one shared Stephen's wonder other than a group of peasants. They were standing round a small chalet in the company of a herd of cows, 'a priest in tattered garments sprinkling [the animals] with holy water'. Stephen's party was welcomed by the locals

much as we might have been received in the least frequented of European districts . . . We seemed to have stepped into the

Middle Ages, though I fancied that some shade of annoyance showed itself on the faces of the party, as of men surprised in a rather superstitious observance. Perhaps they had a dim impression that we might be smiling in our sleeves, and knew that beyond their mountain world were sometimes to be seen daring sceptics, who doubted the efficacy of holy water as a remedy for rinder-pest.

In these circumstances Stephen found it hard to remember that 'he was within a short walk of the main route and Mr Cook's tourists'. Yet so he was. For, remote though much of the Alps still remained, by the time of Stephen's ascent of the Rothorn and Whymper's of the Matterhorn, the age of the package tour had arrived.

The creator of what was to become the most important industry in the Alps was then in his mid-fifties. Born in 1808, Cook was the son of a Derbyshire farm labourer. He left school at the age of ten to become a gardener's boy, wood-turner and, in due course, printer, before creating virtually single-handed the industry he called 'excursionism'. Of medium height, dark complexion and slight build, Cook – in the words of an early biographer – had 'the black piercing eyes of the fanatic'. The driving-force of his personality lay in his Christianity, his business career being paralleled by a vocation as an observing Baptist. At his Sunday school he became scholar, teacher, then superintendent. By the age of twenty he was a village missionary, by his thirties a leading light in the Midlands temperance movement, aptly described by the company's historian as 'a secular expression of the Non-conformist religious experience'.

It was then that a happy – he would say, miraculous – conjunction of his two careers occurred. His business by 1841 was the printing and publication of temperance tracts. By then he was married, and had settled in the Leicestershire town of Market Harborough. Setting out to walk to the county town on 9 June of that year, he had a vision. He was, as he later wrote, almost half-way along the road, when 'a thought flashed through my brain – what a glorious thing it would be if the newly developed powers of railways and locomotives could be made subservient for the cause of temperance'. It was his belief that temperance was as likely to be achieved by the provision of entertaining – and preferably uplifting – alternatives as by mere exhortations on the evils of drink. An excursion, Cook wrote,

> provides food for the mind; it contributes to the strength and enjoyment of the intellect; it helps pull men out of the mire and pollution of old corrupt customs; it promotes a feeling of universal brotherhood; it accelerates the march of peace and virtue, and love; – it also contributes to the health of the body, by a relaxation from the toil and the invigoration of the physical powers.

With all these advantages it seemed inevitable that the scheme should succeed, although the first excursion on 5 July 1841 incorporated other important elements. The large numbers of people whom Cook transported (some five hundred between Leicester and Loughborough) enabled him to charge less than a shilling, well below the going rate. Entertainment was contrived at the destination in the form of a teetotal lunch of bread and ham. A temperance rally followed, a band played, and the local dignitaries made speeches. Finally, Cook himself made all the arrangements, personally conducting the outing.

From the start his business prospered. By 1845 he was conducting tours from Leicester to Liverpool and Snowdonia, the following year to Scotland; in 1851 he took 165,000 visitors to the Great Exhibition; in 1855 came his first expedition to the Continent. This provided him with invaluable experience of Continental railway porters ('tobacco or onion-scented, blue frocked varlets'), the tiresome weighing of luggage ('bear-garden scenes of rude and rugged conduct, vociferation and vulgar grossness'), and the curious custom of penning passengers in waiting-rooms until a few minutes before the train was ready to depart, leading to a 'tumultuous and disorderly rush' for the carriages, which left women and children behind.

So equipped, Cook prepared himself and his customers for the delights of the mountain scenery which Wordsworth, Byron and Ruskin had done so much to inculcate. His first tour, from 26 June to 15 July 1863, took a party of sixty to Geneva and the Mont Blanc region. Such was the success of this and subsequent trips that season that Cook declared that they marked 'a new epoch in our labours and adventures . . . that which took *teens* of years in Scotland seems to have been acquired at a single bound in Switzerland, where "Cook's Tours" already rank among the institutions of the Confederation'. One of his earliest customers on a party to Geneva wrote: 'It really is a miracle. Everything is organized, everything is catered for, one does not have to bother oneself with anything at all, neither timings, nor luggage, nor hotels. And, do you know, I have met the man who arranges it all. I have even said "Good morning" to him. He is named Mister Cook and they say he is a Saint!'

It was the beginning of a remarkable career, to which this story will return.

If it was true that missionary zeal lay behind Cook and his alpine tours, it was also true that they owed much to the iron horse and the iron road. At first, the railway system to and within the Alps was limited. It penetrated some of the principal alpine valleys, notably the Isère, the Rhône, the Aare and the Rhine, but there were few tributary or distributary lines. On Cook's inaugural Swiss tour, Geneva was reached by rail, Chamonix by diligence, Martigny by mule. As the 1860s progressed, however, so too did the railway network: partly as an extension of the existing system by means of the great alpine tunnels, partly through the creation of a series of entirely new mountain railways. Both were manifested – indeed pioneered – at Mont Cenis.

Linking the Italian province of Piedmont with Savoy and thence Geneva, this pass had been used by Charlemagne's army in the ninth century. Napoleon recognized its strategic importance, and on his orders a great new road was forged between 1803 and 1810. As Whymper remarked on a visit more than fifty years later, this 'changed the rough path into one of the finest highways in Europe, mounting in grand curves and by uniform grades, and rendered the trot possible throughout its entire distance'. It was a carriage-way, though, rather than a railway, and as a high alpine pass it could be paid only the guarded compliment of being 'one of the most practicable in winter time'. Even the enthusiast Whymper was obliged to notice the perils of the descent:

> The horses, reduced in number to three, or perhaps two, were the sturdiest and most sure of foot, and they raced down with the precision of old stagers. Woe to the diligence if they stumbled! So thought the conductor, who screwed down the brakes as the corners were approached. The horses, held well in hand, leant inward as the top-heavy vehicle, so suddenly checked, heeled almost over; but in another moment the brake was released and again they swept down, urged onward by the whip, 'hoi' and 'ha' of the driver.

Yet the days of the great highway – or at least its carriages – were numbered. As Whymper noted on his return in 1869, 'All this is changed. The Victor Emmanuel railway [named after one of the scheme's backers, King Victor-Emmanuel of Sardinia] superseded a considerable portion of Napoleon's road, and the "Fell" railway the rest, while the great tunnel in the Alps will soon bring about another change.'

The problem the Fell railway tackled was simple. At the time, even a most modest gradient, say 1 in 80, greatly slowed the pace of a normal train drawn by an ordinary locomotive. How then, Whymper questioned, 'is a train to be taken up an incline that is *six* times as steep?' – the incline to be traversed if the Fréjus pass below Mont Cenis was to be surmounted. This had long puzzled engineers in England and the Alps alike, various schemes being advanced to solve the problem. One of these was the brainchild of Charles Vignolles, responsible for building the first railway in western Switzerland. Vignolles's idea was for a third rail to be placed between the two normal ones forming the track, raised slightly above them. In addition to the usual vertical driving wheels, the locomotives were to carry two pairs of horizontal driving wheels to grasp this rail. The adhesion of the machine to the track, critical for both ascent and descent, would thus be vastly increased.

Pioneered on the Cromford and High Peak line in Derbyshire, this development was put into practice on Mont Cenis by an entrepeneur named John Barraclough Fell. Running south from St Michel, the small settlement towards the southern end of the Maurienne valley, the line rose some four and a half thousand feet to the Fréjus pass before falling in a much shorter distance over five thousand feet, the gradients at their steepest being 1 in 12. Whymper called it a marvel, demonstrating as it did the ability of the railway to tackle severe gradients. Its drivers, who were all English, were less sure. 'Yes mister, they told us as how the line was very steep, but they didn't say that the engine would be on one curve, when the fourgon [good's van] was on another, and the carriages was on a third. The gradients, too, mister, they say they are one in twelve, but I think they are one in *ten, at the least*, and they didn't say how we was to come down them in that snakewise fashion.'

Whymper was nevertheless right in thinking that the great tunnel being bored to carry a new railway under Mont Cenis would bring about further change. The intention was that the Fell railway should close once the tunnel was open. The Mont Cenis would then be the first of the major alpine tunnels to be completed, the pioneer of a series of engineering feats in the years leading up to the Great War that would revolutionize trans-alpine travel. The line as a whole was built partly with English capital, and engineered by Thomas Brassey, who had been responsible for the Hauenstein tunnel at Olten. The tunnel itself was to run from Modane, a few miles further up the Maurienne valley from St Michel, to the village of Bardonecchia. In boring the tunnel, Brassey and the French engineer Germain Someiller, over a fourteen-year period, developed techniques critical to the success of the subsequent Arlberg, Gotthard, Simplon and Lötschberg routes. These included dynamite rock-blasting, a compressed air drill that made it possible to bore fifteen feet a day, and a ventilation system using air from water-powered fans in which exhaust was drawn from a duct at the top of the tunnel.

There were great celebrations when the tunnel was finally opened – and the Fell railway closed – in 1871. Now there was an iron road that could take travellers and goods straight from Paris to Turin. The barrier that the Alps had so long represented to the speedy passage of people in large numbers had finally been broached.

Whymper visited the works on Mont Cenis four years after the Matterhorn accident. By then he was a changed man. In the immediate aftermath of the tragedy he was obliged to concern himself with the inquest and the controversy that followed, not least with the suggestion that the elder Taugwalder had cut the rope between himself and the unfortunate Hadow, or – foreseeing an accident – had deliberately chosen the weaker line. Thereafter, Whymper found himself in the paradoxical position of being the world's most famous – or notorious – mountaineer, whose alpine enthusiasms were now curtailed. Soon he would write, 'I did not go out wishing to make ascents or passes, having as you may suppose not quite so much appetite for this sort of thing as I had.' Though apparently not greatly moved by the fate of his companions on the Matterhorn, he was to some extent unnerved, and his climbing in the Alps virtually ceased. He made two visits to Greenland, one in 1867, the other in 1872, and later turned his attention to the Andes of Ecuador. In 1888 he made the first ascent of the 20,498-foot Chimborazo and six other peaks of more than 15,000 feet, this exploit inspiring *Travels Among the Great Andes*, published in 1892. He had become a mountaineering lecturer and writer rather than an active mountaineer, a symbol rather than an adventurer.

The ascent of the Matterhorn, the last of the major alpine peaks to be conquered, marked a turning-point. The achievement, marred by catastrophe as it was, raised the question as to what alpinists should do next. There were even those who considered that the Alpine Club should be wound up, its work having been done. By a curious coincidence, however, on the very day of the tragedy, the beginnings of an answer were being articulated on Mont Blanc. It was there that a party also including a father and son – Frank and Horace Walker – together with G. Matthews and A.W. Moore were conquering the massif from the southern side.

It was natural enough that in his pursuit of the Matterhorn Whymper should have spent years investigating the easiest route up the mountain, or at least the line of least resistance. This, after all, had been the strategy by which the other great peaks had been conquered. Yet if the appeal of mountaineering lay in its challenge to the determination, strength, courage and ingenuity of the climbers, was it not also the case that pleasure lay in overcoming the difficulties posed by more difficult routes to peaks that had already been conquered? So thought the Walkers. Ascending Mont Blanc by what had become the established route from Chamonix or St Gervais might be all very well for the likes of Albert Smith, but it was neither novel nor – in decent conditions – especially challenging. The approach from the southern, Italian side of the massif facing the Aosta valley, where the summit lies above the broken Brenva glacier, was another matter. Spectators here, as A.W. Moore would put it in an account published in the 1865 edition of the *Alpine Journal*, were 'overwhelmed by its beauty and by the uncompromising steepness of its glaciers and of the rock walls and spires which towered above them. Dark red granite pillars soar up like petrified flame on each side of the gaps through which fantastically crevassed glaciers pour down into the valley.' Moore, a clerk in the India Office, and later to become Lord Randolph Churchill's private secretary, relates an incident from what has been described as one of the finest alpine tales:

> On most arêtes, however narrow the actual crest may be, it is generally possible to get a certain amount of support by driving the pole into the slope below on either side. But this was not the case here. We were on the top of a wall, the ice on the right side falling vertically (I use the word advisedly), and on the left very nearly so. On neither side was it possible to obtain the slightest hold with the alpenstock. I believe also that an arête of pure ice is more often encountered in description than in reality, that term generally being applied to hard snow.

But here, for once, we had the genuine article, blue ice without a speck of snow on it. The space for walking was, at first, about the breadth of the top of an ordinary wall, in which Jakob [one of the guides] cut holes for the feet. Being last in the line I could see little of what was coming until I was close upon it, and was therefore considerably startled on seeing the men in front suddenly abandon the upright position, which, in spite of the insecurity of the steps and the difficulty of preserving the balance, had been hitherto maintained, and sit down *à cheval* [as one rides a horse]. The ridge had narrowed to a knife edge, and for a few yards it was utterly impossible to advance in any other way . . . I worked myself along with my hands in an attitude safer, perhaps, but considerably more uncomfortable, and, as I went, could not help occasionally speculating, with an odd feeling of amusement, as to what would be the result if any of the party should chance to step over on either side, – what the rest would do, – whether throw themselves over the other side or not, – and if so, what would happen then. Fortunately the occasion for the solution of this curious problem did not arise.

Given the increasing paucity of virgin peaks, the opening up of the Brenva by Moore, Matthews and the Walkers showed that challenge still abounded in the Alps. Charles Hudson, who died on the Matterhorn, had been among the idea's first proponents, publishing a volume with E.S. Kennedy in 1856 on more difficult mountain routes, called *Where There's a Will There's a Way*. Soon Leslie Stephen's adversary Professor Tyndall would follow. Incapacitated by the refusal of Zermatt guides to tackle the Matterhorn in the aftermath of the 1865 accident, in 1868 he made the first crossing of the mountain from Breuil to Zermatt, the route so long championed by the guide J.A. Carrel. Then came A.F. Mummery, the greatest of the climbers of his age, who made the first ascent of the north-western Z'mutt Ridge of the mountain. The allure of the mountains remained undiminished, as the French writer Théophile Gautier, who had come across a triumphant Reverend J.M. Elliot in Zermatt, recorded:

A tall young man, strong and thin, dressed in brown corduroy, with gaiters up to the knees, a soft felt hat pulled down over his eyes, looking a perfect gentleman in spite of the unavoidable carelessness of his clothes. He was a member of the Alpine Club and had just successfully ascended the Matterhorn . . . His guides were walking behind him with their ropes coiled around their shoulders, holding their axes, their iron-spiked poles and all that was required to tackle so wild a peak. These three resolute sunburnt faces were resplendent with the joy of their triumph over great difficulties . . . The guides entered the hotel and the Englishman remained for a few moments on its threshold, leaning against the wall with complete unconcern, looking as if he was just coming from his club in Pall Mall . . . While watching this handsome youth, probably rich and certainly used to comfort and refinement, who had just been risking his life in a useless dangerous enterprise, we thought of the resistless passion which drives men to undertake terrific scrambles. No example can deter them. When going up towards the Matterhorn, this young man had certainly seen the graves of his three countrymen in the Zermatt churchyard. But a peak can exercise the same irresistible power of attraction as an abyss.

During the summer of 1868 Queen Victoria made her first trip to the Alps. Still in deepest mourning for the Prince Consort, she was persuaded of the virtues of the trip by her advisers and her doctors who were alarmed by her continued withdrawal from society and her unrelenting commitment to the affairs of state. Shocked though she had been by the Matterhorn affair, she remembered Albert's love of alpine scenery, and eventually conceded the therapeutic qualities of the scheme.

Her party travelled incognito, the Queen herself being styled the 'Countess of Kent'. Arriving at the beginning of August, they settled in Lucerne at the Pension Wallis. Impressed, Victoria recorded in her diary: 'What am I to say of the glorious scenery of Switzerland; the view from this Hse wh. is *vy high* is most wonderfully beautiful with the lake – Pilatus, the Righi &c – & I can *hardly* believe my eyes – when I look at it! It seems like a painting or decoration – a *dream*!' The Queen was eventually persuaded to venture as far as the peak of Mount Pilatus. This she did by pony, accompanied by her 'highland attendants'. These included the redoubtable John Brown, who allegedly outdistanced the local porters on the climb. The holiday could not of course be kept a secret for ever, and the Queen's stamp of approval provided a further incentive for her subjects to visit the Alps.

As might be supposed, English visitors were increasingly drawn from a class far removed from the Queen herself. This was a process that had begun a generation earlier, but was hastened by the advent of Thomas Cook's tours. Partly a consequence of the awareness of alpine pleasures that the impresario and conqueror of Mont Blanc, Albert Smith, had done much to create amongst the middle classes, it was also a consequence of cost. The least prosperous of Cook's alpine excursionists had an income in the order of £300 a year. When the Queen had come to the throne it would have cost more than a tenth of that to return to Switzerland via the Rhine by carriage. It would also have taken more than a month. Now the whole trip could be accomplished in two weeks at a cost of £9. A wild extravagance had become entirely practicable. As a result the Alps began to attract not only the leading men of the day – aristocrats, scientists, artists, mountaineers, the avant-garde – but also ordinary holidaymakers. According to Cook himself they were 'clergymen, physicians, bankers, civil engineers, merchants, tradesmen, manufacturers, and professional gentlemen' – the middle class.

The new arrivals were not universally welcomed by the cognoscenti, and Leslie Stephen was far from alone in his desire that the Alps should remain an upper-middle class preserve. Henry James, a little later, would write that the new tourists were 'rarely, to judge by their faces and talk, children of light to any eminent degree'. From these elevated perspectives, the issue was moreover not one simply of quality but of quantity. Cook wrote on his first alpine trip that he could 'see no reason why a hundred may not travel together as easily as a dozen, and I guess that the day is not distant when a Centurion's corps may march through some of these Alpine passes, as the first Napoleon crossed the Alps with his grand army.'

Cook, himself soon to be dubbed 'the Napoleon of Excursions', was right. Within a few years he would be taking not dozens or hundreds but – within the four months that was then regarded as the season – thousands on his trips. Soon Switzerland would enjoy the greatest season ever with 'universal crowding'. The Anglicization of the Alps, already proceeding before Cook's arrival, gathered pace. The tourists' demands brought to the snow-line – in the words of a guidebook – those 'cardinal British institutions – tea, tubs, sanitary appliances, lawn tennis and churches'. More practically it led to a boom in hotel-building, the gradual opening up of Stephen's sequestered valleys, and the provision of facilities for travel of every nature.

There were hiccups. The growth of tourism so agreeable to the hoteliers, railway companies and mountain guides was always vulnerable to the vagaries of Continental politics. The year 1860 had seen a crisis over the French annexation of Savoy, a dubious plebiscite consigning the dukedom to Napoleon III, despite the intervention of Queen Victoria herself. Napoleon in effect agreed to accept Cavour's unification of Northern Italy in exchange for Nice and Savoy. The troubles surrounding unification were then at their height, resolution being reached in 1861 with the summoning of the first Italian parliament in Turin.

This was all fairly small beer by comparison with the Franco-Prussian War of 1870–1. Its beginning interrupted the Passion Play at Oberammergau – including the visit by one of Cook's first parties to the event. At once the spectators – and tourists throughout the Alps – panicked and returned home *en masse*, leaving the resorts deserted. The season was ruined.

It was perhaps as a consequence of the truncation of the 1870 season that 1871 saw the publication of an unusual number of alpine books, a product of their authors' enforced leisure. The most enduring and famous of these were to be Leslie Stephen's *The Playground of Europe*, Professor Tyndall's *Hours of Exercise* and Whymper's *Scrambles Amongst the Alps*.

In the previous thirty years a number of important and influential alpine books had been published, ranging from Professor Forbes's *Travels Through the Alps of Savoy* to Alfred Wills's *Wanderings Among the High Alps* and the Alpine Club's *Peaks, Passes and Glaciers*. These had varying qualities, but they were ultimately workmanlike accounts. They instructed and to an extent they entertained, but they were not strictly literature in the highest sense of the word. At a glance, much the same might be said of the works of Whymper, Tyndall and Stephen. Although Stephen was himself, in the phrase of the time, a man of letters, neither he nor his fellow authors had great literary ambitions. Yet in each case the writer's mountain experiences transmuted his intentions and led him to create something greater than he had intended.

Whymper's *Scrambles Amongst the Alps*, which remains the most famous of all mountaineering books, was snapped up on publication, and translated into all the major European languages. Perhaps judiciously, Whymper had kept his audience waiting some time for the full story of the Matterhorn tragedy while he wrote and rewrote the volume.

It was Whymper's first book, and his handling of the material is at times uncertain. Moreover the passages about the Fell railway early in the volume mar the unity and coherence of a narrative which in other respects constitutes a single-minded account of the long process by which he conquered the Matterhorn, culminating in the catastrophe of the descent. Nevertheless, the book soon became a classic, for it captured the pioneering quality of the mountaineers of Whymper's generation, gave a sense of the remoteness of the Alps even after the arrival of the railways, and provided a powerful portrait of Whymper himself as a driven man, relentlessly overcoming the obstacles – human and otherwise – that lay in his path. It is difficult to like the man who so portrays himself. It is equally difficult not to respect his dedication and his courage. There are episodes and anecdotes that stand alone – the fall when climbing alone on the Matterhorn which nearly cost the author his life; the storm on the Col du Lion; and – most striking of all – Reynaud's jump on the descent from the Col de Pilatte, the highest pass in the Dauphiné.

Having successfully crossed the Col, Whymper's party was confronted by a chasm that had to be jumped. It was, as Whymper wrote, a leap of only fifteen or sixteen feet down, forwards seven or eight feet. 'That is not much you will say. It was not much, it was not the quantity but the quality of the jump which gave it its particular flavour. You had to hit a narrow ridge of ice. If that was passed, it seemed as if you might roll down for ever and ever. If it was not attained you dropped into the crevasse below.' Monsieur Reynaud was the local travel agent, perhaps not best equipped physically or mentally for the adventure. The last to attempt the jump, he made his reluctance to do so very clear:

> He came to the edge and made declarations. I do not believe that he was a whit more reluctant to pass the place than we others, but he was infinitely more demonstrative: in a word, he was French. He wrung his hands: 'Oh what a diable of a place!' 'It is nothing Reynaud,' I said, 'it is nothing.' 'Jump!' cried the others, 'jump.' But he turned round, as far as one can do such a thing in an ice-step, and covered his face with his hands, ejaculating, 'Upon my word, it is not possible. No, no, no! It is not possible.'
>
> How he came over I do not know. We saw a toe . . . we saw Reynaud, a flying body, coming down as if taking a header into water, with arms and legs all abroad, his leg of mutton flying in the air, his baton escaped from his grasp; and then we heard a thud as if a bundle of carpets had been pitched out of a window. When set upon his feet he was a sorry spectacle: his head was a great snowball, brandy was trickling out of one side of the knapsack, Chartreuse out of the other. We bemoaned its loss, but we roared with laughter.

Always, though, these episodes are part of the greater story that we know will culminate in the writer's final attempt on the mountain. As Arnold Lunn wrote: 'There is no book which has sent more climbers to the Alps ... the book has the genuine ring of Alpine romance. Its pages are full of those contrasts that are the stuff of our mountain quest, the tragic irony that a Greek mind would have appreciated. The closing scenes in the great drama of the Matterhorn move to their appointed climax with the dignity of some of the most majestic passages in the Old Testament.'

Tyndall's *Hours of Exercise* enjoyed much the same contemporary popularity as *Scrambles*. Fragmentary in form, it was drawn together from a series of papers written over ten years. As such it had few apparent pretensions to the coherent drama of *Scrambles*, and might be said to comprise no more than a series of anecdotes. Tyndall, however, was a more evocative writer than Whymper. Here is the Matterhorn:

> The alternations of sun and frost have made wondrous havoc on the Southern face of the Matterhorn; but they have left brown-red masses of the most imposing magnitude behind – pillars, and towers, and splintered obelisks, grand in their hoarseness – savage, but still softened by the colouring of age. The mountain is a gigantic ruin; but its former masonry will doubtless bear the shocks of another aeon.

Or the ascent of the Eiger:

> No trace of cloud was visible in the heavens, which were soon broadcast with stars. Those low down twinkled with exhilarating vivacity, many of them flashing lights of different colours. When an opera glass was pointed to such a star, and shaken, the line of light described by the image of the star resolved itself into a string of richly coloured beads: rubies and emeralds hung together on the same curve. The dark intervals between the beads corresponded to the moments of extinction of the star. Over the summit of the Wetterhorn the Pleiades hung like a diadem, while at intervals a solitary meteor shot across the sky.

Yet underlying both fine descriptive passages and dramatic narratives lies the more profound coherence that Tyndall himself claimed for the book, its quality of illustrating 'the mode in which a lover of natural knowledge and natural scenery chooses to spend his life'. Whymper's imagination was limited and he was a man of little culture. As Claire Engel writes in her history of alpine mountaineering, 'He never meditated about mountains; he did not try to peer into their timeless past or their future. Their geology interested him only in one respect: if the rocks were rotten, then the stones were likely to fall.' By contrast, Tyndall found moral and spiritual uplift in the mountain scenery:

> There is assuredly morality in the oxygen of the mountains, as there is immorality in the miasma of a marsh, and a higher power than mere brute force lies latent in Alpine mutton. We are recognizing more and more the influence of physical elements in the conduct of life, for when the blood flows in a purer current, the heart is capable of a higher glow. Spirit and matter are inter-twined; the Alps improve us totally, and we return from their precipices wiser as well as stronger men.

Inconceivable in Whymper, this response was certainly one which was shared by Stephen. Like *Hours of Exercise*, Stephen's *The Playground of Europe* was a collection of papers and speeches put together over a considerable period with, yet, an underlying theme. Stephen had married – married indeed William Thackeray's daughter – in 1867, and thereafter much restricted his mountaineering. As a consequence the volume, with its various 'additions and alterations' to previously published material, in a sense constituted the writer's farewell to the Alps. Stephen was also Whymper's superior as a prose-painter of mountain scenery, his writing having a uniform excellence unmatched anywhere by Whymper. And there is in Stephen a combination of adventure with wit, charm and intelligence. For his contemporaries, though, Stephen's chief achievement in the book, in the aftermath of the Matterhorn tragedy, was to make mountaineering respectable once again. As his great successor Geoffrey Winthrop Young would remark, Stephen showed that it was 'not a series of foolhardy pranks, but a laborious, hardy and ennobling pursuit'. Stephen wrote:

I will not undertake to sum up the conclusions which might be drawn from these rather desultory remarks. My readers – for I may assume that my readers are mountain-lovers – will agree that the love of mountains is intimately connected with all that is noblest in human nature. If so formal a demonstration of that truth be not possible, our faith in it will not be less firm, and all the more meritorious. The true faith in these matters is not indeed a bigoted or exclusive creed. I love everything in the shape of a mountain from Mont Blanc down to Hampstead Hill, but I also have regard for the Fen Country and the flats of Holland. Mountain scenery is the antithesis not so much of the plains as the commonplace. Its charm lies in its vigorous originality; and if political philosophers speak the truth, which I admit to be an exceedingly doubtful proposition, the great danger of our modern times lies in the loss of that quality. One man, so it is said, grows more like another; national costumes die out before monotonous black hats and coats; we all read the same newspapers, talk the same twaddle, are bound by the same laws of propriety, and are submitting to a uniform imposition of dull respectability . . . The Alps, as yet, remain. They are places where we may escape from ourselves and from our neighbours. There we can breathe air that has not passed through a million pairs of lungs; and drink water in which the acutest philosophers cannot discover the germs of indescribable disease. There the blessed fields are in no danger of being 'huzzed and mazed with the devil's own team'.

Not only do these three books merit the title of literature, but they were the exceptions – English exceptions – to the rule. As Claire Engel was later to put it, 'Few mountain classics have been written by continental writers . . . England is practically the one country where this blending of literary skill with the description of climbs has led to constantly felicitous results.'

Chapter Five

Wider Still and Wider

'Alpine Club members conquered the Alps in a leisurely but confident way ... their enjoyment, they freely admitted, was the main reason for the expenditure of so much energy for so little visible result; their observation was the vestigial remnant of their scientific inheritance; and the almost proselyte fervour with which they acclaimed the virtues of their new pastime sprang from national pride that the last outposts of Europe were falling to the British.'

Gavin de Beer, *Alps and Men* (1932)

It was in the last quarter of the nineteenth century that the ethos of empire fully gripped the British people. In opposition to the imperialist ambitions of France and the newly unified Italy and Germany, the 1870s were to see the British acquisition of a major shareholding in the Suez Canal, the Queen's assumption of the title Empress of India, the reannexation of and subsequent revolt in the Transvaal, and the outbreak of the Zulu War.

A similarly expansionist spirit was abroad in the Alps. The attention of foreign – and particularly English – visitors had long been focused on the triangle formed by Mont Blanc in the west, the Matterhorn in the east, and the peaks of the Bernese Oberland to the north. Yet the great age of mountaineering brought with it the desire to investigate the less frequented districts. The results of this began to be seen in the sixties but found their fullest expression in the last thirty years of the century. To the east, west and south of the more frequented heartland of the great mountain chain, the pioneer mountaineers travelled first to explore and then to conquer. In due course they were followed by Mr Cook and his tourists.

In some respects the Dauphiné Alps south-east of Grenoble, standing apart from the main alpine chain, represented the greatest prize. At 13,458 feet, the magnificently glaciated Barre des Écrins is the highest mountain in France outside the Mont Blanc group. Nearby, La Meije, similarly glaciated, with three distinct peaks, the highest 13,067 feet, looked no less formidable. The region's third highest peak, the 12,900-foot Mont Pelvoux, completed a group every bit as challenging as their Bernese counterparts of the Eiger, Mönch and Jungfrau. They had the appearance – often borne out in reality – of inaccessibility so dear to the mountaineer's heart.

Although Thomas Gray had done something to contribute to the fame of the Grande Chartreuse in 1742, as late as 1860 the region remained a lost world. It was well off the main routes between France and Italy, there were few villages, fewer roads, and the only map was more than a century old. The French locals, too, had little more interest in their own mountains than the Swiss.

Professor Forbes in 1839 was the first mountaineer to visit La Bérarde, the hamlet that is now the heart of the region's moun- taineering. In 1841 he returned to traverse two glacier passes, the Col du Says and Col du Sella. Then, more than twenty years later, came Whymper, who wrote that 'the district contains the highest summits in France, and some of the finest scenes. It has not perhaps the beauty of Switzerland, but has charms of its own: its cliffs, its tor- rents and its gorges are unsurpassed, its deep and savage valleys present pictures of grandeur, and even sublimity, and it is second to none in the boldness of its mountain forms.' In August 1861 Whymper conquered the highest peak of Mont Pelvoux. He returned three years later to La Bérarde, which he found a 'miser- able village, without interest, without commerce, almost without population'. It was nevertheless the nearest habitation to the Barre des Écrins, the peak he had conquered as a preliminary to his assault on the Matterhorn.

It was on this trip that Whymper encountered the Reverend Thomas George Bonney, traveller and mountaineer, who did much to popularize the region in 1865 with his book, *The High Alps of*

Dauphiny. Like Whymper and Professor Forbes before him, Bonney was a great enthusiast for the climbing in the Dauphiné. About its other attractions he had reservations:

> On the great high road from Grenoble to Briançon there is fair accommodation at one or two places. Off this, everything is of the poorest kind; fresh meat can only be obtained at rare intervals, the bread and wine are equally sour, the auberges filthy, and the beds entomological vivaria. It is hardly possible to conceive the squalid misery in which the people live; their dark dismal huts swarming with flies, fleas and other vermin, the broom, the mop and the scrubbing brush are unknown luxuries; the bones and refuse of a meal are flung upon the floor to be gnawed by dogs, and are left to form an osseus brecia.

In modern terms, the Dauphiné was unspoilt.

Into this fastness in 1870 came an incongruous party of three. It comprised a young, short-sighted and short-breathed American; his aunt Meta Brevoort, once described as a 'grosse hollandische-amerikanische Miss'; and a mongrel bitch called Tschingel. To this trio is owed much of the credit for putting the Dauphiné on the mountaineer's map.

Coolidge, born in New York in 1850, was a distant relative of the future President Calvin Coolidge. Sent to Europe as a teenager in the care of his aunt, supposedly for his health, he first visited the Alps in the summer of 1865, reaching Zermatt a couple of months after Whymper's departure. As much inspired as moved by the tales he heard of the accident, he spent the next five years in an apprenticeship which took him and his aunt – in the company of the leading guides of his day – on a series of major climbs. It was by way of consolation for a failure on the Eiger that in the course of the

1868 season he was presented by the guide, Christian Almer, with Tschingel. Then, in 1870 – at the remarkably young age of twenty – he was elected to the Alpine Club, a triumph which coincided with his realization of the opportunities afforded by the Dauphiné. Here remained the last of the great virgin peaks, and here a man – and a woman and a dog – might make their names. 'There was a whole world for us to explore there', wrote Coolidge, 'and that was good enough for us.'

It turned out to be the first in a splendid series of seasons. In the company of Christian Almer, Coolidge and Miss Brevoort conquered the 13,038-foot Pic Central of La Meije. They then progressed to the village of Monastier, where their abrupt appearance, equipped with the curious tools of their trade and a dog, caused the locals to assume they were wizards. There followed the third ascent of the Barre des Écrins, the first of the heavily glaciated 12,969-foot Ailefroide, and the second non-French ascent of the Pelvoux.

Following the interruption of the Franco-Prussian War, Coolidge and his aunt returned to La Bérarde. There the whole party had to make do with sleeping in a local barn, in company with the animals. Their host's grandfather was one of Professor Forbes's guides, whose party piece was the tale of a journey to the Midi, in the course of which he had seen monocular men, their single eyes set centrally in their foreheads. The following year culminated in the ascent of La Grande Ruine, the 12,352-foot peak to the east of La Meije. Then came the first ascent of Mont Thuria and the 12,037-foot Pic de la Grave, high above the hamlet at the foot of La Meije.

By the summer of 1876, when Miss Brevoort – at fifty – felt unable to join her nephew in the Dauphiné, Coolidge had become a legendary figure, 'the young American who climbs with his aunt and his dog'. For Coolidge, though, 'American' was perhaps a misnomer. In his own account of the Dauphiné he notes with some pride that 'almost all the other high summits and passes have been first climbed by English mountaineers, if the writer (a New Yorker by birth) may be reckoned amongst English climbers'. The brown-coated, white-chested dog herself made sixty-six major climbs, was inspired by the mountaineers' standbys of red wine and weak tea, and became the only honorary lady member of the Alpine Club. Despite this, and the many puppies she bore, Miss Brevoort invariably referred to Tschingel as 'he'.

As a female climber, Miss Brevoort herself was a rarity. The Alpine Club was vehemently and exclusively male, the very idea of women climbing being anathema to its members. Women were thought to have neither the physical nor the moral stamina required for such activities. Scrambling up mountainsides was strictly contrary to Victorian notions of propriety, and climbing was thought unsuited to the female frame and likely to lead to an ungainly carriage. There were also practical issues, the most important of which was clothes. The skirt was ill-adapted to clambering up mountains, yet nineteenth-century manners – even in the high Alps – required that such costume be worn on entering and leaving a hotel. Women were thus obliged either to suffer the considerable inconvenience of skirts or to follow some such expedient as wearing riding breeches underneath and removing and replacing their skirts when occasion demanded. Some were stoned for not doing so.

For others these were merely impediments to be overcome. The first woman to conquer Mont Blanc was an eighteen-year-old chambermaid from Chamonix, Maria Paradis, in 1809. She was followed in 1838 by a French aristocrat, Mademoiselle Henriette d'Angeville, who said that 'what a man has done a lady can do'. Generally, these adventures remained sporadic until the arrival of the English, who brought their womenfolk with them in the form of wives and sisters. Lucy Walker was the daughter of Frank and sister of Horace, the pair who had pioneered the Brenva route up the south face of Mont Blanc. Miss Walker began climbing at the relatively late age of twenty-eight, in 1859. She was a bespectacled, sophisticated and well-read young woman, whose other physical recreations were limited to croquet. By no means an athlete in the conventional sense of the term, in partnership with the guide Melchior Anderegg she would make almost one hundred ascents. In 1862 she encountered an astonished Belgian, the historian and writer Emile de Laveleye, at the Théodule hut above Zermatt:

> We were extremely surprised when, creeping into this dark den we saw a young woman endeavouring to dry her garments, soaked with water and crisp with frost, in front of a wretched fire. The guides told us she was a young English lady . . . she was coming from the top of Mont Blanc and was going to the top of Monte Rosa; indeed, she climbed it a few days later. Her name was Miss Walker. A moment later, we saw her going away. She had two guides. One was going in front of her, the other behind, and a thick tope tied round her slender waist bound both hardy mountain natives. She was walking quickly, though floundering in the snow, and she was very soon out of sight behind a thick mist of sheets of drizzle driven by the blizzard.

Walker and Coolidge's aunt undertook the most important of the climbs made by women in the 1870s, and inevitably they became rivals. Great secrecy attended Coolidge and Brevoort's plans for their assault on La Meije in 1870 so as to prevent Walker gaining the prize. The Pic Central went to Coolidge and Brevoort. That same summer was further brightened by the news that Walker had been obliged to turn back on the great 14,295-foot Dent Blanche, a few miles to the west of Zermatt. In 1871 the Matterhorn became the next point of contention between the two women. Miss Brevoort had failed in an attempt on the Italian side two years previously, and was utterly determined not to turn back again. Unhappily for her, one of her guides incautiously mentioned to Melchior Anderegg that an assault was being planned in Breuil by Brevoort, Coolidge and Tschingel. Anderegg, knowing where his loyalties lay, at once set out for Zermatt. There, as he had anticipated, he found the Walker family. Echoing Whymper's own tale, a rival expedition was at once thrown together, led by Anderegg himself. It comprised Lucy, her brother Francis, her 63-year-old father, and a Liverpool neighbour, Frederick Gardiner. On 21 July they reached the summit.

Miss Brevoort, Coolidge and the dog, arriving in Zermatt two days later, took rooms as usual at the Monte Rosa. Within minutes they heard the terrible news: 'A young lady has climbed the Matterhorn.' Only the nineteenth ascent of the peak, it caused a sensation. All, however, was not quite lost. On 5 September Brevoort in the company of Coolidge and three guides reached the summit of the Matterhorn from the east and descended its western side, thus completing the first ever traverse of the peak by a lady. It was some compensation. Later that month, she climbed the 12,907-foot Bietschhorn, the great peak on the southern slopes of the Oberland. Benighted on the descent, the party was forced to bivouac in a cave on the edge of the glacier. To sleep in such circumstances could have been fatal. All night Christian Almer kept them awake by yodelling. This Miss Brevoort had the pleasure of relating in 'A Day and a Night on the Bietschhorn', though Alpine Club rules obliged her to publish her account in the *Alpine Journal* under her nephew's name.

Lucy Walker continued to climb until the end of the seventies. By then she had been joined by a pair of sisters, Anna and Ellen Pigeon. They had made their name in 1869 by taking over from their failing guides the leadership of an expedition crossing the 14,436-foot Sesiajoch pass, between two of the Monte Rosa summits into Piedmont. To Coolidge in 1892 Ellen Pigeon wrote, 'In days gone by many A.C.s [Alpine Club members] refused to speak to us.'

Then there was the small, delicate, green-eyed Kathleen Richardson, who made 116 major ascents over eleven years, and whose guides remarked, 'She does not eat and she walks like the devil.' Isabella Stratton, born in 1838, first visited the Alps in 1861. She took up climbing seriously in the year of the Matterhorn tragedy. Endowed with a comfortable £4,000 a year, she took as her first climbing companion Emmeline Lewis-Lloyd. Miss Lloyd then brought the guide Jean Charlet of Chamonix to her home in Nantgwyllt to act as a groom. Soon he was accompanying the pair on their alpine adventures. In due course he married Miss Stratton. The pair lived happily near Chamonix, producing two sons. Continuing the family tradition, one climbed Mont Blanc at the age of thirteen, the other at eleven.

Finally, from the 1880s onwards, there was Elizabeth Hawkins Whitshed. Early in her career she had conquered Mont Blanc, her companions discovering in the course of the ascent that she had never before put on her own boots. 'For several years longer it did not occur to me that I could do without a maid, and it was not until one of the species eloped with a courier that I gained my independence of all assistance of the sort that they did, or more often did not render.' Severally married to Messrs Burnaby, Main, and Aubrey le Blond, the former Miss Whitshed wrote extensively of her mountain travels and eventually, in 1908, became the founding president of the Ladies' Alpine Club.

In an age that had scarcely seen the start of the social and political emancipation of women, these climbs represented a remarkable achievement. Miss Whitshed once wrote that she owed 'a great debt of gratitude to the mountains for knocking from me the shackles of conventionality'. It might be said that women mountaineers did the same for the wider world.

By the middle of the 1870s, with only the highest peak of La Meije among the great Dauphiné heights still to be conquered, Coolidge and his contemporaries began to look east for alpine challenges. There, beyond the great peaks of the central highlands of Savoy and Switzerland, the Alps were less lofty. Height still mattered, of course. As R.L.G. Irving later wrote of the Tyrol: 'It is better to visit the Tyrolese Alps before you know the Pennines and Mont Blanc. Beside these giants of the west, the eastern snow peaks have a slightly crushed, subservient look; you will not notice this if your mind is not possessed by the revelation of these greater, prouder Alps.' Similarly, Baedeker in his handbook on the Tyrol and the Dolomites writes rather patronizingly of 'the lower Alps'. Yet difficulty, and with it challenge, could still be found on many of these nominally more modest peaks. In the Tyrol ascents were beginning to be discovered that would do a good deal to test the ingenuity and will-power of contemporary climbers.

As Coolidge himself noted, the term 'Tyrol' was for long used 'commonly and inexactly as more or less equivalent to the Eastern Alps'. By this was normally meant those east of the Brenner pass, including those of Germany's southern province of Bavaria, those of Austria in the province of Tyrol itself, and the Dolomites. Like the 'Tyrolese', the English had for some time interested themselves in these ranges of mountains. Leslie Stephen's first visit to the Alps was a Tyrolese trip, and in the first number of the Alpine Club's periodical, the *Alpine Journal*, in March 1863, there appeared a query from A.W. Moore about the Ortle. This was the highest massif – 12,812 feet – east of Switzerland. An English party successfully scaled the peak the following year, some thirty years after the last ascent. It went on to make the first ascent of the neighbouring 12,638-foot Königspitze, the second highest in the area. By 1865 there were sufficient English visitors in the region to justify Murray publishing a *Knapsack Guide to the Tyrol*. Then, in 1875, there came to the Tyrolese capital of Innsbruck a young man called Martin Conway.

Born in 1856 and educated at Repton and Trinity College, Cambridge, Conway first visited the Alps as a sixteen-year-old in 1872. Rich and well connected, he had been inspired to sample alpinism by Professor Tyndall, and took to it at once. Of his first ascent he wrote: 'It was not so much what I saw as the fact that I had climbed a real peak that kindled my enthusiastic joy. I knew what I wanted to do – to climb peak after peak, all the peaks in the Alps, all the mountains in the world. Every other occupation seemed trifling compared with that. I came down from the Mythen [the 6,240-foot peak on the shores of Lake Lucerne] like Moses from Sinai, bearing with me the law of my life.' From then until 1901, he scarcely missed a season.

The Tyrol, however, came early in his alpine career. His first climb there in 1875 was the 11,499-foot Zuckerhütl, the highest mountain in these Alps wholly on Austrian territory. In the course of the story of this ascent, he drew attention to the limitations of the local guides:

It should be observed that there are no proper guides in this valley at all. The men who act as guides are only miners and chamois hunters, who show you the way but do not regard themselves as responsible for you. They cannot climb slopes of ice or hard snow but must avoid them by detours. They understand something of the use of the rope, but all their ropes that I saw were thin and rotten . . .

The scenery was altogether a different matter:

An astonishing view opened at a sudden corner. The black snow of the Ebrener glacier appeared in the depths of a gloomy gorge, pouring forth with deafening roar the muddy streams from its dark ice-cave. Away back above the shadowed end of the glacier stood the fine Serac – towers and spires of the great ice-fall, white and dazzling in the sunshine and projected against the dark sky.

He then proceeded to the 10,686-foot Botzer, close to Ridnaun. Here, despite the occasion on which his guides 'cast into the frying pan bacon, butter, flour, eggs and milk and stirred all up together with the point of Braunhofer's *Bergstock* [alpenstock]', he succeeded. He was to fail only on the 12,378-foot Wildspitze, the second highest peak in Austria, when poor weather forced him to turn back.

Conway was among the pioneers. Thomas Cook, ever alert to new opportunities, had proposed a trip to Austria and the Tyrol as early as 1870. His inclination was to take a small party of perhaps twenty-five, to leave London on 19 July. The thirty-day trip would cost 35 guineas, including all hotel charges and drinks. This does not appear to have materialized. However, a year later on 6 September 1871, Cook's periodical, *The Excursionist*, reported that Mr Ripley was half-way through a tour to the Rhine, Bavaria, the Tyrol, Switzerland and France. Amongst his party were 'noblemen and ladies and gentlemen of distinction'. By 1875 Cook's Tyrolese tours, taking in Vienna and returning via St Moritz, were firmly established.

It was on the ascent of the Botzer that Conway saw the sun setting 'grandly on the Dolomites, which looked like masts of sunken ships standing out of a sea of cloud'. The comparison is apposite, for these were curious mast-like structures. Dolomite is a particular form of limestone, which is far more susceptible to erosion than the majority of the harder rock forms in the Alps. Largely free from snow, and crafted by wind and rain into fantastical towers and pinnacles, the Tyrolese Dolomites are in most respects unlike the rest of the Alps. As Leslie Stephen was to put it, they constitute

> shapes more like dreams than sober realities; they recall quaint Eastern architecture, whose daring pinnacles derive their charm from a studied defiance of the sober principles of stability. The Chamonix aiguilles . . . inevitably remind one of Gothic cathedrals; but in their most daring moments they appear to be massive, immovable, and eternal. The Dolomites are strange adventurous experiments, which one can scarcely believe to be formed of ordinary rock. They would have been a fit background for the garden of Kubla Khan.

John Ball had visited the region, perched across the Austrian and Italian border, as early as 1857. He conquered the 10,393-foot Monte Pelmo, a few miles south of Cortina d'Ampezzo, now the region's principal resort. Its twin peaks had inspired the name 'Throne of the Gods', for like several mountains in the region they look completely unclimbable. Then came Josiah Gilbert and George Churchill. Gilbert was a portrait painter, Churchill a solicitor; both were fascinated by the Dolomites, but more as travellers than climbers. They journeyed extensively in the region between 1861 and 1863, and subsequently produced a popular travelogue *The Dolomite Alps*. The great Quaker traveller and mountaineer Francis Ford Tuckett was there in 1863. Ball himself returned in 1865 to conquer the Cima Tosa, at 10,335 feet the highest of the Brenta Dolomites, to the west of the main range. In 1866 Elijah Walton produced a series of pen and wash drawings described by the traveller and climber Douglas Milner as 'the most vivid representations of these mountains that have ever been achieved'. Tuckett made the first ascent of the 10,564-foot Civetta in 1867.

Then, in 1869, came Stephen himself. At the time he wrote, 'Some strange magic had held the Alpine Club at a distance, and, what was more provoking, had cast a profound drowsiness over the dwellers at their feet, and almost prevented them from raising their eyes to the wild summits, or bestowing names on them.' Remedying this deficiency of ambition, Stephen conquered two of the most difficult of the Primiero peaks on his own, though he ran into difficulties on one of the descents:

> At one point, as I was letting myself carefully down, a pointed angle of rock made a vicious clutch at the seat of my trousers, and, fatally interfering with my equilibrium, caused me to grasp a projecting knob with my right hand and let my ice-axe fall. With a single bound it sprang down the cliff, but to my pleasure lodged in a rocky chasm some one hundred and fifty feet below me. In regaining it I had some real difficulty. I was forced to wriggle along a steep slope of rock where my whole weight rested on the end joints of my fingers inserted into certain pock-marks characteristic of this variety of rock, and, to be candid, on my stomach.

Tourists then began to explore the regions, among them the adventurous Egyptologist Amelia Edwards. Ball, visiting Cortina while preparing his Alpine Guide, describes it as the chief village of the large and wealthy commune of Ampezzo. He found three inns to recommend: 'The Stella d'Oro, managed by the Sisters Barbara, remarkably clean, quiet and comfortable; Aquila Nera, kept by Ghedina, father of a distinguished Venetian painter; Kruez, also well spoken of.' Edwards, wishing to avoid the popularity of Switzerland, visited Cortina in 1872. Perhaps more exacting than

Ball, she found a 'tolerable' inn only with much difficulty. Continuing east, she was in due course obliged to abandon her carriage because of the poverty of the roads, which were in the process of being improved. Proceeding by mule she encountered some of the road-makers, who were astonished to find a woman travelling in such a remote area. 'You must be Inglese!' they exclaimed. For Edwards the privations were worth the escape 'from hackneyed sights, from overcrowded hotels, from the dreary routine of table d'hôtes, from the flood of Cook's tourists'.

Three years later, in 1875, when Coolidge was elected Fellow of Magdalen College, Oxford, he decided to treat himself to a trip to the Dolomites to celebrate the event. 'A veil of mystery', he wrote later, 'still shrouded the Dolomites, even amongst those who did not count themselves to belong to the vulgar crowd . . . they were not yet fashionable, and were therefore especially attractive to an energetic climber like myself in search of fresh Alps to conquer.' The following September he spent three weeks in the region, tackling a clutch of the great Dolomite peaks, the Cima Tosa, the Cimone della Pala, the Marmolata and – above all – Ball's Monte Pelmo. Never, he later wrote, had he seen 'rocks twisted into such nightmare-like shapes, or splashed with such startling colours'. Yet ultimately he was disappointed. 'The almost complete absence of ice and snow in the Dolomites marks them off very distinctly from the rest of the High Alps, and cannot, in my opinion, quite compensate for the other advantages.' Gradually his interest returned to the more westerly Alps, even though he still wrote of his occasional longing 'for that marvellous region', the Dolomites.

The southern skirts of the Alps – those mountains now comprised by the Swiss Canton Ticino and the northern borders of Italy – had also attracted the English.

The Berninas were described by Baedeker in 1875 as 'a group of mountains scarcely inferior in grandeur to that of the Monte Rosa', and they also bore comparison with the peaks of the Oberland. Forming the border between Switzerland and Lombardy, the group separates the valleys of the Engadine and the Bregaglia, and is accessible from the Val Bernina to the east. The Piz Bernina itself, at 13,184 feet, is the only peak above four thousand metres east of the St Gotthard. In the 1860s these peaks had attracted mountaineers such as Francis Ford Tuckett and D.W. Freshfield, and a little later John Ball. In 1850 the Piz Bernina itself had been climbed by the Coire mountaineer Herr J. Coaz. The Reverend J.F. Hardy and Thomas Stuart Kennedy, two of the founder members of the Alpine Club, were to follow in 1861. Leslie Stephen was the first to climb the 12,067-foot Monte della Disgrazia, the peak just to the south of the Bregaglia mountains. Falling respectively to Freshfield and Coolidge between 1862 and 1867 were the remaining three major peaks in the Bernina's western range: the 11,155-foot Cima di Castello, the 11,070-foot Cengalo, and the 10,853-foot Piz Badile.

To the west were what Coolidge and Ball called the Lombardy Alps, running from the head of Lake Como to Trent. These culminate in the Adamello-Presanella massif. Of the three greatest individual peaks, the 11,661-foot Monte Adamello was conquered by the Austrian Herr Payer; the 11,369-foot Care Alto and the highest peak in the region, the 11,694-foot Cima Presanella, by Freshfield. John Ball would write in his guide, *The Eastern Alps*, that it was 'on the southern side of the main chain of Alps that the mountain traveller derives the greatest advantage for railway communication. All the primary valleys open into the main valley of the Po.' Nascent in the 1860s, by the time Ball published a revised edition of *The Eastern Alps* in 1871, the Italian network was spreading its tentacles towards the hills, bringing with it the usual tally of English travellers.

Much the same would happen to the north-east in Canton Ticino, the most Italianate of the Swiss cantons, when the St Gotthard tunnel opened in 1882. Samuel Butler had made his name with his novel *Erewhon* ten years earlier, and just before the tunnel opened, wrote a holiday book about Piedmont and Ticino entitled *Alps and Sanctuaries*. Already there were signs of English influence. At Monte Bisbino Butler came across a curious phenomenon, a man 'who had lived many years in London and had now settled at Varenna, just below the lake at Como. He had taken a room here and furnished it for the sake of shooting. He spoke perfect English, and would have none but English things about him. He had Cockle's anti-bilious pills, and the last numbers of the *Illustrated London News* and *Morning Chronicle*, his bath towels were English, and there was a box of Huntley and Palmer's biscuits on the dressing-table.' Then there was the Englishman at Sacro Monte who, when drunk, 'kept abusing all he saw and crying out "Manchester's the place for me"'. Coolidge attributed the increasing number of travellers of all nationalities in this region to the opening of a comfortable inn in the Binn valley in 1883, this forming a 'natural headquarters for a traveller in these parts'. He continued, 'As his train thunders down from Airolo to Bellinzona by that most amazing and daring of all railway lines, he may find a minute to consult his guidebook (let *me* hope that it is a Murray and not a Baedeker).'

To the south-west of Ticino was the old principality of Piedmont itself. After 1861 part of a larger Italy, this had for long been a staging-post for the English on their way to Rome. It abutted Savoy on its north-western border, and as early as 1843 *Murray's Handbook* was recommending it with enthusiasm. The accommodation was equal to any in Switzerland, the practice of 'fleecing the traveller' was not yet systematic, the roads were excellent, and the wines were 'generally wholesome, often fine, and sometimes of great celebrity'. It was true there were 'no maps . . . upon which implicit confidence could be placed', and smuggling was so endemic as to cause 'vexatious delay' at the borders with the customs. Even so, here 'a traveller may devote more time and visit more sublime scenes, at a less expense and with nearly as much facility as in Switzerland'.

In Piedmont's northern quarter was the Val Tournanche, the mirror image of the St Nicholas valley, running up to the southern side of the Matterhorn. Breuil, used by Whymper for his initial attempts on the peak, merits in 1843 only passing mention. It would take Whymper's accident to bring notoriety to the Matterhorn's environs, and the opening of the Mont Cenis tunnel in 1871 to attract English tourists in any numbers. Even in 1875, Baedeker marked Breuil as consisting of only a few chalets, and Whymper's base, the Hôtel du Mont Cervin, as the only accommodation. Further west, the spectacle of Mont Blanc, known in Piedmont as Monte Blanco, brought rather more visitors to the village of Courmayeur. Regarded as the head of the Val d'Aosta – with its reputation for goitre and cretinism – this area's principal attraction in 1838 was still the local mineral waters. It was, however, possible to force a route through to Chamonix on the north side of the peak by the Col de Géant, and according to Murray such a journey had been made in 1823 by a Mrs Campbell and her daughters, 'an adventure not yet forgotten in the neighbourhood'.

Despite Murray's compliments, by the time of Ball's journeys in the southern Alps the inns seem to have deteriorated. 'It is generally known', wrote Ball, 'that no country in Europe is so well provided with inns as Switzerland . . . those in the more frequented places leave very little to be desired by the most fastidious . . . the beautiful valleys of the Italian Alps are far from being equally well supplied.' In particular, Ball found it disappointing that so little progress had been made in the use of water-closets. 'Even when they exist,' he wrote, 'they are frequently in offensive condition. In France these places are perfectly horrible, forming an unaccountable exception to the general advance of civilization. Italy stands next lowest in the scale.'

While the English were fanning out from their bridgehead in the central Alps, they were also busy formulating a mountaineering philosophy, a rationale for their pursuit.

In the early years climbers found various attractions in the peaks. In the first instance scientific curiosity about the world above the snow-line had driven men such as de Saussure, Forbes and Tyndall to the alpine peaks. They were exploring the many varieties of alpine phenomena, from glaciers and avalanches to crystal and marmots; and they were also more broadly curious about a world within their sight but beyond their experience. Thereafter, Alfred Wills's ascent of the Wetterhorn in 1854 was widely held to have ushered in the notion of climbing as a sport, pleasure being derived from the physical challenge of mastering the mountain and proving oneself against a powerful adversary. And alongside curiosity and the sense of enjoyment that even the earliest mountaineers acknowledged as part of the alpine experience, the divinity of the mountains also counted with some. Like many early alpinists, Wills regarded the mountain scenery as a manifestation of God's work, feeling himself on the Wetterhorn's summit 'in the more immediate presence of Him who had reared this tremendous pinnacle'.

To others like the Reverend J.F. Hardy there was, finally, an element of chauvinism in the experience. Along with other early members of the Alpine Club, he made the first ascent of the 14,889-foot Lyskamm, one of the peaks to the south of Zermatt forming the border with Piedmont. To celebrate, he and his party sang the National Anthem. As Hardy described it: 'the noble old anthem fills our English hearts with happy thoughts of home and fatherland, and of the bright eyes that will sparkle, and the warm hearts that will rejoice, at our success.' The conqueror of Mont Blanc, Michel Paccard, summarized several of these motives when he said he climbed for France, for science, and for his own satisfaction.

To test these simple pieties of the early alpinists there came not only the Matterhorn accident but also Darwinism. As the historian of the Fabian Society, E.R. Pease, remarked:

> It is nowadays not easy to recollect how wide was the intellectual gulf which separated the young generation of that period from their parents. *The Origin of the Species*, published in 1859, inaugurated an intellectual revolution such as the world had not known since Luther nailed his thesis to the door of All Saints Church at Wittenberg. The older folk as a rule refused to accept or to consider the new doctrine . . . the young men of the time grew up with the new ideas and accepted them as a matter of course . . . Our parents, who read neither Spencer nor Huxley, lived in an intellectual world which bore no relation to our own; and cut adrift as we were from the

intellectual moorings of our upbringing, recognizing, as we did, that the older men were useless as guides in religion, in science, in philosophy, because they knew no evolution, we also felt instinctively that we could accept nothing on trust from those who still believed that the early chapters of Genesis accurately described the origin of the universe.

No member of the Alpine Club remained untouched by the impact of Darwinism on religious belief. Indeed, given its member-ship, the Club appears to have been especially affected by the great schism. Men like Forbes, Ball and Tyndall were among the leading scientists of the day; Stephen, Coolidge and Hardy himself were representative of the many in Holy Orders. And in 1874, Tyndall was to make a famous speech to the British Association at Belfast in which he defended the legitimacy of science enquiring into matters of religion. The decade, and the disputes it threw up, resulted in a move among members of the Alpine Club – and other mountain-eers – to formulate an altogether more coherent and comprehensive rationale of their activity.

If the physical benefits of the alpine experience were by now received wisdom, in an age which strongly associated the healthy mind with the healthy body, the Alps were seen to be therapeutic to both. Francis Ford Tuckett, who had done much to encourage Coolidge's exploration of the Dauphiné, declared:

> I have returned to them every year and found among them refuge and recovery from the work and the worry – which acts with far deadlier corrosion on the brain than real work – of London. Herein consisted the fascination of the Alps for me; they appealed at once to thought and feeling, offering their problems to one and their grandeur to the other, while confer-ring on both the soundness and the purity necessary to the beautiful exercise of both.

For this reason the mountaineering experience was felt to be health-ful. Yet it was also supposed to be morally formative, Stephen himself declaring that 'we return from their precipices wiser as well as stronger men'. With the rise of imperialism there came, too, a heightened sense of the national achievement gained by mountaineering exploits. Whymper saw himself as Whymper first and an Englishman second, but he was still determined that the English rather than the Italians should be the first to conquer the Matterhorn. Lucy Walker felt likewise. Coolidge as a mountaineer regarded himself as more an Englishman than a denizen of New York. As the alpine scholar R.W. Clark commented, 'The almost proselyte fervour with which [Alpine Club members] acclaimed the virtues of their new pastime sprang from national pride that the last outposts of Europe were falling to the British.'

For many, though, matters went deeper. If Wills and his contemporaries continued to acclaim the Alps as an expression of the Divine will, for the younger generation their meaning was rather different. Many of those who had lost their faith saw the mountains as a spiritual substitute. Stephen, who resigned from Holy Orders in 1870, wrote:

> If I were to invent a new idolatry . . . I should prostrate myself, not before a beast, or ocean, or sun, but before one of those gigantic masses to which, in spite of all reason, it is impossible not to attribute some shadowy personality. Their voice is mystic, and has found discordant interpreters; but to me at least it speaks in tones at once more tender and more awe-inspiring than any mortal teacher. The loftiest and sweetest strains of Milton or Wordsworth may be more articulate, but do not lay so forcible a grasp upon my imagination.

Thus it was that Arnold Lunn – a notable Christian controversialist – saw Victorian mountaineering less as an expression of patriotism than as a spiritual pilgrimage. Indeed, he explained its rapid growth as a response to the tribulations of the age: 'Men lifted up their eyes to the hills to rediscover the spiritual values which were clouded by the smoke and grime of the industrial revolution.'

For its early adherents mountaineering seems to have fulfilled various profound human needs. As many of the early mountaineers themselves remarked, it was less a sport than a way of life.

Stimulated though he had been by the Dolomites, Coolidge returned to Oxford in the autumn of 1876 still hankering for the Dauphiné. La Meije, the main peak of which was still unconquered, had become for him as much of an obsession as the Matterhorn was to Whymper. His plan to return to the mountain in December was, however, interrupted by the sudden death of his aunt, on the 19th of that month, from rheumatic fever. The assault on La Meije was thereafter devoted to her memory.

Once again he travelled out to the Dauphiné and, in the company of Christian Almer and the dog Tschingel, made several first ascents. (One of these was of the 12,382-foot Pic du Vallon — now known as Pic Coolidge.) He then turned to La Meije, and the challenge of its Grand Pic. The French, notably the co-founder of the Club Alpin Français Henri Duhamel, were interesting themselves in this mountain. So, too, was Lord Wentworth, who made two unsuccessful attempts in June. A month later Coolidge set out on his own attempt, in the company of Christian Almer and his son. This failed, and on his return to La Bérarde, Coolidge was none too pleased to find a young Frenchman, Henri Boileau de Castelnau, in residence. This twenty-two-year-old aristocrat had made his name at the age of eighteen on Mont Blanc. Disquieted, Coolidge nevertheless supposed that what had defeated him was unlikely to be surmounted by such a youngster. He accordingly returned to England.

A month later Coolidge was appalled to hear that on 17 August the Grand Pic had been scaled by the Frenchman and two Dauphiné guides, Pierre Gaspard and his son. It was the greatest disappointment of Coolidge's life. He returned to the Dauphiné the following year, reaching Boileau's peak at 1.20 p.m. on 10 July: 'It was a moment of my life which I can never forget. Yet my feelings were very mixed. The pleasure of having attained a long wished-for goal was very great, but at the same time my thoughts recurred to my dear companion . . . one of whose cherished wishes it had been to stand on this lofty pinnacle, a wish which was doomed to remain forever unsatisfied.'

Two years later, Coolidge wrote in a letter to a friend: 'I am at present in great affliction at the death of my dear old dog Tschingel . . . she was so much more a companion than a mere dog and I feel her loss very deeply.'

Chapter Six
Winter Holiday

'Dark at tea-time and sleeping indoors: nothing ever happens in the winter holidays . . .'

Arthur Ransome, *Winter Holiday* (1933)

In July 1877 a man just entering middle age was despatched to Egypt for the sake of his health. He was a victim of tuberculosis, and his condition was such that he reached no further than Davos, where his sister was living. He seemed unable to go on. Given the benefits that mountain air was increasingly believed to confer, there appeared to be nothing to lose by his staying and, as it turned out, there was much to gain. For the journalist and historian John Addington Symonds, both by his personal example and by his writings, was to popularize not simply the cure but the whole notion of wintering in the Alps. By doing so, he was to give the impulse to the winter sports movement.

To many of Symonds's generation, the notion of spending the winter in the Alps was anathema. In summer, with their pleasant lakes and mountains, fine walks and equable temperatures, the Alps were a delight. In winter it was assumed that the region, even if it could be broached, could not be safely traversed. *Murray's Handbook* of 1843 recorded of the Great St Bernard pass:

The perilous passage of this mountain is more frequently undertaken in the winter than is generally imagined: it is difficult to conceive the necessity or urgency of affairs which can lead persons at such a season through scenes of such peril. They are generally pedlars or smugglers who traverse these dreary and dangerous solitudes in defiance of the snows, tourmentes [storms], and avalanches, which always threaten and often overwhelm them. During the severe cold, the snow at this elevation falls like dust; the particles are frozen so hard that they do not attach and form flakes as in lower regions, nor consolidate on the surface where it lies; a storm of wind, therefore, lifts it, and the air is filled with a mist of snow which the eye cannot penetrate; and the poor wretch exposed it to wanders from the landmarks, which in clear weather would guide him, to some fatal spot where he is destroyed.

Then as now, these passes were reliably clear of snow only in June, July, August and September, and the season for travelling for pleasure in the Alps was restricted to that period. Dangerous enough in the summer, mountaineering was regarded as inconceivable in the winter, when for the ordinary traveller the hotels and auberges were almost invariably shut, and many of the passes and routes – even the lower ones – impassable. For practical purposes, the Alps in winter were closed.

From the earliest days, though, there were exceptions. Those obliged to travel in winter through the region, or those who came by chance, saw the incomparable beauties of the winter scene; saw too, that it was often accompanied by spells of remarkably fine weather. Ruskin was early in bringing to the public's notice the pleasures of the Alps in winter. In 1861 he remarked, 'I have made up my mind that the finest things one can see in summer are nothing compared to the winter scenery among the Alps.' Travelling in the Alps, though, always difficult and slow, was doubly so in the winter. Sleighs and toboggans might have a certain romance, but they progressed at little more than walking pace. The coming of the railways, however, made the slopes accessible in winter, and by the early 1860s the alpine foothills were within reach of the foreign traveller winter or summer. Indeed, it was in 1860 at one of the two great shrines of the Alpine Club, the Bear at Grindelwald, that a winter season was inaugurated when a party of Englishmen persuaded the Bosses that they should open the hotel for their convenience on Boxing Day.

Once the first winter visitors had arrived at their destination, they then faced the question of how best to occupy their time. Skating had thrived since medieval times on canals in the Low Countries, and in England since the sixteenth century. Samuel Pepys in his diary describes skaters on the canal in St James's Park in 1662. The first skating club was established in Edinburgh in 1742. The British introduced the sport to America in the middle of the nineteenth century, by which time it was in England the main winter sport, particularly popular in the Fens. The early English alpine winter tourists took their skates with them to the Alps, and before long artificial rinks were established, one of the most famous private ones being that of the Bear itself which gave rise to 'The Bear' skating club, an exclusive and highly English institution.

Inevitably, though, visitors also turned their eyes to the mountains. Hitherto, mountaineering had been a summer pastime, and few thought the peaks could be tackled in winter. Indeed, the absurdity of the notion was perfectly conveyed by Whymper's comments on Thomas Stuart Kennedy's assault on the Matterhorn in the winter of 1862. To Whymper, it was an extraordinary idea that the peak might prove less impracticable in January than in June, and he wrote derisively that Kennedy (one of the founders of the Alpine Club) would find 'that snow in winter obeyed the ordinary laws, and that the wind and frost were not less unkind than in summer'. A.W. Moore, who had found fame on the Brenva, found similar discouragement in the Dauphiné. There, crossing the Col de Valloise, he encountered a Frenchman who asked him why he was travelling. 'Pour plaisir,' said Moore; whereupon, he recounted, the Frenchman 'threw up his hands and, with a glance round at the dreary snow covered landscape and the gathering clouds, exclaimed in a tone suggestive of his own intense antipathy to his surroundings, "que diable de plaisir!" And then fled . . . as though escaping from a dangerous lunatic.' Moore remained undiscouraged. On 23 December 1866, in the company of Horace Walker, he set out from Grindelwald, crossed the Finsteraarjoch and returned via the Strahlegg. This achievement paved the way for Coolidge who soon began a series of winter adventures in the Bernese Oberland. These took him and his aunt first to the peak of the Wetterhorn, then the Jungfrau, neither previously tackled in winter. In due course they were followed by the pioneer lady climber, Elizabeth le Blond, the former Elizabeth Whitshed. Mrs le Blond's winter climbing included Mont Blanc, the Monte Rosa and the Matterhorn. She would also write the first book devoted to winter mountaineering, *The High Alps in Winter*, published in 1883.

Another early winter enthusiast was Leslie Stephen. To him, this was the season

> when the whole region becomes part of the dreamland . . . the very daylight has an unreal glow . . . the pulse of the mountains is beating low . . . the peaks are in a state of suspended animation . . . they are spell-bound, dreaming of dim abysses of past time or of the summer that is more real to them than life. They are in a trance like that of the Ancient Mariner, when he heard strange spirit voices conversing overhead in mysterious murmurs.

By the end of the seventies, the practice of winter mountaineering had been established.

Mountaineering would always remain an esoteric pursuit, the enthusiasm of the few. Previously, though, where the mountaineers had led, less adventurous travellers had followed. So it happened with the winter season.

Along with the Bernese Oberland, the Grisons – the easternmost canton of Switzerland – witnessed the first establishment of winter custom. There, St Moritz in the Engadine valley had enjoyed a reputation for its waters since the time of Paracelsus in the sixteenth century, a spa with its own drinking-room being established in 1831.

For some years, though, it remained undeveloped. *Murray's Handbook* of 1838 noted that 'the village had only 160 inhabitants', its pastures were let to 'Bergamesque shepherds', and its accommodation was 'of the homeliest kind'. On a recent visit an English traveller 'on repairing to church on a Sunday . . . found the parish fire-engine drawn up by the side of the pulpit – the church, in this and other villages, being somewhat profanely used as an engine-house'.

With its proximity to the Bernina range, the Engadine had found favour with climbers from the 1850s. For tourists St Moritz, like Chamonix, Zermatt and Grindelwald, was popularized by the founding father of one of the great alpine hotel dynasties. Johannes Badrutt had established the Engadine Kulm in St Moritz in 1855, and the hotel quickly acquired a clientele amongst the all-pervasive English, one of whom Badrutt married. Anxious to use his premises for more than the traditional four months of the year, Badrutt persistently sang the praises of the Engadine winter. Eventually, in 1864, he struck a bargain with a party of four Englishmen, the agreement being that if they were disappointed by the winter weather Badrutt would pay for their return journey. The genial hotelier won his wager, his guests benefiting from their escape from the English winter. Thereafter he kept his hotel open for the winter season of January to March. Along with the opening of the Bear at Grindelwald in 1860, this marked the beginning of winter tourism in the Alps. By the end of 1873 the new arrangement had proved so successful in St Moritz that the winter season was busier than the summer.

Badrutt's brother-in-law was the English doctor Peter Berry, who lived in the village. By advertising his services the Kulm had been able to exploit the village's reputation as a station for alpine cures. With its somewhat warmer, drier climate, nearby Davos was by now benefiting considerably from the pioneering work on consumption of Alexander Spengler. In its early days as a cure-station the village had been populated by the 'steady, plodding German and Dutch patients'. This was to change with the arrival of Symonds in the winter of 1877.

Like Leslie Stephen, Symonds was a man of letters, like Ruskin at Oxford he had won the Newdigate Prize for poetry, and like Coolidge he was a Fellow of Magdalen College, Oxford. Born in

1840 in London, the son of a doctor, he was educated at Harrow. Aloof and shy, he disliked the school, and only flowered when he went up to Oxford in 1858. There at Balliol he won a double first in classics and, failing at Queen's College, achieved a Fellowship at Magdalen. He then suffered a breakdown and went to Italy to recover. Married in 1864, he was increasingly obliged to travel abroad in an attempt to cure what emerged as tuberculosis – first to the Riviera in 1867, then to Corsica in 1868, these journeys inspiring a series of essays published in 1874 as *Sketches in Italy and Greece*. Then, after a tour of Italy in early 1877, he broke down with a tubercular haemorrhage. His condition by the summer was serious; permanent residence in a more sympathetic climate represented more or less the last hope. As Davos's reputation as a cure-station held good for the summer season alone, his intention was to settle in Egypt.

For weeks after his arrival in early August, he thought he would die. Gradually, though, the cure did its work, as Symonds described:

> The method of the cure is very simple. After a minute personal examination of the ordinary kind, your physician tells you to give up medicines, and to sit warmly clothed in the sun as long as it is shining, to eat as much as possible, to drink a fair quantity of Valtelline wine, and not to take any exercise. He comes at first to see you every day, and soon forms a more definite opinion of your capacity and constitution. Then, little by little, he allows you to walk; at first upon the level, next up-hill, until daily walks begin to occupy four or five hours. The one thing relied upon is air. To inhale the maximum quantity of the pure mountain air, and to imbibe the maximum quantity of the keen mountain sunlight is the *sine qua non*. Everything else – milk-drinking, douches, baths, friction, counter-irritant applications, and so forth, is subsidiary.

Three years later, Symonds's health had so improved that he thought it worthwhile to settle in Davos, building the home, Am Hof, that was to become the centre of the village's English community.

That same year his fellow consumptive, Robert Louis Stevenson, visited the village with his wife and stepson. Of Symonds he remarked to a correspondent, 'Beyond its splendid climate, Davos has but one advantage – the neighbourhood of J.A. Symonds. I dare say you know his work, but the man is far more interesting.' Stevenson, obliged to winter in Davos to husband his own health, found the village claustrophobic and the life monotonous. These sentiments were shared by Symonds and some of the other English visitors, and they cast around them for some form of distraction. It was true that there was skating, for which a rink had been established in the year of Symonds's arrival. This, though, Stevenson thought pedestrian. He was altogether more taken by the toboggan. This was simply a small-scale sleigh, the *schlitten*, used by the locals as a means of transport. The English invalids, with time on their hands, thought it a source of pleasure. Wrote Stevenson:

Perhaps the true way to toboggan is alone and at night. First comes the tedious climb, dragging your instrument behind you. Next a long breathing space, alone with snow and pine woods, cold, silent, and solemn to the heart. Then you push off; the toboggan fetches way; she begins to feel the hill, to glide, to swim, to gallop. In a breath you are out from under the pine-trees, and a whole heavenful of stars reels and flashes overhead. Then comes a vicious effort; for by this time your wood sled is speeding like the wind, and you are spinning round a corner, and the whole glittering valley and all the lights of the great hotels lie for a moment at your feet; and the next you are racing once more in the shadow of the night, with close shut teeth and beating heart. Yet a little while and you will be landed on the highroad by the door of your own hotel. This, in an atmosphere fighting with forty degrees of frost, in a night made luminous with stars and snow, and girt with strange white mountains, teaches the pulse an unaccustomed tune, and adds a new excitement to the life of man upon his planet.

By 1883 there was sufficient enthusiasm for the new pastime for Symonds to form the Davos Tobogganing Club. Symonds himself was elected president, purchased some cups as prizes, and encouraged races between residents at the various hotels on a run established on the road between Davos and Klosters. The following year there was a highly successful week of races. Word of this soon reached what had become a significant English colony in St Moritz, where most of the colonists were experimenting with the winter cure. With a passion for organizing, some of those resident in Badrutt's Kulm hotel thought that their hitherto spasmodic sporting activities could be given focus by the formation of two committees, one indoor, one outdoor. The latter assumed responsibility for creating a toboggan run, the Badrutt family in the form of Johannes's son Peter providing the pioneers with a good deal of free labour and much encouragement.

This was the genesis of what was to become the Cresta Run, an exhilarating course of some 1,800 metres running between St Moritz and Celerina, via the hamlet of Cresta. When it was completed in January 1885 a challenge was issued to the Davos Club. Symonds put together a team of ten for the purpose. He recorded the journey in his diary: 'Going to St Moritz we crossed the Julier [pass] by starlight in open sleighs. Most impressive. Such stars, and long into the night a fan was sent up from the buried sun, aloft among the constellations.' Come the great day, 18 February 1885, all of St Moritz turned out to see the race.

It was Davos's day. Riding conservatively on an unfamiliar course, they easily outdid the more ambitious St Moritzers, who suffered a series of accidents. Arnold Lunn would comment of the whole phenomenon:

> The evolution of tobogganing at Davos from a mere mode of transport, among the Swiss, into an organized sport, among the British, is a characteristic episode in Anglo-Swiss relations. Whenever the British appear the organization of sport begins. Clubs and tournaments and championships and codes, written and unwritten, emerge from the vague background of somewhat shapeless activity.

It was the beginning of the whole winter sports movement, in which the English would play a pioneering role at almost every point.

Coincident with the early days of the winter season was the brilliant climbing career of A.F. Mummery, whose fame rests on his pioneering ascent of the Z'mutt Ridge of the Matterhorn, and his defeat of the most difficult of the Chamonix Aiguilles. It was said of Professor Tyndall and even Edward Whymper that they simply walked uphill. Mummery climbed.

Born in 1855, the son of a highly successful Dover tanner, like so many of the early mountaineers Albert Frederick Mummery was a man of independent means. He was first taken to the Alps as a sixteen-year-old, there to be astonished by the Matterhorn. 'It was shining in all the calm majesty of a September moon, and in the stillness of an autumn night it seemed the very embodiment of mystery, and a fitting dwelling place for the spirits with which the old legends people its stone-swept slopes.' At a stroke he had found his vocation, which he would pursue despite suffering from short sight and a marked weakness of the spine.

Now that all the major peaks had been climbed, Mummery took as his mission the call to 'leave paths that common sense, custom, or the average mountain sheep would point out . . . and go in some other direction where the chances appear to be in favour of breaking your neck'. Having climbed the Matterhorn by Whymper's own route along the north-east ridge, at the age of twenty-four he decided to tackle the mountain's north-west face above the Z'mutt glacier. This was the glacier on to which Whymper's companions had fallen, and which divides the Matterhorn from the 13,684-foot Dent d'Hérens. Of the face above it, Whymper himself wrote that it 'looks, and is, completely unassailable'. Most of Mummery's contemporaries thought the same. In the company of three splendid guides – Alexander Burgener, Augustin Gentinetta and Benedikt Venetz – Mummery set out before dawn one summer's morning in 1879 to prove the contrary.

For an hour the party struggled across shale to reach the snow arête that – seen from Zermatt – comprised the right-hand profile of the mountain. Roped together, they followed the arête past precipice, pinnacle and 'rickety piles of frost-riven rock' until it steepened to the perpendicular. After traversing briefly on to the north face, they rejoined the arête and passed carefully over an area of powder snow where the rock was frighteningly unsound. Here, wrote Mummery, 'a slip of one meant the destruction of all', and the guides took the lead. At last they regained a firmer surface, albeit one of heavily fissured steep rock. Here Burgener's pipe was plucked from his pocket by a rock splinter and clattered down to the Z'mutt glacier below. This made the whole party think twice. For a time they made steady progress on the arête, till an overhang forced them round on to the western face. Soon, though, they were back on the skyline, and an hour later on the summit. The climb had taken them nine hours. 'The pipe', said Burgener, 'is avenged.'

In establishing this route, the inter-war alpinist Stanley Snaith wrote, 'Mummery laid the climbing world under his debt . . . on sunny days the fairways of the Matterhorn might creak and groan under the massed weight of tourists, but the elite will always be sure of finding a breathing-space on this grand course.'

Mummery then turned his attention to the Chamonix Aiguilles. These are the great gothic needles that guard the approaches to Mont Blanc. Not startlingly high, they are generally regarded as the most difficult peaks in the Alps. For visitors to Chamonix, then as now, they look like something out of a fairy tale. To Mummery's generation they represented the same sort of challenge as the Matterhorn did to Whymper's. Although the 12,609-foot Midi was climbed in 1856, the remainder would fall much later to – in Coolidge's words – valiant Englishmen. Mummery's prizes were the Aiguille des Grands Charmoz in 1880, and the Grépon the following year. Each climb was attended by high adventure.

On the 11,293-foot Charmoz, Mummery, Burgener and Venetz found their way blocked by a forty-foot vertical slab which had broken away from the mountain. Ascent was only possible by means of the resulting chimney, which was coated with a thin layer of ice. Through this – some fifteen feet up – protruded green-iced rock. To surmount it Burgener thrust Venetz upwards by means of an ice-axe against his backside – 'that portion of the guide's costume most usually decorated by patches of brilliant and varied hue'. Venetz grasped the ice just below the bulge. Burgener then drove the axe into the ice below his companion to act as a step, Venetz throwing himself over and above the bulge. Voilà! Burgener and Mummery then followed on to the ledge formed by the top of the bulge. Again their way seemed entirely barred, the ice walls of the cliff merely narrowing into a cleft. A desperate measure was required. Clasping their hands in front of them, the climbers drew them to their chests, jammed their elbows against the walls, and proceeded upwards by jerks of the knees.

Thereafter the work was merely hard going till just short of the summit. Here the party tried to overcome a steep slab by the expedient of Mummery clambering on to Burgener's shoulders, Venetz on to Mummery's. Eventually they were obliged to use a short ladder they had brought. Their arrival on the peak was observed from Chamonix, and cannon were set off in celebration. 'The men', wrote Mummery, 'rejoiced greatly at the reckless waste of gunpowder . . . Burgener, as fitting recognition of this attention, planted our ice-axe on the highest point.'

With the Charmoz behind them, its neighbour the 11,423-foot Grépon remained. In Mummery's words, it was 'the most difficult climb in the world'. Here the mountaineer in 1881 was to give his name to the crack that has since become renowned and which forms the chief barrier to the ascent of the aiguille, the crack being formed where a flake of granite some seventy feet high has partially broken off from the body of the needle. Too narrow to accommodate the human frame, perpendicular, and with the lower section overhanging, its ascent marks the true climber. To get up it was simple so far as Mummery was concerned: it merely involved putting his right hand and boot into the crack, leaving the remaining limbs free to slide up the flake. 'The climber', he wrote, 'thus levers his way upward, the body being kept in situ by the hands, which pull against the edge of the flake as if to rip it away from the face of the mountain.' The footholds diminish as the climber ascends, the crack becoming 'a stiff trial of strength'. Even to the most experienced mountaineers of Mummery's day, the crack seemed unassailable. To his delight, Mummery confounded them, and when the party reached the summit they enjoyed the 'sundry half-bottles of Bouvier' secreted in Mummery's knapsack.

Eleven years later, Mummery returned to the Grépon. He wrote: 'In 1892 I once again started for the mountain. This time we were without guides, for we had learnt the great truth that those who wish really to enjoy the pleasure of mountaineers must roam the upper snows trusting exclusively to their own skill and knowledge.'

In doing so Mummery was not setting a precedent, but he certainly popularized the idea. Although the guides' *raison d'être* was firmly enough established from the early days of mountaineering, there had always been a few adventurers like Mummery keen to test their own skills. Amongst them had been the Reverend A.G. Girdlestone, who caused a good deal of controversy by the practice. The very idea, encapsulated in the title of his 1870 book *The High Alps Without Guides*, seemed to many the height of foolhardiness and irresponsibility. Still, there were practical reasons for going it alone. As mountaineering became more popular, the better guides became booked long in advance. Accordingly, rather than chance their luck with the less able, both English and Continental climbers started to climb unguided in significant numbers. Where they were competent, this proved a success; when they fell to their deaths, less so. Mummery, though, was a man whose reputation could withstand the stigma attached to guide-less climbing. By tackling safely such exceptional climbs as the Brenva route up the south side of Mont Blanc, the first traverse of the Grépon, and the first ascent of the Dent du Requin, he legitimized guideless mountaineering.

Regarded as the greatest climber, English or otherwise, of his day, Mummery would publish just one book on mountaineering, the 1895 classic *My Climbs in the Alps and Caucasus*. Widely read and highly influential within the growing climbing community, it was notable for formulating the memorable division of peaks into three: inaccessible; the most difficult ascent in the Alps; an easy day for a lady. He was lost in 1895 on the 26,000-foot Nanga Parbat in the Himalaya, in the course of one of the earliest attempts on a high peak in that great range. The mountaineer and writer F.S. Smythe remarked: 'Long after many famous names are forgotten simple natives will point upwards to the shining snows of Nanga Parbat and say "Here Mummery Sahib lies". Who could wish for a better epitaph or grander resting place?'

Mummery was a man who found sufficient challenge in the Alps in the summer not to be troubled by the allure of winter climbing. During the remainder of the 1880s, however, the winter habit continued to grow in the Bernese Oberland and the Grisons, not least because of the latter's association with Symonds. His health at least in part restored and away from the distractions of England, he was prolific. The first year of his stay saw a study of Shelley. There followed biographies of Sir Philip Sidney, Ben Jonson and Michelangelo. He translated the latter's sonnets, and produced prose translations of the autobiographies of Benvenuto Cellini and Count Carlo Gozzi which were regarded by his contemporaries as outstanding. At the same time he published with his daughter Margaret a series of articles on the Alps which were collected into the volume *Our Life in the Swiss Highlands*, published in 1891. This, in the words of an early biographer, 'powerfully stimulated the formation of English colonies not only at Davos but elsewhere in the Engadine'.

Davos as a cure-station was certainly booming, with purpose-built sanatoria now beginning to be established for tuberculosis patients. Coinciding with the arrival of Symonds in the village was that of Sir Thomas Allbutt, who came to investigate Spengler's claims for the curative qualities of the climate for consumptives. His enthusiasm was such that ten years later his fellow practitioner E. Symes Thompson wrote: 'It is a fact now generally accepted by the profession and by the public, that a winter spent in the high Alps is often productive of great benefits in the cases of chest disease.' As a consequence, the village had become 'quite a town, with its baths and gas works and large shops, perfumiers and hotels'. The latter, once empty, were now in winter overcrowded. This, however, had unfortunate consequences. As A.T. Tucker Wise, a fellow physician of Symes Thompson, was obliged to point out:

> When a small village, even in a healthy locality, with a scanty population and scattered dwellings, develops into a little town, unless sanitary matters go hand in hand with building and increase in population, disaster results. For the sake of Davos and the number of sick who frequent the place with the object of prolonging their lives, it is earnestly to be hoped that the new drainage system will soon reach completion. Before it is completed, however, let us trust that some hotel proprietors be encouraged to make a little outlay *on airing their houses*.

According to *Murray's Handbook* of 1892, in the winter of 1889–90 seventeen hundred visitors wintered in Davos. In Davos-Platz the Kurhaus boasted 180 bedrooms, five separate villas or annexes, and a theatre. There was also Dr Turhan's Sanatorium, with sixty bedrooms, and the Kurhaus Clavadel. In Davos-Dorf there was the Kurhaus Davos Dorfli. Dr Haggard was noted as the English physician, and the 'comforts required . . . for patients with delicate lungs . . . are generally obtainable'.

With growing numbers of visitors with time on their hands, winter sports in Davos and St Moritz grew apace. Who introduced precisely what, and when, is now a matter of speculation. Curling is native to Scotland, and its legislative body was founded as the Grand Caledonian Curling Club in 1838. It seems to have been introduced to Switzerland for the pleasure of his English guests by Johannes Badrutt at Kulm. It then grew rapidly throughout the few winter resorts. In St Moritz by this time there was also a skating rink, the Cresta toboggan run and sleighing. Writing after the Second World War of this forgotten pastime, Monk Gibbon wrote:

> Sleighing is almost an amusement of the past. It is a pleasant anachronism today to climb into a horse-drawn vehicle at a station, pull a fur rug over one's knees, and be driven off to an

hotel a few hundred yards away. But when I first went to Switzerland sleighing parties were still fairly popular. The long line of connected luges swung about like a great snake behind the horse-drawn vehicle, and people shouted and laughed and fell off in the snow and enjoyed it all.

Then, in 1888, Colonel C.C. Napier became the first Englishman to ski at Davos.

The notion of some form of extension to the human foot to spread the load of a man's weight on soft surfaces was an ancient one. There are many parts of the world where for several months of the year it is impossible to move off the beaten track without plunging knee-deep in snow. Snow shoes or skis – in reality variants – effectively address this problem, and were adopted independently in many of the areas affected, from Tibet to the Pennine region of England. From the Middle Ages date records – indeed depictions – of skis being used for military purposes, and by the seventeenth century there is evidence of widespread usage throughout northern Europe. It was in Scandinavia, however, that the long snowy winters encouraged their development. The village of Telemark in the Morgechal valley of Norway, in particular, was noted in the early nineteenth century for its use of skis for the everyday purposes of marketing, going to church and to work, and on Sundays for recreation and pleasure.

These early skis and the technique that went with them were crude. The skis were little more than thin planks, attached to the skier's foot by the simplest of bindings. It was fairly easy to run straight, but difficult either to turn or stop. Without sharp edges the skis would not grip on the snow, and sharp turns generally resulted in the foot coming out of the binding. The usual way of stopping was to lean heavily on the single long ski-pole which it was then customary to use. The breakthrough came in 1866 when the Norwegian Sondre Norheim invented an improved binding. This enabled him to perfect two sorts of turn, later to become famous: the 'telemark' and the 'christiana'.

With the opening up of the winter season in the Alps in the late sixties and seventies, the Scandinavians brought their skis to central Europe, anxious to try them elsewhere. The Norwegian Konrad Wild took a pair to Switzerland in 1868, Henri Duhamel of Grenoble imported some Swedish skis at much the same time, and another Norwegian presented a pair to the monks of the St Bernard Hospice. The Austrian Mathias Zdarsky also experimented with Norwegian skis in Lilienfeld in the Black Forest and soon had a large following of enthusiasts from Vienna, and from England. He developed his own type of ski, rather shorter than the Scandinavian prototypes. Like most of the pioneers he also experimented with bindings, in his case rigid metal rather than the cane or rope frequently used. Finally, Colonel Napier's Norwegian manservant brought skis to Davos. Their use in the village during the winter season of 1888/9 inspired a number of tales, including that of the servant skiing into town with a tea-tray perched on his shoulder.

As it turned out, the Scandinavian style of skis, adapted to more modest slopes and more consistent snow quality, proved ill-suited to alpine conditions. Coolidge, too, grumbled. Now as much alpine scholar as mountaineer, he called them 'modern imported distractions'. Napier, however, late of the Bengal army, Companion of Honour of the Indian Empire, was a pioneer. Just a year after Queen Victoria celebrated her Silver Jubilee, he began a vogue in Davos that was to grow to an extent he cannot possibly have imagined.

As alpine skiing was taking hold, so too was burgeoning an activity that would do more than any other to popularize the region. Hitherto, strangers to the Alps had relied on the artist's hand to convey something of their majesty and grandeur, and visitors from the painter Turner to the engraver Whymper had succeeded in doing so. Neither these artists nor their contemporaries, however, could achieve the realism that the extraordinary medium of photography would introduce.

The projection of an image from nature on to a dark screen had been practised since classical times by means of the *camera obscura*. The problem lay in fixing such an image. The Renaissance had seen a number of attempts to master this, all of which failed. It was not until the beginning of the nineteenth century that Thomas Wedgwood, son of the potter Josiah, first demonstrated the possibility; and only as Professor Forbes was first exploring the high Alps that the Englishman William Fox Talbot and the Frenchman Daguerre simultaneously demonstrated photography in practicable form. John Ruskin was at once struck by this means of accurately representing nature, and in 1854, in the course of one of his alpine tours, took what he described as 'the first sun-portrait of the Matterhorn'. This set the fashion for alpine photographs.

For some years, however, the equipment remained extremely bulky and cumbersome, not least because of the need to sensitize the plates with liquid before exposure, and to process them immediately afterwards. Auguste Bisson, on his 1861 expedition to photograph the panorama from the summit of Mont Blanc, needed twenty-five porters to carry his cameras, mobile darkroom, heavy glass negatives and chemicals to the peak. Still, by the time Whymper conquered the Matterhorn, the Reverend Hereford George had visited the Bernese Oberland and, in *The Oberland and Its Glaciers Explored and Illustrated with Ice-axe and Camera*, published in 1866, he displayed the results of his photographic endeavours. Thereafter Whymper's art of engraving was gradually eroded, photographs slowly replacing engravings in periodicals and books.

With the invention of dry plates by an English physicist in 1871, the modern era of photography began. The 1870s accordingly saw a number of talented photographers at work in the Alps, and images of that strange world became more commonplace. In 1880, William Frederick Donkin exhibited at the Alpine Club winter dinner a panorama taken from the summit of the Dom, at 14,910 feet the highest peak entirely within Switzerland. His obituarist Coolidge wrote that this 'excited the admiration of all who knew the Alps, and must have revealed a new world to those who did not'.

Donkin was an Etonian and a graduate of Coolidge's own Oxford college, Magdalen. He had suffered tragedy as a young man when his wife died in childbirth and their infant survived only two days. If this overshadowed his life, it scarcely restricted his climbing, undertaken perhaps as a distraction. By the 1880s he was both an energetic mountaineer and, along with the Italian Vittorio Sella, the greatest exponent of alpine photography. He went on to climb in the Caucasus – the 750-mile range dividing Asia from Europe – in the season of 1888, but on 30 August the entire party was lost. Subsequently an exhibition was mounted jointly by the Photographic Society and the Alpine Club at the Gainsborough Gallery in Bond Street. Coolidge wrote:

> these exquisite photographs . . . have enabled everyone who visited the Gainsborough gallery to study at their leisure the secrets of the snows. In the absence of some such opportunity most tourists cannot ever form any accurate idea of the great, strange world above their heads, a world where every prospect pleases, without a touch of vileness, where sky as well as earth seem to open out into 'a nobler, purer air' in a never-ending succession of distance behind distance, and where each quality of light and colour seems more refined than it is below.

Donkin used a camera which, with its plates, weighed fifteen or twenty pounds. In the year of his death, Kodak introduced roll film and the hand-held camera, both of which were instrumental in bringing photography to a much wider public. In England photography became something of a craze. By the turn of the century one in ten of the population was said to own a camera, and there were more than two hundred and fifty photography clubs. This compared with less than one hundred in America, and less than twenty-five in the whole of Continental Europe. The humorist Jerome K. Jerome would complain that 'the amateur photographer is the curse of Switzerland . . . I noticed in my early skiing days, that whenever I did anything graceful the Kodak crowd was always looking the other way. When I was lying on my back with my feet in the air, the first thing I always saw when I recovered my senses was a complete circle of Kodaks pointing straight at me!'

It was on his first tour of the Alps in 1878 that Mark Twain reflected on the extraordinary transformation of the region:

> What a change has come over Switzerland, and in fact all Europe, during this century! Seventy or eighty years ago Napoleon was the only man in Europe who could really be called a traveller; he was the only man who had devoted his attention to it and taken a powerful interest in it; he was the only man who had travelled extensively; but now everybody goes everywhere; and Switzerland, and many other regions which were unvisited and unknown remotenesses a hundred years ago, are in our days a buzzing hive of restless strangers.

There might have been a degree of writer's licence in his remark, 'everybody goes everywhere'. Nevertheless his description fairly reflected the revolution in the nature and number of people visiting the Alps, and Napoleon's Helvetic Republic, since the turn of the century, and more particularly since the accession of Victoria. As late as the 1830s the Alps had remained, for the most part, the preserve of aristocrats and artists. Artists it still continued to attract, and Leslie Stephen some fifty years later complained of the presence in his hotel in St Moritz of 'a genuine king'. There, though, in the same hotel, Stephen was distressed to encounter quite a different species, 'the genuine British cockney in all his terrors'. To Stephen the king was no more appealing than the cockney. They were both 'very objectionable neighbours at an hotel. They raise prices and destroy solitude and make an Alpine valley pretty nearly as noisy and irritating for the nerves as St James's. Was it worth while to travel some hundred miles to find one's self still on the very brink of civilization?'

Ruskin, too, by now at the height of his fame, found time in his autobiography *Praeterita* to deplore the vulgarization of the Alps, and to indulge his nostalgia for the land of his early manhood: 'Difficult enough for you to imagine, that old travellers' time when Switzerland was yet the land of the Swiss, and the Alps had never been trod by foot of man . . . steam, never heard of.' As to numbers, Switzerland alone by the 1880s was estimated to be attracting about a million visitors a year. These were figures the Dauphinois, Savoyards, Piedmontese and Tyrolese were keen to emulate, though they had not yet done so.

The irony remained that it was the writings of Ruskin and Stephen that had popularized the alpine world, while, as Ruskin recognized, the technology of steam had brought the Alps within the financial reach of the many, albeit with the active promotion of Thomas Cook and his competitors.

Cook was by now far and away the world's largest travel agency, virtually an institution of the British Empire, within the Alps as elsewhere a power to be reckoned with. In 1880 the Egyptian government had ceded to Cook the management of all steamers operating in the country. The *Daily Mail*'s star correspondent G.W. Steevens was able to write, almost without exaggeration, that 'The nominal suzerain of Egypt is the Sultan. The real suzerain is Lord Cromer. Its nominal governor is the Khedive. Its real governor is Thomas Cook.' Of course, more settled political conditions in Europe had greatly encouraged alpine tourism. So too had the development of what would today be called the alpine infrastructure – railways, roads, hotels, telegraph post offices, restaurants. *Murray's Handbook* of the period spoke of the 'developments in facilities for travelling which have effected a complete revolution in the means and mode of travelling'.

At the same time, it could not overlook the package or 'circular' tours whose agents were 'Messrs Cook & Co. of Ludgate Hill Circus, E.C., by whom they were established'. The popularity of such tours may be inferred from the *Handbook*'s disdain for 'systems . . . sprung into existence to meet the case of persons more or less incapable, from want of experience in travel or ignorance of foreign languages, of taking care of themselves while abroad'. Murray was prepared to concede that 'the hotels designated are, as a rule, good', and that 'the system may be worked so as to effect a small saving in money'. Ultimately, though, the tours were arrangements ill-suited to the purchasers of the *Handbook*, being 'only for those who would otherwise be altogether excluded from the advantages of foreign travel, many of which, however, are necessarily lost by such a system'.

Vulgar though some may have considered them, such travellers had arrived; and vulgar or not, they would continue to come. For as Twain himself said, the Alps were now entrancing the sophisticated and unsophisticated alike:

> I met dozens of people, imaginative and unimaginative, cultivated and uncultivated, who had come from far countries and roamed through the Swiss Alps year after year – they could not explain why. They had come first, they said, out of idle curiosity, because everybody talked about it; they had come since because they could not help it, and they should keep on coming, while they lived, for the same reason; they had tried to break their chains and stay away, but it was futile; now they had no desire to break them. Others came nearer formulating what they felt; they said they could find perfect rest and peace nowhere else when they were troubled; all frets and worries and chafings sank to sleep in the presence of the benignant serenity of the Alps; the Great Spirit of the Mountain breathed his own peace upon their hurt minds and sore hearts, and healed them; they could not think base thoughts or do mean and sordid things here, before the visible throne of God.

The Alps – in winter now as well as summer – were exerting their intangible spell.

Belle Époque

'My bedroom is filled in the style of the great cosmopolitan caravanserais of a city. It is Turkey-carpeted, radiator-warmed; it has a dressing-room with hot and cold water, and a marble-tiled, nickel-plated, private bathroom; its furniture, if not by 'Maple', is the product of some other artist equally suave and decorative in his ideas; and finally (this, I begin to think is the hall-mark of the modern hotel), there is a telephone at the head of my bed, so that I can languidly order breakfast without rising. Downstairs we have splendid entrance halls, lounges, reading-rooms, smoking-rooms, two billiard rooms . . . a sun verandah, and a ball-room-cum-theatre. There is a writing room on every floor, electrically controlled clocks in every corridor; every room, including the writing rooms, has its telephone. Liveried servants operate the elevators, hover about the billiard rooms, attend on the skittle players, open and close doors, and are ready to run errands on every conceivable excuse. I might be in the Savoy in London or the Adelphi in Liverpool; only outside the proud portals there is a humble village of chalets half-buried in the drifts.'

Ward Muir

1. Edward Whymper, the engraver who rapidly developed into the leading
mountaineer of the 1860s, and who was to conquer what was regarded as
the last remaining great alpine peak in his twenty-sixth year

2. Gustave Doré's imaginative rendition of the Matterhorn tragedy of 14 July 1865 in which four of Whymper's companions fell to their deaths: speculation as to the cause of the accident haunted Whymper for the rest of his life

3. Mountaineering, Victorian style: a party of ten complete the crossing of a crevasse, using a light wooden ladder carried for the purpose. The group is roped closely together according to the custom of the day, and the two ladies wear veils to protect them from the sun

4. 'The Club-Room of Zermatt, in 1864': Whymper's most famous engraving depicts the leading climbers and guides of the day, against the backdrop of Alexander Seiler's Monte Rosa hotel. This was the Alpine Club's summer home

5. 'The Chamouni polka' was part of an extravaganza devised by Albert Smith to celebrate his own ascent of Mont Blanc on 12 August 1851. His entertainment dramatizing the triumph ran for nine years and introduced the middle classes to the Alps

6. The new tourists in the Alps were often surprised by the precipitous nature of
the mountain paths. Here the cartoonist Sydney Hall caricatures a gentleman
tourist 'cutting off a fearful corner'

7. Having pioneered 'excursionism' – the package tour – in England in the 1840s, in the summer of 1863 Thomas Cook took his first party of tourists to the Alps. Not everyone was happy with the subsequent influx, Henry James remarking that the new visitors scarcely seemed 'children of the light to any eminent degree'

8. Despite the growing tide of visitors, many of the alpine resorts retained their unspoilt qualities until the coming of the mountain railways. This is Grindelwald in 1864, before the arrival of the railway in 1890 led to its being 'besieged by throngs'

9. Leslie Stephen, founder of the *Dictionary of National Biography*, and father of Virginia Woolf and Vanessa Bell, also had a series of virgin peaks to his credit. His *The Playground of Europe,* published in 1871, remains one of the wittiest books on mountaineering

10. The advent of Thomas Cook's continental tours saw the Mer de Glace in Chamonix established as an essential part of the tourist itinerary. The Alps' most famous glacier, it had first been investigated by a party of Englishmen in 1741

11. W.A.B. Coolidge (*second left*) established himself in the 1870s as 'the young American who climbs with his aunt and his dog'. Although dogs were acceptable, the Victorian public was much shocked by the spectacle of female mountaineers. The party is flanked by its guides

12. A.F. Mummery was the first great climber to emerge after the major alpine peaks had been conquered. He defined his mission as 'to leave the paths that common sense, custom, or the average mountain sheep would point out, and go in some other direction where the chances appear to be in favour of breaking your neck'. Following his maxim, he was lost on Nanga Parbat in the Himalayas in 1895

13. An Edwardian mountaineering party: Geoffrey Winthrop Young (*far left*) would lose a leg in the Great War but continued to climb; his protégé, the dazzling George Leigh Mallory, is on the far right

14. Four generations of the Lunn family, to whom the Alps owe the popularity of downhill skiing: the pioneer winter sports travel agent Henry S. Lunn is seated right; his son Arnold, father of British skiing and Christian controversialist, stands

15. The Arnold Lunn medal, the talisman of the English gift to winter sports

16. Zermatt: once little more than a 'crowded assemblage of dank, dirty-looking wooden houses', by the Great War it had become 'an alpine village that has almost lost its identity among a colony of hotels'

17. The Oberland village of Mürren owed its development partly to the arrival of the railway, partly to Henry Lunn's insistence that the system should be opened for the winter season of 1910/11. A contemporary wrote: 'One might imagine from the illustrated press that Mürren's winter visiting population was composed of ski-ing duchesses, skating lords and curling bishops'

18. 'There is one Mecca, there is one St Peter's, there is one Cresta. As Mecca is to the Mohammedans, as is St Peter's to the Catholic, so is the Cresta Run to the tobogganer'. A lady competitor in 1908

19. Horse-play in St Moritz, New Year's Day, 1938

20. Leni Riefenstahl with camera crew on the summit of Mont Blanc, 1929: later chosen by Hitler to film the 1936 Olympics, she treated mountaineering as melodrama

21. The Cambridge University ski team in 1938, preparing to do battle with Oxford in the Italian Alps. For the first time the sport merited a half-blue

22. Hitler at the Winter Olympics at Garmisch-Partenkirchen, February 1936. Arnold Lunn deplored the politicization of skiing and, in his broadcast at the closing ceremony, said: 'Germans, may I tell you a little secret. There are still people who ski for fun.'

23. The Alps at war: a French alpine soldier on the Franco-German border, January 1945

24. The epitome of English alpinism: George Mallory, here on Everest with E.F. Norton in 1922. In 1924 Mallory and Andrew Irvine made a further attempt on the mountain, in which they both perished

Chapter Seven
White Leprosy

'The French revolutionists made stables of the cathedrals of France; you have made race-courses of the cathedrals of the earth. Your one conception of pleasure is to drive in railroad carriages round their aisles, and eat off their altars ... [There is no] foreign city in which the spread of your presence is not marked among its fair old streets and happy gardens by a consuming white leprosy of new hotels.'

John Ruskin, *Sesame and Lilies* (1864)

In the early hours of 16 August 1892 a stray spark from the kitchen fire in the Bear hotel at Grindelwald started smouldering. Soon there was a blaze. Despite its international fame, the community still consisted of little more than a few dozen picturesque wooden chalets. Means of controlling such a conflagration were no more sophisticated than at St Moritz, where the fire engine nestled cosily in the village church beside the pulpit. It was not long before the whole west end of Grindelwald was alight. Lucky to escape with their lives were two young boys named Arnold and Hugh Lunn.

Three generations of the Lunn family were to have a remarkable influence on the development of the Alps. The boys' father, Henry Simpson Lunn, was aptly described by his son Arnold as 'a queer mixture of merchant adventurer and mystic'. Born in Horncastle, Lincolnshire, in 1859, in modest circumstances, he was still a youth when he discovered that he could profitably barter mice through the columns of the second-hand goods' paper *Exchange and Mart*. By early manhood he was a successful businessman, eventually selling his shares in his company to finance a career as a medical missionary in India, the jewel in Queen Victoria's imperial crown. For this purpose in 1886 he was ordained a Methodist, and took a degree in medicine and surgery at Trinity College, Dublin. However, like others before him he found his constitution unequal to the demands of the subcontinent and, returning to England in 1888, he founded the *Review of the Churches*, a journal devoted to the ecumenical movement. To further the great project, Lunn proposed an annual meeting of divines representing the various different Protestant churches, Anglicans, Methodists and Nonconformists alike. His choice of venue eventually fell on Grindelwald. This was partly because St Bernard of Clairvaux had once had a retreat in the vicinity; partly because the new mountain railway up from Lauterbrunnen, opened in July 1892, made it the most accessible of the principal alpine winter resorts.

The objective of these conferences – the reunification of the Protestant churches – was ambitious, so much so that they might be considered to have been doomed from the start. The artist Neville Lytton once ironically remarked: 'Sir Henry Lunn is a courageous man – once he set out to convert the Pope of Rome to Protestantism.' However, the complex organization that went into these meetings was to interest Lunn in the business of travel, and inspire the travel agency that still bears his name. So impressed were his first guests with the standard of arrangements that they asked him to organize a party for the following autumn in Rome. Expecting to take fifty or sixty pilgrims, he finally had a group of four hundred and forty under his wing.

It was the Alps, though, that really intrigued Lunn. Like the invalids to the east in the Grisons, he noticed that 'mid-winter in the high Alps is an earthly paradise – the gloom and fog and damp are left in the valley below, while up in the eternal snows the sun is often too hot to bear, and the sparkling atmosphere is more of a tonic than the finest champagne.' Although Thomas Cook – then in the hands of his son John Mason Cook – had been bringing visitors to the summer Alps for more than a quarter of a century, it was Henry Lunn who was to develop the mountains for winter tourism. Indeed, Neville Lytton could be forgiven for saying, with only a little exaggeration, that 'The great popularity of winter sports dates from the Grindelwald Conference.'

This, however, lay in the future. For the present certain social niceties had been transgressed. As Arnold Lunn was later to write, 'The old Bear, like the Monte Rosa at Zermatt or Couttet's at Chamonix, was one of the shrines of the Alpine elect. It was not exactly a club, but those who were not accepted by the habitués felt slightly chilled as they crossed the sacred threshold.' So it was with the twenty-six divines who attended the first Grindelwald conference in 1892. The Bear's guests were much of a class, and had made the hotel their own. In winter it was perhaps yet more exclusive, the coterie of guests devoting their days to tobogganing parties and skating. When the divines arrived, personally conducted by Dr Lunn, 'it was as if Mr Cook himself had descended with his tourists. The Bear lost caste when the pilgrims arrived.'

This was a problem Lunn would have to solve if he were to succeed. It was also one he shared with the second great alpine competitor of Thomas Cook, Quintin Hogg and his Polytechnic Touring Association. Born in 1845, Hogg was an Etonian who at a relatively young age had made a fortune in the sugar trade. In the tradition of the great Victorian philanthropists, he then devoted himself to the disadvantaged, founding successively a school for the poor at Charing Cross, a Youth's Christian Institute and, in 1882, the Regent Street Polytechnic. At a time when provision for self-improvement among the working classes was extremely limited, this would offer – in the words of Hogg's daughter – 'facilities for mechanic artisans to improve . . . their knowledge of their trade and their technical education'. In doing so he started the whole polytechnic movement in the capital.

In line with these aspirations and the contemporary popularity of the Alps, Hogg then established the Polytechnic's Continental holidays. Given his bent towards philanthropic 'improvement', the organization aimed to provide as much instruction as it did pleasure. The first party consisted of sixty schoolboys under the supervision of three masters, and the group spent twenty-seven days touring the Alps and improving the boys' grasp of history and geography. All this was achieved at the remarkable cost to each of £5 19s. od. –

inclusive. Such benevolence, though, was not welcomed by all. In the summer of 1892 a well-known English clergyman was enjoying the beauties of Meiringen in the Bernese Oberland when, as he recorded:

> One evening there trudged into the hotel garden a party of unmistakable London lads, clerks and shopmen mainly, weary somewhat with the long walk from the Furka Pass. They were from the Regent Street Polytechnic, and when I found that a fortnight in Switzerland had cost under eight pounds, I first marvelled at what co-operation and contrivance and contracts could effect; then, turning my thoughts to grimy Woolwich, I began to wonder whether 'Woolwich in the Alps' was an impossibility.

To the Reverend Canon John William Horsley – as to Leslie Stephen before him – such intrusions marked an ominous erosion of the exclusivity of the Alps.

Among Arnold Lunn's earliest memories were those of the Grindelwald fire. He was only four at the time. Later, he spent many of his childhood holidays in the chalet his father had acquired in the village. There was inculcated a passion for the mountains that – in the tradition of Forbes, Ruskin, Tyndall, Stephen and Mummery – would inspire his whole life. He wrote, 'When I was a small boy I had no ambition to be a soldier or an engine-driver. Life, to me, began and ended with mountains.' *Murray's Handbook* of 1892 noted that the village pastor, Herr Strasser, spoke English and 'may be appealed to in cases of difficulty'. For Lunn, Gottfried Strasser was a difficulty in himself. He was 'Grindelwald's most imposing figure', who regarded the advent of tourism with horror. 'The favourite theme of his Sunday sermon was the baneful influence of the tourist. His congregation, many of whom had spent the week on the distant cow Alps, nodded solemnly as he warned them against the rising tide of luxury.'

To Strasser, this was most obviously manifested in the local hotels. By 1893 the charred remains of the Bear had been rebuilt on altogether ampler lines than its predecessor, and since the arrival of the railway from Lauterbrunnen, further pensions and inns had proliferated. For many visitors to the Alps, however, these provisions were neither unwelcome nor premature. Although accommodation of a passable quality had long been a feature of the principal alpine towns and cities, standards had been minimal elsewhere. The early scientific explorers venturing into the remote alpine valleys of Savoy, the Dauphiné, the Oberland, Piedmont, the Grisons or the Tyrol had at first been obliged to throw themselves on the hospitality of the local priests. Fleas and bedbugs were as abundant as fresh meat was rare, and the ceremony of bread-baking would typically take place once a month – in areas where there was little firewood, once a year. The wine was sour. With the exception of the oldest resorts, inns and hotels arrived only in the 1850s, and offered no more than basic facilities. Alexandre Seiler's original Monte Rosa hotel in Zermatt boasted three bedrooms, lighting by candle, and sanitation of the most primitive kind. According to *Murray's Handbook*, at inns in other remote areas 'manoeuvres are sometimes resorted to for the purpose of retaining the guests'. Of the hotel at the summit of the Rigi above Lucerne, Murray famously wrote:

During the height of summer, when travellers are most numerous, the Culm inn is crammed to over-flowing every evening; numbers are turned away from the doors, and it is difficult to procure beds, food, or even attention. The house presents a scene of the utmost confusion, servant maids hurrying in one direction, couriers and guides in another, while gentlemen with poles and knapsacks block up the passages. Most of the languages of Europe, muttered usually in terms of abuse or complaint, and the all-pervading fumes of tobacco, enter largely as ingredients into the Babel of sounds and smells, and add to the discontent of the fatigued traveller. In the evening the guests are collected at a table d'hôte supper; after which most persons are glad to repair to rest. It takes some time, however, before the hub-hub of voices and trampling of feet subside; and not infrequently, a few roystering German students prolong their potations and noise far into the night.

The coming of the railways to the foothills of the Alps at last stimulated the multiplication of hotels, and brought to them some of the amenities of modern accommodation. In the 1860s and '70s the great alpine hotel dynasties – the Seilers, the Bosses, the Couttets – were in the process of expansion; in Switzerland alone the number of beds available in tourist hotels doubled in the ten years preceding Lunn's first conference at Grindelwald.

By then the Victoria at Interlaken, at the heart of the Bernese Oberland, was remarkable for its size and the provision of electric light. In the Grisons, at Maloja, a few miles from St Moritz, the Kurhaus was 'an enormous establishment', boasting some three hundred and fifty beds and an orchestra. The Trois Rois in Basel possessed a fine view, was very large, and was 'one of the best appointed hotels in Switzerland'. In Davos, the Kurhaus had one hundred and eighty bedrooms and its own theatre. At Neuchâtel the amenities of the Bellevue included a 'very obliging landlord'. At Poschiavo, just on the Italian side of the Bernina pass, the Croce Bianca was 'a curious old house, good and reasonable'. Soon electric light, along with carpets, hydraulic lifts, telegraphs and telephones, would be as obligatory as English water closets – the variety where the user could sit rather than squat.

In France things were less satisfactory. Returning to the Dauphiné in 1895, W.A.B. Coolidge recorded his astonishment at the recent improvements made for the comfort of visitors, praising in particular the sanitary arrangements, 'to which English travellers attach great importance'. More generally, though, 'hotels of the highest class were to be found only in large towns, the inns elsewhere retaining their primitive provincial characteristics, which might prove rather attractive than otherwise were it not for the shameful deficiencies of the sanitary arrangements'. In the Tarentaise, the valley of the Isère in Savoy, Baedeker predicted that Tignes would become one of the area's chief excursion centres. In the meantime, though,

> everything is still very primitive. Owing to the rigour of the winter, those of the inhabitants who do not migrate share their dwelling-room with their stock. In such quarters light and air are scarce and the only division between man and beast is a trench. Even when there is a guest-chamber on the first floor, it is in a common-room such as described that the hotels receive their visitors.

Nearby Val d'Isère did not even merit a mention.

Similarly in Italy, although first-class hotels were to be found in all the principal alpine resorts, elsewhere Baedeker found matters less satisfactory.

> The popular idea of cleanliness in Italy is behind the age, dirt being perhaps neutralized in the opinion of the natives by the brilliancy of the climate . . . those who go off the beaten track should be prepared for privations. Iron bedsteads should if possible be selected, as they are less likely to harbour enemies of repose. Insect powder (*polvere insetticida*) and camphor somewhat repel their advances.

Murray's *Knapsack Guide to the Tyrol* complained that the Germans adulterated their guests' coffee with chicory, and that tea was unknown 'except in hotels on the great routes'. Yet the concerns of Grindelwald's pastor were ultimately justifiable. For the purposes of meeting the ever-increasing demands of the tourists, luxury was indeed engulfing the Alps.

It was this phenomenon that John Ruskin some years earlier had called 'white leprosy', identifying his compatriots as the source of the infection. Even in the 1890s, as the Alps began to attract a highly cosmopolitan clientele, the English remained the basic cause of the trouble. *Murray's Handbook* of the time still reiterated the old refrain that 'the wants, tastes and habits of the English are more carefully studied in the Swiss hotels than in those of any other part of Europe'. There was the late table d'hôte dinner so insisted upon by the English, and 'tolerably good tea'. In the Tyrol, Baedeker told hotel-keepers that those 'who wish to commend their houses to British and American travellers are reminded of the desirability of providing the bedrooms with *large* basins, foot-baths, plenty of water, and an adequate supply of towels. Great care should be taken to ensure that the sanitary arrangements are in proper order, including a strong flush of water, and proper toilette paper.'

The English language, too, was becoming increasingly wide-spread. In the Tyrol itself, Baedeker remarked that 'those who do not deviate from the beaten track will generally find that English or French is spoke at the principal hotels in the usual public resorts.' In the French Alps, although the native language was 'indispensable in remote parts', on the usual trails visitors 'will generally find English spoken'. As to Grenoble, the city that now billed itself as the capital of the French Alps, a pamphlet written in 1896 recorded that 'L'Angleterre est bien, en effet, le pays qui tourne le plus de touristes à notre région.'

If the English in the 1890s were still contributing significantly to what was then generally seen as the civilization of the Alps, they were also continuing to be great publicists of the varied joys of alpinism. Indeed they were universally recognized as alpinism's greatest proponents.

Publicity of course came in many forms. The cynic might say that the Matterhorn tragedy was devised to exemplify the maxim that all publicity is good publicity. Then there was Coolidge, who had first visited Zermatt soon after Whymper's disaster. He had forged his reputation in the early seventies as a mountaineer. Following his election as a Fellow of Magdalen College, Oxford, in 1875, he added to this the aura of the pioneering alpine scholar. He was the first to put the study of the Alps' history, culture, peoples and development on a systematic scholarly footing, publishing in the remaining fifty years of his life a spate of articles, essays and books on alpine matters. Indeed, he became such an authority that he was once called upon to review one of his own books, taking the author to task for a number of minor errors. Stemming from this came his reputation as a controversialist. As his biographer Ronald Clark was obliged to concede, Coolidge as he grew older became burdened with the 'certain, constant and often insupportable assertion that he alone could be right'. With the Alps and particularly the Alpine Club full of men of high academic standing, it was inevitable that many chose to take issue with Coolidge, or Coolidge with them. Sometimes the matters were of substance. Very often – whether or not a peak had been climbed on a particular day, or by this or that route – they were not. Arnold Lunn called him simply 'the Lord of the Battles, the man who had the highest opinion of the one Alpine historian with whom he had never quarrelled, himself'.

In his capacity both as climber and scholar Coolidge was appointed in 1879 editor of the *Alpine Journal*, and as such attracted the attention of the brilliant young alpinist Martin Conway. Conway had explored the Tyrol in 1875. Now just down from Cambridge, he applied to Coolidge for help in publishing a mountaineer's guide-book to Zermatt. Coolidge at once recognized the merit of a book focusing in some detail on a locality so rich in challenging climbs, and drafted by a man whose gifts with a pen were of the same order as those with his ice-axe. Coolidge helped Conway revise and refine the book, and thus began perhaps the only unclouded friendship of the scholar's life. With his patrician manners and easy charm, Conway was adept at handling the prickly Coolidge. He steered his irascible partner adroitly through the production of what were to become the first proper climber's guides. He was also adept in handling a publisher well aware of Coolidge's reputation and – in his biographer's words – 'worried by the possible length, unreadability, and general unmanageability of what might be prepared by way of copy'. Credited to them both, the series began in 1892.

The value of Conway's contribution was underscored the following year when Coolidge was asked by John Murray to revise his father's *Handbook for Switzerland, Savoy and Piedmont*, the elder Murray having died the previous year. Coolidge conceded that he was the only man in a position to handle the task competently, and accepted 100 guineas for doing so. In due course he produced a very lengthy and detailed introduction. Of this Murray said 'a large part of the information is thrown away on the herd of travellers'. Then there was a passage libelling a well-known Geneva hotel. Finally, when the book was at proof stage, Coolidge returned with such a mass of minor corrections and amendments that the publisher despaired. Taking umbrage, the scholar for long refused to associate his name with the version finally published.

Soon Coolidge was to be involved in another squabble, this time with Whymper over the accuracy with which he had described one of his climbs, 'Almer's Leap'. Published in *Scrambles Amongst the Alps*, this was Whymper's account of a jump over a deep notch by the guide Christian Almer, on the descent from the Barre des Écrins in 1864. Coolidge had long been sceptical of Whymper's description, and he took advantage of Almer's death to ventilate these doubts. A first-class row ensued that led to Coolidge's resignation from the Alpine Club and Whymper threatening a libel action.

Conway, meanwhile, had come up with the notion of an expedition which would make his name, the record of which appeared in 1895 as *The Alps from End to End*. With the exploration and mapping of the Alps by now nearing completion, Conway – like Whymper and Mummery before him – had already begun to investigate ranges elsewhere. His exploration of the Karakorams in the western Himalaya in 1892 was one of the first European expeditions to the greatest of the world's mountain ranges. It had given him a taste for long journeys, and in an age when tours of the Alps were becoming shorter rather than longer, he now designed a route which would take him from Limone in the French Maritime Alps almost to Vienna. He was to be accompanied by two of the Gurkhas from the 5th Gurkha Rifles who had been with him in the Karakorams, his intention being to instruct the two soldiers so they could disseminate their knowledge amongst their fellows on their return.

The party assembled in Turin on 1 June 1894, and the subsequent journey proved a remarkable adventure. The three men walked more than eight hundred miles in eighty-six days. They climbed twenty-one peaks, including Mont Blanc and the Jungfrau. They traversed thirty-nine passes. The Gurkhas, tentative at first, ended up fine mountaineers with a penchant for discussing the niceties of the native cheeses with the local inhabitants. Published in instalments in the *Pall Mall Gazette*, the resulting book drew much of its freshness from the diary account that Conway kept. On 27 July, the party reached the summit of Mont Blanc. Here, Conway reflects on the huts and observatories that local alpinists had begun to establish on the high peaks:

> It was just noon when we stood on the top, arriving there all together. The first thing we looked at was not Europe at our feet, but M. Jansen's hut – a dreadful disfigurement. The last time I was here, the surface of the snowy dome was one unbroken curve of snow, aloof from man. Now man has rooted the evidences of his activity deep into the icy mass and strewed its surface with shavings and paper, so frozen that the storms of a whole year have not yet been sufficient to move them. I cannot however say that we felt any resentment against the hut-builders, for we took shelter behind the observatory from the blasts of the cold gale.

The Alps from End to End was the best book on the subject since the *annus mirabilis* of 1871, which had seen publication of those classic works by Stephen, Whymper and Tyndall. It also contributed to Conway's knighthood, awarded the following year 'in recognition of his remarkable work as a traveller'.

On Conway's great trek poor weather had precluded an attempt on the Matterhorn. A little later in the 1894 season, though, a young man arrived in Zermatt and tackled the famous peak with success. This was Leopold ('Leo') Amery, who in the years up to the Second World

War was to win fame as a mountaineer, writer and politician, and as such – like Lunn, Coolidge and Conway – was to be a notable publicist for the Alps.

Born in India, and educated at Harrow, Amery in 1894 was enjoying his first year at Oxford. A scholar at Balliol College, he wrote that his summer term was 'almost entirely given over, when I was not sailing or idling on the Cherwell in punt or canoe, to all the other innumerable diversions that can make Oxford so delightful to those who wish to study books rather than life'. Belatedly mindful of his studies, in the manner of the day he decided to take a packing-case full of books to the Continent for the long vacation. He was, though, a talented gymnast, this combining with his stature to give him the nickname at Harrow of 'Pocket Hercules'. In the company of a schoolfriend, he ended up one fine August day in Zermatt. By now the old wooden houses had been joined by a series of hotels, and what Murray described as the usual kind of shops and lawn tennis courts. Amery recalled:

> The heroic generation of mountaineering in which all the great Alpine peaks were first scaled, and chiefly by Englishmen, was over, but still a very living memory. Its conquerors, both guides and amateurs, were mostly still alive, and many, like Whymper, still climbing. They could be seen, like ordinary human beings, sitting on the wall opposite the Monte Rosa hotel, or at tea on the terrace at the Riffelalp, or even met on a climb, when they would treat the awe-struck beginner with genial encouragement. A new generation was actively finding, if not new peaks, at least new routes, or causing much shaking of heads among their elders by the daring innovation of climbing guideless. Far off still were the days when impossible precipes were to be pegged with pitons, or formidable snow summits treated as ski-runs. The giants of the Alps, by what are now called the 'ordinary routes' were then still real adventures, to two boys at least adventures supremely worth essaying.

At once contracting the services of a guide, Amery made a trial run on the 11,149-foot Unter Gabelhorn, one of the tributary peaks to the Monte Rosa. Passing the test satisfactorily, within days he had conquered the 13,848-foot Rothorn and the 14,780-foot Weisshorn. Then came the Matterhorn. Less than thirty years had passed since the first ascent, and its tragedy – so Amery recalled – was still fresh in men's minds. By now, though, the route up the north-east ridge had been established, and it was regarded in good weather as a challenging though by no means overwhelming summit. Put on his mettle by encountering Miss Lily Bristow, a highly accomplished climber tackling the far trickier north-west route pioneered by A.F. Mummery, he reached the summit with ease. A 'new and delightful chapter had been opened in life, full of fresh air and strenuous exertion with just enough savour of adventure and risk to spice the whole'.

That same month a schoolfellow of Amery's, who was also to follow a political career, arrived in Zermatt. Like Amery, he had attended a lecture by Whymper at Harrow, later recalling his 'wonderful pictures of guides and tourists hanging on by their eyelids or standing with their backs to precipices which even in photographs made one squirm'. This was Winston Churchill. So inspired, Churchill determined to climb the Monte Rosa. At 15,203 feet, this was the highest alpine peak wholly within Switzerland. Despite suffering from mountain sickness, and sunburn which stripped the skin from his face, he reached the summit. It was his only attempt at mountaineering, although his love for the Alps endured. Amery later expressed regret that such a combination of adventurer and writer should not have pursued the sport.

Yet if Churchill passed up some of the pleasure of the mountains, Arthur Conan Doyle did not. Such was the all-encroaching fame attached to the creator of Sherlock Holmes by the early 1890s that Doyle, paradoxically never one of Holmes's greatest enthusiasts, was contemplating his destruction. His hand was temporarily stayed by the stupendous offer from his serial publisher, the *Strand Magazine*, of £1,000 for a further dozen stories. In 1893, just as 'Silver Blaze', 'The Reigate Squires' and 'The Naval Treaty' were appearing, Doyle and his wife made a tour of Switzerland. Here was the inspiration of the last tale in the collection, that of Holmes's struggle with the archcriminal Moriarty at the Reichenbach Falls, recounted by the faithful Watson:

For a charming week we wandered up the Valley of the Rhône, and then, branching off at Leuk, we made our way over the Gemmi Pass, still deep in snow, and so, by way of Interlaken, to Meiringen. It was a lovely trip, the dainty green of the spring below, the virgin white of the winter above, but it was clear to me that never for one instant did Holmes forget the shadow which lay across him. In the homely Alpine villages or in the lonely mountain passes, I could still tell, by his quick glancing eyes and his sharp scrutiny of every face that passed us, that he was well convinced that, walk where we would, we could not walk ourselves clear of the danger which was dogging our footsteps.

At a critical moment, Watson was lured away from Holmes's side to attend an Englishwoman in the last stages of tuberculosis. Within months, Doyle's wife Louise was diagnosed as being in the early stages of a serious form of the same disease. The couple's doctors vacillated between sending them to St Moritz or Davos, eventually settling for the latter. The pair wintered at the Kurhaus hotel, moving on to Maloja for the summer. Then, towards the end of 1894, they returned to Davos and the Hotel Belvedere, the most popular in the town amongst the English.

Like Stevenson, Doyle found the life there rather dull, remarking that 'as our life was bounded by the snow and fir which girt us in, I was able to devote myself to doing a good deal of work, and also to taking up with some energy the winter sports for which the place was famous. In the early months of 1895 I developed ski-running in Switzerland.' Doyle was of course preceded in this by Colonel Napier some six years earlier, and probably by others. Nonetheless there is some justice in his claim, for that year he made a fifteen-mile journey on skis from Davos across the Furka pass to Arosa.

Doyle was an accomplished sportsman who – like many others – was inspired to experiment with skis by an account of their use by the Norwegian explorer Fridtjof Nansen in his classic record, *The First Crossing of Greenland*, published in English in 1890. Doyle induced two local tradesmen, the Branger brothers, to obtain several pairs of skis from Norway. When they eventually appeared they were 'two strips of elm wood, eight feet long, four inches broad, with a square heel, turned up toes, and straps in the centre to secure your feet'. The three men set about learning how to use them, for some weeks affording 'innocent amusement to a large number of people who watched our awkward movements and complex tumbles'. Within a month, Doyle felt himself ready for a challenge. The trio climbed the Jacobshorn at the south end of the village and then skied down. The flags in the village were dipped in honour of the accomplishment, Doyle writing of the thrill of 'getting as near flying as any earth-bound man can. In that glorious air it is a delightful experience, gliding over the gentle slopes, flying down the steeper ones, taking an occasional cropper.'

The 7,976-foot Furka pass was sterner stuff. Arosa had established itself as a health resort somewhat in the shadow of Davos. It was scarcely twelve miles away as the crow flies, but could be reached in winter only by a circuitous railway journey or by the snowbound pass. Doyle set out before dawn one March morning in the company of the faithful Branger brothers, who had undertaken the traverse on foot the previous year. The journey was not without incident. The first occurred when the three were obliged to traverse a steep slope too deeply frozen to afford any grip for the wooden edges of the skis. It declined precipitously into a chasm, from which – in Doyle's words – 'a blue smoke or fog rose in the morning air'. Without a rope between them, the three had to hope for the best as they edged tentatively towards safety. Later they

came to an absolute precipice, up which no doubt the path zig-zags in summer. It was not of course perpendicular, but it seemed little removed from it, and it had just the slope enough to hold the snow. It looked impassible, but the Brangers had picked up a lot in some way of their own. They took off their skis, fastened them together with a thong, and on this toboggan they sat, pushing themselves over the edge, and going down amid a tremendous spray of flying snow. When they had reached safety they beckoned to me to follow. I had done as they had, and was sitting on my skis preparatory to launching myself when a fearsome thing happened, for my ski shot from under me, and vanished in huge bounds among the snow mounds beyond. It was a nasty moment, and the poor Brangers stood looking up at me some hundreds of feet below in a dismal state of mind. However, there was no possible choice as to what to do, so I did it. I let myself go over the edge, and came squattering down, with legs and arms extended to check the momentum. A minute later I was rolling covered with snow at the feet of my guides, and my skis were found some hundreds of yards away, so no harm was done after all.

The party eventually reached Arosa at 11.30, after a journey of seven hours. On arriving at their hotel Tobias Branger paid Doyle the compliment of registering his profession not as author but as 'sportsman'.

In his contemporary account published in the *Strand Magazine*, Doyle remarked that 'skiing opens up a field of sport . . . which is, I think, unique. This is not appreciated yet, but I am convinced the time will come when hundreds of Englishmen will come to Switzerland for the skiing season between March and April.' When his memoirs were published in the aftermath of the Great War, he wrote that 'skis are, no doubt, in very general use, but I think I am right in saying that these and other excursions of ours first demonstrated their possibilities to the people of the country and have certainly sent a good many thousand pounds since then to Switzerland.'

Doyle was right. His own activities showed the way for the Richardson brothers, who in the new century would make Davos the cradle of English skiing.

By 1897 Henry Lunn had abandoned his courageous attempt to reunite the churches. The skills that he had developed in organizing the annual winter conferences at Grindelwald and escorting his pilgrims to Rome could nevertheless be employed elsewhere, and he accordingly set up shop as a travel agent. But like Thomas Cook before him, he soon found that his charges were stigmatized for putting themselves in the care of 'Lunn's Tours'. It was not the done thing, and the enterprise was in danger of failing.

As Arnold Lunn later explained, the appeal of the older alpine hotels lay in their exclusivity. They catered not simply for Englishmen, but a certain class of Englishmen, who 'liked to preserve their social environment while changing their physical environment . . . those who wished to climb Swiss mountains by day, and dine with congenial Englishmen by night'. Recognizing this problem, the elder Lunn was in many respects well placed to solve it. He was a man who, despite the extent of his European travels, never bothered to learn more than a smattering of French or German, and who, like so many Englishmen of the time, insisted that foreigners adapt their customs to the English rather than vice versa. Within his wide acquaintance was John Stogdon, Leo Amery's housemaster at Harrow. Stogdon had the reputation – according to Amery – of having climbed the Dent d'Hérens alone in tennis shoes and flannels between a morning and an afternoon game of tennis at his Zermatt hotel. Like A.F. Mummery a famous proponent of guideless climbing, Stogdon was persuaded by Lunn to write to Etonians and Harrovians endorsing Lunn's winter sports tours – this at a time when the majority of the members of the Cabinet were drawn from one or other of these two schools.

The first of Lunn's trips with his new-found clientele was to Chamonix, in the year of Queen Victoria's Diamond Jubilee. Chamonix had by now mushroomed into a village of two and a half thousand inhabitants, with more than twenty hotels, an English church, a casino, and numerous souvenir shops, its winter visitors attracted by the opportunities it afforded for sleighing, tobogganing, skating and curling. Lunn's tour was a success. Indeed, it paved the way for the Public Schools Alpine Sports Club (PSASC), the principle of which was the reservation of hotels for the exclusive use of its members. The problem was brilliantly solved, and in the process Lunn established himself as the pioneer winter sports travel agent.

Later, Arnold Lunn would remark that 'the peculiar character of our contribution to winter sports can only be fully appreciated against the background of the period. When I began to ski, the great Victorian age, with its Augustan qualities, was drawing to a close. The Boer War had not yet revealed our weakness, and the Diamond Jubilee had reinforced our pride.' Lunn was right in implying that a turning-point was at hand. Of the great pioneers, Forbes, Tyndall and Ball were dead, Ruskin and Stephen shortly to die. Coolidge that very year of 1897 made his last major ascent.

Conway followed suit on 19 August 1901, taking his daughter up his own first major peak, that of the Breithorn in Zermatt. At a time when the presence and influence of the English in the Alps was reaching its apogee, a new generation were anxious to prove themselves worthy heirs to the great Victorians. Whether they would do so was another question.

Chapter Eight
The Tables Turn

'The English branch exists not to attempt interference in Swiss affairs, but solely to express English sympathy with the aims of the Vereinigung für Heimatschutz [the League for the Preservation of Swiss Scenery] and to refute the assertion that schemes of desecration are desired by tourists and are necessary to attract them; that in the words of a Swiss patriot, "it is for you English that these things are done".'

Alpine Journal, 1909

John Barraclough Fell's railway over Mont Cenis and Thomas Brassey's tunnel under the same mountain had set great precedents. Although the opening of the latter had been marred by the international uncertainty arising from the Franco-Prussian War, thereafter enthusiasm mounted for both trans-alpine tunnels and mountain railways. By the summer of 1899, of the Mont Cenis's four great successors, the St Gotthard and Arlberg tunnels were already open, the Simplon was under construction, and the Lötschberg already planned and partly financed. There was also what amounted to a mania for the construction of mountain railways.

The St Gotthard, like the Mont Cenis, was of strategic significance, for it penetrated the main chain of the Alps south of Lucerne, and provided an international main line from Germany to Italy via Switzerland. It also replaced the St Gotthard pass between Cantons Ticino and Glis which, until the construction of the roads over the Simplon and the Splügen, was the most frequented of the passes. Rather more than a mile longer than its prototype, the St Gotthard proved difficult to bore because of the steepness of the approach valleys, both to the north at Goschenen and to the south at Airolo. This was overcome by laying out the railway in a series of spirals near Wassen Faido and Giornico, thus gaining height at the relatively modest gradient of 1 in 40. The surveying precision required to locate and build these structures was quite unprecedented. *Murray's Handbook* described them as 'the most marvellous features of a wonderful railway line', and added that while 'traversing the tunnel the traveller may amuse himself by watching the strange shiftings of the compass'. When it was successfully completed, the line opened the way for other such tunnels both in the Alps themselves and in the Canadian Rockies. The work of an entire decade, the main bore when completed lay six thousand feet below the ridge above, and there were no fewer than fifty-six associated tunnels.

Coincident with the opening of the St Gotthard was the beginning of work on the Arlberg. This provided a route from Switzerland to the Tyrol. Leaving the Rhine at Feldkirch in the Vorarlberg, it ran due east into the Inn valley at Landeck, the small settlement of St Anton marking the tunnel's eastern end. Built between 1880 and 1884, the tunnel employed three thousand workers on its six-mile bore, and a factory devoted to the production of dynamite was established at the nearby hospice of St Christopher.

The projected Simplon route was altogether more ambitious. It would turn south from the main line running east from Geneva at Brig, through a tunnel twelve miles in length to Iselle, and thence to Milan. By this means it short-circuited the St Gotthard, and created a direct route from Paris and Lyon to Italy. A distinguished English engineer, Francis Fox, was one of a team of three international experts called in to advise on the project. In 1899 the workings were a year old, and already problems were beginning to be encountered. In places, the rock reached temperatures of 127 degrees Fahrenheit, and the surfaces had to be sprayed with ice-cold water to provide sustainable working conditions. As both time and money then began to run out, 24-hour working was introduced, split into three shifts.

When at last the line was completed in 1905, Edward VII sent his congratulations to the Swiss Federal Council, and even after the Great War it was still described as a 'stupendous engineering feat'.

Then came the Lötschberg, which would take advantage of the Simplon by linking Bern with Brig, a nine-mile tunnel under the great peaks of the Bernese Oberland connecting the Aare and Rhône valleys. Despite the experience acquired on its predecessors, this was to prove the most difficult bore of all, very high rock temperatures being compounded by a water break-in which killed twenty-five men and led to the tunnel being diverted; an avalanche killed thirty more. It would eventually be finished only a year before the First World War.

These tunnels opened up great European strategic routes between north and south, east and west, and the resulting reduction in cost and improvement in the convenience of reaching the mountains created what contemporaries regarded as a revolution in alpine travel. Famous services like the Blue Train between Paris, the Côte d'Azur and Rome, and the Orient Express to Constantinople were inaugurated – both in the year 1883, the latter using the Simplon from 1906. Moreover, in helping to bring visitors in large numbers to the mountains, the routes also encouraged the construction of lines to take travellers up and in some instances over the Alps; the tourist – in Murray's words – was now able to 'reach by railway places which were almost inaccessible to the pedestrian half a century ago'. By the close of the century dozens of such schemes were being mooted or were under construction, from the Maritime Alps to the Tyrol.

These were inspired not only by the Fell railway but also by the financial success that accompanied the construction of lines on two summits in the Alps that combined spectacle with relative accessibility – the 5,906-foot Rigi and the 6,990-foot Pilatus, on opposite sides of the lake above Lucerne. Both used the rack and pinion system, in which a cog-wheel or pinion attached to the locomotive engages with a series of teeth – the rack – on the central rail, enabling it to tackle both steep inclines and steep declines. Devised by John Blenkinsop, the manager of a Leeds colliery, the system was revived by the Swiss Nikolaus Riggenbach, who successfully installed it on the Rigi. As *Murray's Handbook* would put it:

The gradients vary from 1 in 20 to 1 in 4, i.e. to every 4 ft of length the line rises 1 ft, the utmost allowed in ordinary railways being 1 in 25. This is exceedingly steep, much steeper, in fact, than would be practicable for horse-carriages or ordinary roads, and in this consists the extraordinary character of the railway. To ascend or descend such gradients by ordinary railway appliances would be impracticable; stationary engines and ropes would be difficult of application and highly dangerous, and it has therefore been necessary to adopt a system of propulsion which, though it was tried in the infancy of railways . . . has never been used in their practical development.

The first engines on the Rigi came from works at Winterthur northeast of Zürich, founded by the English engineer Charles Brown. The Pilatus line tackled even steeper gradients by adding a second rack to the system. Climbing from the lake itself up 1,629 metres in only two and a half miles, the track, opened in 1888, had a gradient of 1 in 2.75, a remarkable feat.

These two highly successful schemes provided much food for thought elsewhere in the Alps. In Zermatt, a line of five miles running up the Gornergrat was opened before the turn of the century, providing magnificent views of the most famous alpine panorama of eighteen heavily glaciated peaks, including the Monte Rosa, the Lyskamm, the Breithorn, the Weisshorn, the Täschhorn and the Matterhorn itself. Plans were also gestating for an assault on Whymper's peak. The line up the Rochers de Naye, high above Montreux, opened in 1892. In the Tyrol there was a scheme that would materialize as the line between the Mendel pass and Bozen, at the time the steepest in the world. In the Bernese Oberland, the line up the 7,706-foot Brienzer Rothorn was completed a few years before the turn of the century.

Further south in the Oberland the railway already snaked its way up to Grindelwald. A far bolder project – brainchild of Friedrich Seiler of the hotel dynasty – was under way to extend the line from the old resort right up inside the Eiger, almost to the peak of the adjoining Jungfrau. Initially it was thought that the pneumatic railway built in 1864 near the Crystal Palace at Sydenham in South London, would offer a suitable model. This railway, however, had proved itself unsatisfactory over relatively flat terrain, let alone on a steep incline, and the project was eventually taken over by the Zürich industrialist Adolph Guyer-Zeller. As was customary by now, the scheme met a great deal of opposition, not least from those who thought that construction workers and passengers would suffer from the altitude. Guyer-Zeller was obliged to conduct an experiment to refute this belief. This took the form of transporting seven test passengers by individual litter up the 13,865-foot Breithorn, with eight construction workers manning each litter. The doubters being half-persuaded, on 27 July 1896 work began at Kleine Scheidegg. Two years later, mainly by virtue of pick and shovel, the line had reached the Eiger Glacier station. Work then started on the bore within the mountain itself. Grindelwald's pastor Gottfried Strasser, despite opposing the railway on the nearby Wengernalp, was induced to preach a sermon on the occasion. By 2 August 1899 the temporary station at Rostock was operating, and the bore had reached as far as the Eiger Wall.

Strasser was of course by no means the sole objector to schemes of this nature. Admittedly they were potentially lucrative and brought employment to places that were often extremely poor. As one pragmatic local later remarked to the English mountaineer and writer F.S. Smythe: 'It may be ugly, this railway, but it will bring more tourists and more money to this valley. As for scenery, there is plenty elsewhere.' Yet these schemes could equally well be seen as projects that desecrated the natural scenery, destroyed traditional ways of alpine life, and brought to the remote places those who – it was sometimes felt – scarcely appreciated them. The line up to the Kleine Scheidegg was vehemently opposed. It would erode the alpine meadows, the engines would frighten the cattle, and the guides escorting visitors up from Lauterbrunnen would lose their livelihood. Since the English were still the most prominent of foreign visitors to the Alps, it was also easy for alpine conservationists to blame them for inspiring these developments. One such critic went so far as to state publicly, 'It is for you English that these things are done.'

If this was in some respects manifestly true, it was by no means the case that the English universally applauded such developments. Following in the footsteps of Ruskin, Coolidge was among the first to object to a proposal for a railway to the top of La Meije in the Dauphiné, where travellers would be welcomed in an 'Hôtel Observatoire'. Coolidge had resigned his Magdalen fellowship and retired to Grindelwald in 1896, and took care to marshal his arguments. Leaving aside moral or aesthetic objections, he focused on the practical, pointing out that few of the line's backers had had any experience of the conditions on the peak itself. 'Those who have will, however, try to imagine the *Hôtel Observatoire* filled with guests – say on 1 January – with a snow storm raging furiously around, and will be tempted to believe that though consumptive patients may get cured in that fine air, yet the nerves will be severely tried by a stay at this new *séjour d'hiver*, and that they will return to their homes no longer sick in body, but very sick in mind indeed.' Similarly, at the opening of a section of the Jungfrau line, while the British minister to Switzerland Sir Frederick St John made some complimentary remarks, he noted privately, 'I sincerely hope that this insensate scheme will be abandoned, and that the process of vulgarizing the "playground of Europe" will be arrested.'

But whether inspired by the English or opposed by them, the mania for railways raged on.

Now that it was so much easier to reach the Alps, both the number and the nature of alpine visitors changed rapidly. This was not, however, simply a consequence of the new ease of travel. Reflecting on the changes since he had begun to climb, the veteran alpinist Frederic Harrison remarked on the smaller proportion of English to be found there, noting that the social and economic conditions that had first sent the English to the Alps were now being replicated elsewhere. This was entirely true, for the nation states of Italy and Germany were growing rapidly and flexing their muscles. The Kaiser's Germany had seen a fifty per cent rise in population since unification, and between the turn of the century and the war her industrial output quadrupled. She also had colonial ambitions, seeking what she famously termed her 'place in the sun'. Italy, too, aspired to be a great power, and busied herself with creating a large conscript army and a new navy. Soon, she too would seek to express her national identity by spreading her wings abroad. As Harrison put it: 'Other nations, especially the German and Italian, have gained in half a century enormously in facilities and access, and also in wealth and energy and ambition.' Alpinism was simultaneously an expression of that prosperity, of the desire to escape the claustrophobia of industrialization, and a manifestation of imperialism. It was hardly surprising that alpine enthusiasm in Germany and Italy should be on the increase.

This was most obviously manifested in the foundation of national alpine clubs. The Swiss in 1863 were the first to follow the English foundation of 1857, the Italians only a few months later. Then came the German and Austrian clubs, both founded in 1869. The French followed in 1874, the generally more overt nationalistic ethos of the Continental organizations being expressed in the motto of the Club Alpin Français, 'Pour la patrie par la montagne'. Yet if they were more chauvinistic, they were also more democratic than their English prototype. Enthusiasm for the alpine experience rather than expertise tended to be regarded as sufficient qualification. Nor were these clubs socially exclusive (A.F. Mummery had allegedly been blackballed at first from the London club on the grounds that he was 'in trade').

The result of this more catholic approach was that by the 1890s membership of the Continental clubs numbered not hundreds but tens of thousands. With funds to match, these clubs were able to do a great deal in a practical way to encourage alpinism. The first step was the building of mountain huts. Hitherto those wishing to ascend the high peaks early in the day when the snow was at its hardest and safest had been obliged to make do with the natural shelter of rock or cave, or to carry a tent. In the days before portable stoves, both systems required the party to carry its own firewood. Now small and primitive huts were provided – often little more than caves – provisioned with a stove, utensils and blankets. By 1890, the Swiss Alpine Club had built thirty-eight such structures, the French thirty-three, principally in the Dauphiné. Further measures included the siting of fixed ropes on some of the more exposed parts of frequented ascents, particularly in Chamonix and Zermatt – an idea that the Austrians later took over with what contemporaries regarded as excessive enthusiasm. The clubs' other activities were similarly practical. In the early days guides had been self-taught; now they took it upon themselves to provide more structured and professional training. In the days before proper national surveys, many of the local clubs also organized map-making. Finally they signposted the mountain paths.

The consequences of this were predictable. In his youth, Harrison had reckoned that three-quarters of alpine travellers were English, whereas 'the Alps now – even the high Alps – are thrown open to people of every age, nation, sex, class, and purse'. What had once been regarded as the Englishman's playground now seemed the German's *Kurhaus*.

There was more to come. Transatlantic sailings had, since the 1860s, become a regular event, so much so that the services were dubbed the 'Atlantic ferry'. Dominated by British shipping companies, the transatlantic market continued to grow rapidly. Then, in 1897, the Irish engineer Charles Parsons introduced the steam turbine on his revolutionary yacht *Turbinia*, doing away with the traditional reciprocating arrangement of cylinders and dramatically increasing both speed and efficiency. As the new century approached, the Cunard line was designing its great ships *Lusitania* and *Mauretania*; the White Star line would follow with *Olympic* and the doomed *Titanic*. These vast liners brought Americans to Europe in such numbers that they were regarded as an invading army. Often through the good offices of Thomas Cook and Son, many of these newcomers found their way to the Alps.

Hitherto amongst the poorest of regions, the Dauphiné, Savoy, Piedmont, Lombardy and the Tyrol began to prosper. And inevitably, since it possessed the greatest peaks and the most famous resorts, Switzerland benefited even more. There, from the seventies onwards, occurred the economic expansion known as the *Grunderzeit*. By a virtuous circle, the explosion in tourism financed the construction of railways. New lines then brought in tourists in such numbers that the whole infrastructure of railways, lake steamers, restaurants and hotels was once again stimulated. Not only did this result in the tourist industry fast becoming the country's economic mainstay, but it also brought with it incalculable commercial benefits. These ranged from the establishment of a capital-raising and banking system capable of financing the whole tourist infrastructure to the growth in manufacture and transport of the country's leading products, among them milk and watches, first within Switzerland itself, then abroad. Tourism through the Alps was now an industry in its own right.

It was not long after the turn of the century that Bishop T.E. Wilkinson recorded in his diary: 'Drove to Château d'Oex, where I consecrated the new English church.'

Victorian England was of course religious to an extent unfamiliar today. Nonconformist congregations, especially Henry Lunn's Methodists, were still attracting large numbers; the census of 1851 suggested that something like a third of the population were regular worshippers; the Ten Commandments were still seen by many as legitimate guides to life, for some as dictates to be absolutely obeyed. At least in the country, the parish church stood alongside the 'big house' as one of the two principal institutions of the community. Attendance there on Sunday, sometimes twice or three times, was more or less obligatory. Such services provided opportunities for exchange of news and gossip, and were the chief social event of the week. If not quite a day of prayer, the Sabbath was kept free for worship and no sport or other leisure activity was allowed. Reading was restricted to the Bible or to the collections of sermons then popular. If a number of clergymen took their duties as lightly as Ernest Pontifex in Samuel Butler's *The Way of All Flesh*, many were genuinely committed to the saving of their parishioners' souls.

It was hardly surprising that people were reluctant to abandon such customs when abroad, and from the earliest days of English exploration of the Alps, provision had been made for religious observance. In his first edition of the *Handbook*, Murray remarked that some of the wealthier alpine innkeepers arranged for local clergymen to perform church services on Sundays for their English guests. As the English began to arrive in larger numbers, the practice grew up of providing free or subsidized accommodation for English clergymen, in exchange for divine service. Then came the establishment of churches and chapels for the English congregations in a remarkable number of the alpine resorts.

Typically, these came about through a concatenation of circumstances, involving different parties with quite different motives. Meiringen in the Bernese Oberland was the first resort in the Alps to provide regular Church of England services. First held in 1851 in the Hôtel du Sauvage, they were conducted by the Reverend Dr C.T. May under the auspices of the Society for the Propagation of the Gospel, one of several English organizations supporting missionary or quasi-missionary work abroad. Dr May himself for many years combined duty with pleasure, taking services when holidaying in the resort. These arrangements were however somewhat ad hoc, so in 1864 he persuaded the local authorities that it was in their interest to let him hold his services in a deconsecrated church in the village. Dating from 1486, this was 'out of repair, dirty and comfortless'. It was nevertheless a church and not a hotel, and would suffice until something more satisfactory could be contrived. This materialized in 1868, when an entirely new church, dedicated to the English congregation, came into use. In a further manifestation of enlightened self-interest, Monsieur Baud, proprietor of the Hôtel du Sauvage, provided the site in the grounds of the hotel itself; the local authorities the stone and labour; the Society for the Propagation of the Gospel the benefice for the chaplain. As was often the case, the church's architect was English.

The arrangements were similar at Aigle, just south of the head of Lake Geneva. The Reverend R.D. Lanson first held services at the Grand Hôtel des Bains in 1885 and was soon collecting for the erection of a church, for which the SPG purchased a site in the grounds of the hotel in 1894. The building, dedicated to St John the Evangelist, was subsequently erected at the expense of the hotel proprietor. At Montana, perched beneath the 10,643-foot Wildstrubel on the southern slopes of the Bernese Oberland, St Luke's was long associated with the SPG and the Palace Hotel. When the latter was acquired by Henry Lunn, the chaplain became his nominee. In due course Lunn had a church built in the hotel's grounds at his own expense, and made himself responsible for the subsequent costs, including the chaplain's stipend.

Alongside the SPG was the Colonial and Continental Church Society (CCCS), an organization with comparable objectives to the SPG but of lower church ethos. Although by the turn of the century churchgoing in England had begun to diminish significantly, Bishop Wilkinson might have been excused for assuming that between them the two organizations had the high Alps pretty well covered. *Murray's Handbook* of the time noted that at Adelboden the CCCS provided an English service in the Swiss church; at Aigle the SPG sponsored the St John's English church, though rivalled by the CCCS with its service at the Hôtel Beausite; at Arolla the CCCS church had an 'outside pulpit for use in fine weather'; in Courmayeur at the head of the Aosta valley on the southern side of Mont Blanc the SPG ran a service at the Hôtel Royal; at Davos there was St Luke's; at Saas-Fee in the Valais not far from Zermatt, a CCCS English church; at Griessbad Falls, not far from Reichenbach, a service at the Grand Hotel; at Kandersteg the SPG church was – appropriately – close to the Hotel Victoria; at Montreux there was both an English church and a Scottish Presbyterian benefice; at Pontresina in the Grisons the Holy Trinity; at Stresa a CCCS service at the Hôtel des Iles Borromées; at Vevey on Lake Geneva, All Saints. Finally in Zermatt, there was the CCCS Church of St Peter's, often described as the parish church of the Alpine Club.

The SPG had originally set out 'to settle the State of Religion as well as may be among our *own people* there . . . and then to proceed in the best Methods towards the *Conversion* of the *Natives*'. Not only was its message being propagated throughout the Alps, but the architectural expression of that message was increasingly visible. Leaving aside the alpine cities where English churches had long been established for local English residents, by the time Bishop Wilkinson consecrated the elegant little church in the newly fashionable resort of Château d'Oex in the western Oberland, there were something like seventy such structures to be found in the Alps. Although in many cases their congregations have disappeared, the vast majority of these buildings remain to this day.

'The history of the alpine winter resorts is the story of the mountain railway and Swiss enterprise – roused to activity by the Englishman's craze for exciting sport.' So stated the traveller and writer Charles Domville-Fife a few years after the Great War. If to Swiss enterprise is added that also of the French, Germans and Austrians, then this is true enough. For with the arrival of the mountain railways in the early years of the twentieth century came the proper establishment of winter sports. Hitherto there were only four winter resorts in the whole of the high Alps: St Moritz itself, Davos, Grindelwald and Arosa. The next few years saw the emergence of dozens of rivals, almost without exception in the wake of the railway's arrival or as a result of the introduction of winter services along existing lines.

Henry Lunn was among the first to make use of these services. His exploratory winter sports tour to Chamonix in 1898 had proved a success. The following year he placed his business in jeopardy by publicly opposing the Boer War – a stance that he shared with the Continental newspapers, which painted England as an evil imperialist aggressor. At the end of that war, Lunn discovered in Adelboden, in the Bernese Oberland, a village which he thought might make a better winter resort than Chamonix. Within easy reach of Frutigen and its railway, it was high and sunny, set in a fold between two great ridges, and with magnificent views of the 10,643-foot Wildstrubel to the south. At the time, the village consisted of little more than a couple of inns and a cluster of chalets, its inhabitants alleviating the poverties of pastoral life with matchbox-making. With the promise of prosperous visitors, however, the place was transformed. The Grand Hotel and Kurhaus were opened, and Lunn's party of Etonians and Harrovians brought *fin de siècle* English style to the little Oberland village. Arnold Lunn remembered that on the occasion of the first tour in 1902 the hotel had

> something of the same atmosphere as the 'Monte Rosa' at Zermatt in the seventies. Instead of isolating ourselves at small tables we dined together at two long tables, and people did not wait for the formality of an introduction before speaking to each other. Evening amusements were . . . varied. We danced three or four times a week, and devoted the remaining evenings to indoor gymkhanas and amateur theatricals. The polka and lancers were just dying out, and it was still considered rather fast to reverse. Young people who had tobogganed together usually addressed each other not as Miss Smith or Mr Brown but as Miss Mary or Mr Bobby, which was considered a real advance in intimacy. To dance more than twice with the same partner was faintly compromising.

The small party at Adelboden proved a success, and in 1903 the elder Lunn decided to extend his experiment by founding the Public Schools Alpine Sports Club. This took block bookings of its favoured hotels, excluding anyone other than a member of an English public school or university, or those holding service commissions. In addition were permitted, in the Victorian fashion, the 'wife, daughter or sister of a person so qualified'. Foreigners were only admissible in small numbers, and only if 'distinguished'. Perhaps lacking in egalitarian spirit, in the pre-war years the club was instrumental in opening up more than a dozen villages as winter sports centres, amongst them Mürren, Wengen, Villars, Montana, Lenzerheide, Kandersteg, Klosters, Maloja, Morgins, Sils-Maria and Pontresina, all chosen as much for their proximity to the railway as for their suitability as winter sports resorts.

In the days when Thomas Cook was only just beginning to offer ten-day winter sports holidays for ten guineas, Arnold Lunn always made large claims for the influence of his father's company in developing the winter Alps. True of many of the Swiss resorts, it was in fact so only in conjunction with the railway. Château d'Oex, Gstaad and Saanenmoser in the western Bernese Alps all grew up in the wake of the narrow gauge railway that rises so spectacularly from Montreux. St Moritz's great popularity dates from the arrival of the railway from Chur in 1904. The Dauphiné resorts depended on the light railways laid out at the turn of the century. Resorts like Bardonecchia at the southern end of the Mont Cenis tunnel and St Anton at the eastern end of the Arlberg benefited enormously from their proximity to the main lines. The pioneer winter travel agents and the new railways were mutually dependent.

It was at Adelboden in 1903 that Arnold Lunn first fell in love with skiing. Although the sport was very much the bridesmaid among winter pastimes, it was by now spreading rapidly, its appeal lying in the speed that it shared with tobogganing, and enhanced by the variety of direction that tobogganing lacked. Together with Lunn, its earliest twentieth-century proponents were E.C. Richardson and, to a lesser extent, his brother C.W.R.

'E.C.', as he was invariably known, was born in Hartfield Cove, Dumbarton, in 1871. Educated locally, then at Harrow, he took a degree in law at Trinity Hall, Cambridge. From 1894 he and his brother spent their Easter holidays in Norway and Sweden. It was here that they apprenticed themselves in the local traditions of cross-country skiing and competitive ski-jumping. In the season of 1901/2 they appeared in Davos, where – despite Colonel Napier and Arthur Conan Doyle – they were told that neither the terrain nor the snow was suited to the sport. Undeterred, they pursued their enthusiasm with such success that by the following year there were sufficient adherents in the resort to form the nucleus of a Davos English ski club, which they themselves founded. Lunn called 'E.C.' the father of British skiing, a title better suited to Lunn himself. Richardson was nevertheless a great pioneer skier and all-round sportsman, who died – aged eighty-seven – after a game of tennis. Golf he dismissed as a game for old men.

Also prominent in the development of the sport was the

Anglophile German W.R. Rickmers, who had been taught by Mathias Zdarsky, the king of Lilienfeld. Addressing the Alpine Club in May 1903, Rickmers manifested an enthusiasm shared by the Richardsons and Lunn himself:

> Today the exhaustion of the Alps is a trite story . . . the great, the obvious problems are gone, and we are thrown upon new means to find new results. Tobogganing and cycling are such means, among others, but the intensity of the movement is more than compensated by the limitations of locality. There is, however, one instrument which has come as a revelation, which bids fair to rejuvenate the Alps, and that is the Norwegian snowshoe, the skee . . . the skee has begun to promise new life; it will keep that promise beyond our most hopeful expectations.

Given the immaturity of the sport, these remarks were prescient. Despite the inventions of Sondre Norheim, most skiers were still using equipment little better than that of Arthur Conan Doyle – primitive bindings and normal walking shoes or boots, and detachable sealskins to prevent the ski sliding back when going uphill. Without the benefit of today's ski-lifts, the sport also involved a good deal of climbing. Except in the rare instances when it was possible to use the mountain railways, the skier went down only as far as he had climbed up, often with his skis on his back, and he would be lucky to do a couple of runs in the course of a day. The runs, too, were rarely established trails and certainly not prepared pistes. Skiing on virgin snow, the early exponents took pot luck with crevasses, avalanche slopes, broken branches and farmers' fences.

For the pioneers, however, the challenge of mountaineering and the thrill of skiing itself combined to make the sport wonderfully appealing. As J.A.R. Pimlott, author of *The Englishman's Holiday*, put it:

> To these men and the disciples who collected round them, skiing was more than a sport, more even than an art; it was a spiritual exercise which brought its reward in an unbelievable exhilaration and exaltation of mind and body. Inspired by the

same sentiments as the early Alpinists, this small group of young Englishmen set to work in collaboration with the Continental pioneers to evolve a scientific technique out of the crude traditional methods and equipment to propagate their tremendous discovery.

Suiting their deeds to their words, Rickmers and the Richardsons in 1903 founded the Ski Club of Great Britain. Its inaugural meeting was at a dinner in the Café Royal in Regent Street on 6 May, then a byword for elegance and style. Yet, as perhaps suited an increasingly democratic age, the club was to have a modest subscription, to require no qualification for entrance, and to admit lady members. Unlike the Alpine Club, however, it was not the first in its field, being preceded by the Norwegian Ski Association, founded in 1883, and the Swedish, founded in 1892. It was nevertheless to become a considerable force in the promotion of skiing, establishing the notion of tests and standards, and it was instrumental in the development of downhill skiing.

If the English had taken to skiing with remarkable enthusiasm, it was perhaps less surprising that they were also amongst the pioneers of cycling in the Alps.

First the French and then the Germans laid claim to be the originators of the modern bicycle. Invented in the aftermath of the Napoleonic wars, the early bicycles were crude machines that needed to be scooted along on iron wheels, and they never captured the public's imagination. In the year of Whymper's ascent of the Matterhorn, a Parisian invented the well-named 'bone-shaker', the pedal-driven prototype of the modern bicycle. It was not until 1881, however, with John Dunlop's invention of the pneumatic tyre, that the machine came of age. The Cyclist's Touring Club was founded in 1883, and mass production of the safety-cycle soon followed.

In the subsequent cycling boom Britain led the world. Another reaction to the claustrophobia of urban life, the bicycle brought personal mobility at a price affordable even to those of modest means, and personal independence for both men and women in the age before the motor car. 'There is a new dawn, a new dawn of emancipation, and it is brought about by the cycle', wrote an early feminist. 'Free to wheel, free to spin out into the glorious countryside, unhampered by chaperone or, even more dispiriting, male admirer, the young girl of today can feel the real independence of herself, and while she is building up her better constitution she is developing her better mind.'

Tours through the English countryside soon gave way to more ambitious trips, normally in conjunction with the railways. Cook's 'Continental Conducted Cycling Tours' began with a trip in 1896 to Normandy. By 1901 Baedeker's *Swiss Guide* included a long section on the pleasures and pains of alpine cycling, advocating in particular the necessity of fitness. 'German and French cyclists sometimes hire a horse to walk up a steep road, and tie their machines one after the other to a long rope, the end of which is fastened to the animal's traces. They are thus enabled to sit on their machines on the way up but must of course be ready to put foot to earth every time the horse stops. English cyclists usually prefer to plod on foot; hence the necessity for good condition.'

By this time the Cyclist's Touring Club boasted 60,000 members, and provided various services to assist alpine tours: cycling maps, discounts for club members at approved hotels and the like. Soon a handbook was published comprehensively entitled the *Alpine Profile Road Book of Switzerland, and adjacent portions of Tyrol and the Italian Lake District*. As it remarked, 'it was evident, from the number and length of articles on Alpine cycle touring which have appeared in the Touring Club's *Gazette* and elsewhere during the last two or three years that the cult of this most delightful and invigorating method of spending a summer holiday is rapidly spreading.'

Among such enthusiasts was Jerome K. Jerome, who had made his name in 1888 with *Three Men in a Boat*. Its long-awaited sequel, *Three Men on the Bummel*, published in 1900, was the story of a cycling tour of the Black Forest, taken in the company of the narrator's boon companions

George and Harris. In its meandering course Jerome found time to
reflect upon the impact of English visitors to the Continent:

> The man who has spread the knowledge of English from Cape
> St Vincent to the Ural Mountains is the Englishman who, unable
> or unwilling to learn a single word of any language but his own,
> travels purse in hand into every corner of the continent. One
> may be shocked at his ignorance, annoyed at his stupidity, angry
> at his presumption. But the practical fact remains: he it is that is
> Anglicizing Europe. For him the Swiss peasant tramps through
> the snow to attend the English class open in every village. For
> him the coachman and the guard, the chambermaid and the
> laundress pore over their English grammars and colloquial
> phrase books. For him the foreign shopkeeper and merchant
> send their sons and daughters in their thousands to study in
> every English town. For him it is that every foreign hotel – and
> restaurant – keeper adds to his advertisement: 'Only those with
> fair knowledge of English need apply . . .' . . . Did the English
> races make it their rule to speak anything else than English,
> the marvellous progress of the English tongue throughout the
> world would stop. The English-speaking man stands amid the
> strangers and jingles his gold. 'Here', he cries, 'is payment to all
> such as can speak English.' He it is who is the great educator.
> Theoretically we may scold him; practically we should take our
> hats off to him. He is the missionary of the English tongue.

Early in Jerome's book, George, Harris and the narrator are discussing what form their holiday will take.

> 'You won't think of anything better than a bicycle tour', per-
> sisted Harris. I was inclined to agree with him. 'And I'll tell you
> where,' continued he: 'through the Black Forest.'

'Why, that's *all* uphill,' said George.

'Not all,' retorted Harris; 'say two-thirds. And there's one thing you've forgotten.' He looked round cautiously and sank his voice to a whisper.

'There are little railways going up those hills, little cogwheel things that –'

Here Harris was interrupted by the entrance of his wife, from whom he wished to conceal the advantage of the mountain railways. Nonetheless the trio were perfectly happy to take the easy way up the hills, and did so without compunction.

Yet with mountain railway after mountain railway proposed, planned and created, as the new decade got into its stride the opposition became more organized and more vociferous. Local objectors to individual schemes could only do so much, so the next step was to involve the relevant national bodies, most obviously the various alpine clubs. With their often intelligent and articulate memberships, these were at the forefront of attempts at conservation, be it discouraging the establishment of fixed ropes up mountainsides or the building of the Jungfrau railway and its siblings. The English and Swiss clubs were in the vanguard, followed by the French, Italians, Austrians and Germans.

Ultimately, however, the clubs had other matters to concern themselves with, and new organizations were created whose sole purpose was that of mountain conservation. The League for the Preservation of Swiss Scenery was founded in 1905, its English branch shortly afterwards. Soon the English offshoot organized a petition objecting to a proposed railway up the Matterhorn. A public meeting was held at the Society of Arts, chaired by Sir Martin Conway. The petition began, 'The high summits of the Alps are the clear possession of the whole of the Swiss people, and the symbol of Swiss freedom. They are not for sale.' The plea fell on deaf ears.

Equally there were plenty of individuals, English and otherwise, prepared to publish their reservations. Coolidge had the pleasure of seeing the Meije scheme abandoned, only to see it replaced with a comparable project for the nearby 12,497-foot Le Rateau. Then Hilaire Belloc, whose account of his pilgrimage by foot to Rome proved the first alpine classic of the new century, entered the lists. But far from being seen as a civilizing force, the railways to Belloc were about as sympathetic as they were to Ruskin. 'Trains', he thundered in *The Path to Rome*, 'are the trenches which drain our civilization . . . Avoid them by so much as a quarter of a mile and you may have as much peace as would fill a nosebag.'

Besides the Jungfrau and various schemes in the Dauphiné, there was plenty to arouse the conservationists' ire. Mont Blanc had been the subject of all sorts of proposals from as early as the 1860s, and already under construction was a railway which was intended eventually to reach its summit. In the Grisons, the line over the Bernina pass into Italy was half complete. Hardly better was the Matterhorn scheme, which envisaged the piercing of a shaft through the mountain, and the conversion of the summit into a series of 'grottoes and balconies'. Approved by the Cantonal Assembly of the Valais and the Swiss Federal Assembly, this was something that the Alpine Club could only deplore. As its president Charles Pilkington put it:

> The Alps, we may claim, are conquered by the common brotherhood of mountaineers, but victory entails responsibility as well as fame. That the mountains should be a sanctuary for mountaineers is an idea impossible of attainment and it would be selfish to desire it, but now that their slopes are being disfigured with unnecessary railways, their cliffs degraded with iron lifts, and their noblest glacier threatened by a wire sledge run, it is time that Englishmen should heartily co-operate with those who have the right to protect their native mountains, and take a share in the noble work of preserving for future generations the beauty and the mystery that have charmed and elevated their lives.

It was a new century and a new age. The English, so long the proponents of alpine travel, were now beginning to resist its advance.

Chapter Nine
Edwardian Summer

On the idle hill of summer
  Sleepy with the flow of streams
Far I hear the steady drummer
  Drumming like a noise in dreams.
        A.E. Housman

When the Alpine Club celebrated the first fifty years of its existence on 4 February 1908, the speaker Charles Pilkington felt obliged to talk of the new challenges posed to its alpine sanctuary in the half-century that had elapsed since the club's foundation. In that period alpine tourism had undergone a revolution so profound that to Pilkington and his Edwardian contemporaries the very heartland of their sport seemed under siege.

In the days of Alfred Wills, John Tyndall and Leslie Stephen, alpine tourism was still a relatively esoteric pursuit. It attracted scientific mountaineers, poets and painters bent on recording the alpine experience, the aristocracy, the wealthy. In all, these people represented relatively small numbers, tens of thousands at most. There was scarcely a railway meriting the name in the whole of the Alps. The season was confined to the summer alone. Hotels and inns might be passable in the principal centres, but elsewhere were primitive or non-existent. Beyond the Chamonix and Aosta valleys, the Bernese Oberland, the Valais, and isolated parts of the Tyrol, much of the Alps was still largely unexplored. However they might have been romanticized in poetry, prose or paint, the alpine peoples were largely indigent peasants.

Fifty years on, alpine tourism was commonplace amongst a far broader swathe of the English populace. Between the death of Queen Victoria and the outbreak of the Great War the numbers annually crossing the Channel to the Continent, many of whom progressed to the Alps, almost doubled to a million. For much of the Alps, in consequence, as *Murray's Handbook* stated, 'the great annual influx of strangers [was] of the same importance as some additional branch of industry or commerce would be'. In Switzerland itself, tourism had become the linchpin of the economy, and for the alpine regions of France, Italy, Germany and Austria it was scarcely less important. Whilst mountaineers, aristocrats and the rich still abounded, the success of Thomas Cook and his competitors drew many new visitors from the middle classes. The infirm also saw the Alps, with their clean dry air and winter sun, as a lifeline. Everywhere there were hotels, and the best were 'palaces . . . inferior in luxury to no houses of their kind in Europe'. If visitors were now staying for shorter periods – some for as little as a week – the new winter season had in effect doubled the length of the hoteliers' year. Carriages and gigs were still to be found, but for longer distances the railway system now linked all the principal alpine cities and towns.

In the language of the day, the alpine peoples were being rapidly civilized, and goitre and cretinism were gradually disappearing. The exploration of the mountains themselves was nearly complete. They had been comprehensively mapped, the principal peaks and the vast majority of the minor ones had been conquered. Those mountaineers in search of fresh adventure were obliged to seek new ways up old peaks – or to transfer their attentions elsewhere. Far from stepping into the unknown, the successors of Professor Forbes were more likely to discover that the alpine slopes were indeed being 'disfigured with unnecessary railways, their cliffs degraded with iron lifts, and their noblest glacier threatened by a wire sledge run'. As to the remote hamlets that had once served as a base for their exploits, on the higher slopes of the Rigi huge hotels had been built capable of accommodating thousands. Grindelwald was besieged by 'immense throngs'. St Moritz was the largest community in the whole of the Engadine valley, and boasted curling, skating, tobogganing, golf, lawn tennis, a local English society, and an English newspaper. Zermatt would soon be 'an alpine village that has almost lost its identity among a colony of hotels'. The Alps were indeed the playground of Europe, arrangements for the suitable reception of tourists now extending from the southern extremes of the Dauphiné to the eastern edge of the Tyrol.

An age regarded as the *belle époque* of alpine tourism, it was – as Pilkington recognized – an era of extraordinarily rapid development. And as it turned out, it was a boom that had only half a dozen more years to run.

Another agent of change, to which Ruskin would undoubtedly have taken exception, was about to arrive on the scene. James Watt's invention of the steam engine had led to the railway age that transformed the Alps in the last quarter of the nineteenth century. Yet it was also an invention that led – albeit indirectly – to a different sort of transformation in the twentieth.

Although steam carriages had enjoyed a vogue in England as early as the 1830s, the real breakthrough in personal mechanized transport came in 1878 with Nikolaus Otto's invention of the internal combustion engine. Soon, imaginative engineers throughout Europe were installing the new engines in all sorts of chassis. By 1894, when Martin Conway was traversing the Alps from end to end, something entirely recognizable as a motor car was to be seen on the streets of London, Grenoble, Geneva, Bern, Vienna and Turin.

Much as the arrival of the railways had encouraged travel, so now, too, did the motor car. In the early years of the new century the adventurous began to take their cars abroad, ferrying them across the Channel on the packet boats, just as Ruskin's parents had ferried their luxurious carriage sixty years earlier. In 1900 C.L. Freeston had seen a market for his book, *Cycling in the Alps*. Within a few years he thought the time ripe for *The High Roads of the Alps – A motoring guide to one hundred Alpine passes*. Introducing his subject, he remarked that the railway era in the Alps 'for nearly two generations has led people to forget that there are such things as roads'. With the growing popularity of the motor car, though, things were changing.

> The volume is designed to meet a want – a want which is the more pressing now that the power and efficiency of the modern car have made England seem small, and all lowland touring opportunities only too familiar. If there is one place on earth where the tireless qualities of the motor car may justify themselves, it is on the long-drawn but glorious ascent of an Alpine pass.

Freeston was prescient. Although the Swiss themselves fought a long rearguard action against the private car, as the watershed of 1914 approached, such vehicles began to be seen in the Alps in considerable numbers. After the war Freeston wrote that 'No small degree of interest in the subject of road travel in the Alps was aroused between 1910 and 1914, and the cars of British and American tourists were to be seen in large numbers on the passes that were then available.' Soon would come Mussolini's autostradas and Hitler's autobahns, and the transcontinental motorways that would largely supplant rail and, in a curious way, echo the construction of Napoleon's great highways.

It was also the internal combustion engine that had proved the catalyst for powered flight. July 1908 saw the first Zeppelin hovering over Switzerland. In 1909 Louis Blériot flew the Channel, and by the outbreak of war, Oskar Bidar had become the first man to fly over the alpine chain.

If 1909 was Blériot's year, so too, in a more modest way, was it Vivian Caulfeild's, for it was then that he published *How to Ski*.

The early years of the century had seen the sport spread with remarkable rapidity. There were a number of milestones. Most important were the Richardsons' development of skiing in Davos, and the activities of Henry Lunn in Adelboden. Then came the foundation of the Ski Club of Great Britain, followed in 1908 by Arnold Lunn's brainchild, the Alpine Ski Club. The latter was modelled closely on its mountaineering namesake, and was inaugurated under the presidency of Sir Martin Conway. By then W.R. Rickmers, E.C. Richardson and Crighton Somerville had published the first book in the English language on skiing. Then, in 1909, came both Vivian Caulfeild's *How to Ski* and E.C. Richardson's *The Ski-Runner*, books instrumental in introducing growing numbers of Englishmen to the sport. Caulfeild in particular was credited by Continental authorities with being the first to understand and explain the dynamics of skiing.

Born in 1874, Caulfeild was an Etonian whose father had sought to make a man of him first by sending him to Australia as a hand on a square-rigger, then to the Texas oil-fields. When introduced to skis he wrote, 'My real life now began.' At Adelboden he spent a series of seasons experimenting with and refining his skiing technique. At a time when both turning and control of speed were largely dependent on the use of the single ski-pole, Caulfeild was the first to denounce the practice, and preach that turning and slowing should be achieved by shifting weight from one ski to the other. It was this that made *How to Ski* revolutionary. Illustrated with figures and photographs, written in the plainest of styles, the book carries an introductory essay on 'The Englishman as a Ski-runner' (an early term for skier), goes on to deal with equipment, dwells in nine subsequent chapters on the management of skis, covering everything from general principles to the Christiana turn, and concludes with chapters on cross-country skiing, jumping and practice. Full of common sense, Caulfeild is admirably honest about the limitations of his fellow countrymen as skiers:

Whatever may be the reason, the fact remains that the average British skier has little or no idea of the superiority of good running to bad as regards safety, comfort and speed – to say nothing of interest or beauty. He would probably be surprised and somewhat sceptical if told that by learning a good style of skiing he would find it possible to do the downhill portion of his tours in about half the time (or less) with half the fatigue, with just as few falls (if he wished to avoid them) and with less chance of hurting himself when he did fall; that he would thus get infinitely more pleasure, interest and excitement out of his skiing and that, moreover, by going in for jumping he would still further increase all these benefits without increasing the risks.

Caulfeild, together with Lunn, Rickmers and the Richardson brothers, were among a dozen Edwardians who pioneered skiing techniques in these years, principally through the hothouse of competitions. Initially these were affairs that combined skiing with skating and tobogganing, one of the first being held in Adelboden under the auspices of the Public Schools Alpine Sports Club in 1903. That year the club adhered to the practice inherited from the Scandinavian countries of racing over a flat cross-country course, otherwise known as 'langlauf'. Pleasant enough for the young, strong and fit dedicated to the sport, it was less attractive to casual holiday skiers who were beginning to arrive in greater numbers. Such people were discouraged by the relatively strenuous training, and even more by the customary abstention from alcohol and tobacco that was required. Accordingly a downhill section was introduced the following year, involving an initial climb of some five hundred feet, followed by a descent of one thousand feet. It was won by Arnold Lunn.

Increasingly, however, winter sportsmen were becoming specialists in their own sports, and in 1911 the PSASC decided that separate competitions should be run for each of the principal winter activities. Henry Lunn had done an extraordinary job in inveigling the great and the good of Edwardian England to endorse his club, its first president being Lord Carnock, its vice-presidents Neville Lytton, E.F. Benson and Lord Roberts of Kandahar. One of the military heroes of his age, widely credited with winning the Boer War, Roberts was induced to lend his name and title to the downhill ski competition.

The first race for the Roberts of Kandahar Challenge Cup was held at Montana on 6 January 1911. Baedeker in 1875 did not even mention this village, above Sierre in the Rhône valley. By the turn of the century, though, with its fine views across to the Weisshorn, the Zinal Rothorn and the Gabelhorn, it was an established resort. Crans, one thousand feet higher, was still entirely separate. Lunn's competitors left the village the previous evening, carrying their skis up to the Wildstrubel hut on the Plaine Morte glacier. Then, the following morning, at 10 a.m., they crossed the glacier and skied five thousand feet down to Montana, the winner taking 61 minutes. All the competitors had started together, and there was no hard piste, rather – as Arnold Lunn was to put it – a flagged course 'down natural snow, as shaped by sun, wind, and frost'.

Lunn himself, though, had to sit the race out. Mountaineering in Wales, he had fallen on Cader Idris and broken his leg. Only just avoiding amputation, he ended up with his right leg two inches shorter than the left, and an open wound that did not heal for eleven years.

Writing after the war, E.C. Richardson would acknowledge the great contribution of Henry Lunn to the sport, noting that this non-skier was among the first to recognize and promote the virtues of skiing. Lunn, though, did more than simply introduce Englishmen to skiing. The regimes of the hotels booked by the PSASC were tightly controlled by a representative, and a local club committee. An anecdote of Arnold Lunn's illustrates the atmosphere thus created:

> It would have been unthinkable for an Englishman not to dress for dinner at any one of the leading sports centres during the first decade of the century. Such luckless guests as had lost their luggage en route slunk about with a miserable and apologetic mien. It wasn't their fault they had to dine in their ordinary clothes. We knew that. Still, they were under a cloud . . . I remember one miserable outcast whose registered luggage did not arrive for a week. Everybody was kind to him, but he lost caste. He was slipping. He knew it. We knew it. The head waiter knew it. And then the cloud lifted. His luggage arrived.

I shall never forget the expression on his face, when he appeared for the first time in evening dress. He looked like a man who had just been cleared by court martial of a disgraceful charge.

If this was the tone set by the PSASC, it was also that adopted by other leading hotels in the Alps. English mores, English customs, English codes of dress set the standard. As the alpinist Frederic Harrison wrote at the time, 'The English laws of costume now have to be observed by the most lawless plutocrat from Illinois and the most pushful banker from Frankfurt.' Later, J.A.R. Pimlott wrote that although by this time the proportion of English visitors was certainly diminishing, 'English influences remained marked, being exemplified by such institutions as separate tables for meals, dinner jackets, the rule of no conversation with strangers, and to great advantage by such amenities as baths and modern sanitation'.

The disappearance of A.F. Mummery on the Himalayan peak of Nanga Parbat in 1895 for several years created a void in English mountaineering, a void that was filled in the new century by Geoffrey Winthrop Young. This great figure, poet as well as mountaineer, was the epitome of the Edwardian climber. As Arnold Lunn was to put it, like Whymper and Mummery before him, Young was 'the symbol of a particular age in mountaineering, for he stands in much the same relationship to the last decade before the First World War as Whymper to the Golden Age and Mummery to the Silver Age of mountaineering'.

The second son of Sir George Young of Cookham, G.W. Young was born in 1876 and educated at Marlborough and Trinity College, Cambridge. There he interested himself in the new sport of climbing the roofs of the colleges by night, publishing under a pseudonym a *Guide to the Roofs of Trinity*. Graduating in 1898, he became an assistant master at Eton, and from 1905 until the Great War an inspector of secondary schools. For his first visit to the Alps he somewhat perversely chose the Tarentaise, which was as primitive as he might have wished. Thereafter, he climbed every season until the war. As a climber he had an outstanding natural talent, was exceptionally strong in wind and limb, and virtually fearless. Like Coolidge, he formed a brilliant alliance with a guide. This was Josef Knubel, a native of the St Nicholas valley in Canton Valais and a stonemason by trade. Although of modest height and relatively light build, Knubel was remarkably strong and light on his feet. He had known the mountains from an early age, and his skills were spotted by Young, whose protégé he became. (Knubel was also taught to ski by Arnold Lunn.)

Climbing in an age when the great alpine peaks had already been conquered, Young established his reputation by way of a series of exceptionally difficult ascents in the highest of the Alps, few of which were to be repeated within a generation. His most famous was that of the south-west face of the Täschhorn, the 14,758-foot king of the Täsch valley, a few miles north of Zermatt. The party comprised the Irishman V.J.E. Ryan, Knubel, and two other famous guides – the brothers Franz and Josef Lochmatter. The men had been climbing for some hours on extreme pitches and in poor conditions when they reached an overhang six hundred feet below the summit which seemed utterly insurmountable. A retreat in the worsening snow was equally unthinkable. Ryan, an exceptional mountaineer in his own right, asked Young how he reckoned their prospects. Wrote Young, 'I can hear myself answering, "About one in five."'

At length it was agreed that Franz Lochmatter should attempt an ascent, roping himself up to climb to a small blister on the near-vertical face, around which he might belay the rope. 'Advancing almost imperceptibly', Lochmatter moved up the face, and in a few minutes was out of Young's sight. Then:

Suddenly I heard that unmistakable scrape and grit of sliding boot-nails and clothes. Above my head, over the end of the roof to the right, I saw Franz's legs shoot out into space. Time stopped. A shiver, like expectancy, trembled across the feeling of unseen grey wings behind me, from end to end of the cliff. I realized impassively that the swirl of the rope must sweep me from my hold before it tightened on the doubtful belay of the blister.

Yet it was not to be. A moment later, Young saw the guide's boots once again disappearing above him, Lochmatter having 'stopped himself miraculously on the rim by crushing his hands on to ice dimples on the slab'.

Eventually surmounting the overhang, the guide reached a point sufficiently secure for him to be able to hang on with one hand, to leave the other free to pull up the remaining members of the party on the rope. Joined first by his brother, the pair of them were hauling up Ryan when the Irishman realized that his frozen hands could no longer grasp the rope. Young recalled:

> Very coolly, Ryan shouted a warning before he started of the insufficient power left in his frozen hands. Some twenty feet up, the rope tore him from his inadequate, snowy holds. He swung across above our heads and hung suspended in mid-air. The rope was fixed round his chest. In a minute it began to suffocate him. He shouted once or twice to the men above to hurry. Then a fainter call, 'I'm done', and he dangled to all appearance unconscious on the rope. Franz and Josef could only lift him half inch by half inch. For all this hour – probably it was longer – they were clamped one above the other on to the steep face of the dome, their feet on shallow but sound nicks, one hand clinging on, and only the other free to pull in. Any inch the one lifted, the other held. The rough curve of the rock, over which the higher portion of the rope descended, diminished by friction the effectiveness of each tug. The more one considers their situation, the more superhuman do the co-operation and power the two men displayed during this time, at the end of all those hours of effort, appear.

At last Ryan was rescued and, miraculously, resuscitated. Young and Josef Knubel joined them and – by no means without further difficulty – the party reached the summit. They had spent nine hours ascending the last nine hundred feet of climb. There, Young and Franz Lochmatter shook hands. 'You will never do anything harder than that Franz!' 'No,' Lochmatter said reflectively, 'man could not do much more.'

If the Täschhorn was Young's greatest climb, 1911 proved his greatest season. It was a summer of peculiar brilliance, a season of seasons, when hundreds of splendid alpine adventures were enjoyed. Yet with Edward VII's death the previous year, a constitutional crisis threatening the House of Lords, and the Agadir imbroglio raising tension between France, Germany and England, the atmosphere was strained. Joined by H.O. Jones, another outstanding mountaineer, Young spent the early part of the season training in the Dauphiné. The pair then set out for Mont Blanc, Young later remembering how they 'rocked and trembled across the passes of Savoy in hair-breadth motor diligences to Courmayeur'. They would spend the rest of the season scrambling around the Mont Blanc massif, most famously establishing two new routes of exceptional difficulty: the Grépon from the Mer de Glace above Chamonix, and the first ascent of the west ridge of the Grandes Jorasses.

Like the Täschhorn, the Grépon proved the excellence of Young's guides, in this case once again Josef Knubel. Following in Knubel's tracks on one of the steepest of its pitches, Young wrote:

Apart from the rope there was no hold at all. I could but scuffle, and try to spread myself adhesively, like butter – melting butter, on a tilted plate! A microscopic crack sloping steeply upward appeared above me on the left. I reached it. It was too small and shallow to admit even a fingertip. But here and there in it I could see tiny dark spots, where Josef had snicked in the points of his amazing axe, and dragged himself up the slab by its single support. But how he held himself at that angle, and upon that surface, for the seconds during which he was shifting up the pick to a new hold – only he himself and the sky could know! I marvel even now to think of that lonely fight, far up ahead on the blind, leaning wall: a duel with immensity, uncheered, even unwitnessed . . . Somehow it was over at last; and I had hold, panting and rope-crumpled, of Josef's dangling foot.

Leading an ambulance unit in the course of the Great War, Young was to lose a leg. Undaunted, he returned once again to conquer a series of high peaks including the Matterhorn. As the distinguished French mountaineer Alain de Chatellus wrote: 'Misfortunes can only break mediocrities, but reveal their powers to men who are worthy of the name.'

That summer also saw the healing of a long-standing breach. The quarrel between Coolidge and Whymper over Almer's Leap that had threatened to end in the courts had eventually petered out. In the new century the pair had once again begun to correspond, and in the summer of 1911 a meeting was proposed. The grand old man of English mountaineering, now seventy-one, would visit the foremost alpine scholar in his Grindelwald lair. Whymper came one day in early September, writing in advance to Coolidge, 'When I come I shall come up in my old style. Shall walk up, not order rooms in advance, and take my chance as to finding a room. If none can be had, I shall camp out.' The two spent the whole day of 3 September together. Who knows what they talked about? The Matterhorn tragedy, the adventures of the silver age, the great prospects of the Himalayas? Perhaps they even talked of Josef Knubel, who once remarked that if all his climbs were added together they would reach heaven. Whymper then travelled on to Zermatt, back along the Rhône valley to Geneva, thence to Chamonix. There, in the words of Coolidge's biographer, 'he fell ill, refused aid, locked himself in his room and died, alone and friendless, one of the last survivors of mountaineering's heroic age'.

When Young himself returned to England in September 1911, tensions with Germany over the Agadir incident were running high. The

Cabinet had even ordered that the South-East and Chatham Railway be patrolled. As the English climber W.E. Durham recorded in his diary, 'Slept at the Täschalp, where we met Mr A.E.W. Mason [the novelist] and the Lochmatters. Mr Mason had just arrived from England, and told me, on the authority of Lloyd George, how near we were at the moment to war with Germany.' By November, however, the crisis was over.

For that winter season Henry Lunn elected to move the Kandahar race from Montana to Mürren, perched high on a ledge on the western side of the Lauterbrunnen valley in the Bernese Oberland. The village had been transformed by the coming of the railway in 1891. Formerly visited by no more than a couple of hundred travellers a day, it now received two or three times that number by rail. For the next twenty years, however, the village in winter remained as isolated as it had always been. Then, in 1909, however, Lunn induced the railway authorities to open up the system for the winter. This was all that was needed to champion winter sports in Mürren.

With easy access provided, the Kandahar downhill race now proved a great draw for skiers and spectators alike. Within two years, one of the most influential guidebooks of the day, Will and Carine Cadby's *Switzerland in Winter*, noted that the village 'has rushed into fame and become popular so quickly. One might imagine from the illustrated press that Mürren's winter visiting population was composed of skiing duchesses, skating lords and curling bishops.' In due course it would be described as 'practically British territory'.

On a broader canvas this was a far from inappropriate description of the various winter resorts opened up by both the PSASC and Thomas Cook in the two remaining winter seasons before the war. There was Engelberg, high above Lucerne, described by a contemporary guidebook as 'one of the most important strongholds of Messrs Thos. Cook & Son in Switzerland'. Leukerbad, below the Gemmi pass linking Oberland to the Rhône valley, was another Cook resort. Then there was Lenzerheide in the Engadine, and Villars, close to the head of Lake Geneva. The latter was famous for its enormous skating-rink, of which the novelist E.F. Benson was president. The railway had also opened up Château d'Oex, Gstaad and Saanenmoser, all of which became established as skiing centres before 1914. These three contrived for themselves a principally English clientele, not least by advertising in the English newspapers. Outside Switzerland, in Savoy there was Chamonix and Argentières, and in the Dauphiné St Pierre de Chartreuse and Villard de Lans. In Bavaria, Garmisch-Partenkirchen and Kohlgrub were still relatively small, Feldberg substantial. In the Tyrol, Cortina, Kitzbühel and St Anton were by now firmly established. And thanks to Mathias Zdarsky, Lilienfeld in the Black Forest was famous throughout Europe.

Despite the spread of skiing, in the years up to the war skating remained the most popular winter sport in the majority of resorts, one of its curiosities being the squabble it spawned between the English and Continental styles.

Technically distinct – the English skater keeping the non-weight-bearing leg closer to his side than his Continental counterpart – the two styles also diverged in another respect. The English liked to skate together, the Continentals preferred to do so individually. The phenomenon was usually taken as an expression of national character. 'Like all English games', the Cadbys claimed, *esprit de corps* plays a very important part in the sport, and whether or not the playing-fields of Eton had any material influence on the Battle of Waterloo, certain it is that games which foster good fellowship have done a great deal in building up the character of the nation and the proverbial love of fair play which all true English people pride themselves on.'

This, though, posed a problem. As Lunn put it, 'four Englishmen skating a "combined" need more space than fifty foreigners walking in the degenerate Continental style'. In the days when resorts had been opened in winter solely for the benefit of the English this was all very well. But as winter sports became more popular alpine hoteliers became increasingly sensitive to the fact that ice rinks cost money, and that the English were taking up more than their fair share of skating space. The 'politics of skating', as it was called, culminated in the withdrawal of the famous Bear Skating Club in Grindelwald to Morgins in the Rhône valley. In Lunn's words:

In the days of our Imperial power, nobody dared question the English skater's demand for *Lebensraum.* The English skated in the English style, and the great rinks at Grindelwald or St Moritz were seldom troubled by the intrusion of the Continental heresy. But Kipling's England slowly passed away. The 'lesser breeds without the law' began to murmur against the English hegemony of the ice rink, and hotel proprietors began to think in terms of square metres per skater, with the result that the English skaters suddenly discovered they were no longer wanted. English skating gradually faded from the ice rinks of the Alps, and might have disappeared completely, but for the fact that Morgins offered an asylum to the faithful. Humphrey Cobb, the Moses of Anglican skating, led the chosen people out of the bondage of Egypt to the promised land of Morgins, where the law and the prophets were honoured up to the very outbreak of the Second World War.

The old order in the Alps was changing.

On the other side of the Lauterbrunnen valley to Mürren, work was still proceeding steadily on the Jungfrau railway. Starting from Kleine Scheidegg, the line had reached first the Eiger Glacier, then the Eiger Wall and the Eismeer. There were then a series of delays caused by the need to recapitalize the project, the extreme hardness of the rock, and the necessity of running revenue-earning trains on the lower sections of the line. These difficulties culminated in the accidental explosion of thirty thousand kilos of dynamite close to the Eiger Wall station. The explosion was said to have been audible in Germany, but miraculously there were no fatalities.

At last, in February 1912, the tunnellers broke through at what would become the Jungfrau station, 11,401 feet above sea level. The alpinist Claud Schuster was much struck by the enterprise, writing that 'The ice-scenery between the foot of the Bergli rocks and the Eismeer station is more magnificent than that to be met with on any of the ordinary routes round Grindelwald; and the entrance into the internal regions of the Eiger, the galleries and restaurants scooped from the rock, are like nothing but a scene from Jules Verne.' On 1 August 1912, the final section of the line up to the Jungfraujoch was opened to the public. Soon after, the travel writer Charles Domville-Fife described this extraordinary railway, which

> passes by one continuous tunnel carved out into the heart of the mountain, under glacier, precipice, snowfield and avalanche, to the little plateau just below the actual summit of the Jungfrau – a giant of the great range. Here, at an altitude of 11,483 feet, all is barren, just rock, snow, and a range of vision, which, with one sweep of the eyes, embraces the French Alps, the Italian frontier, the Vosges mountains, the Bernese Oberland, the Engadine and the Black Forest.

Despite the new railway, the season of 1912 was not one of the best. Tensions in the Balkans had begun to discourage Continental tourism, and the Kaiser added fuel to the fire by attending Swiss army manoeuvres. Anglo-Swiss relations had never entirely recovered from the Boer War, when the German-speaking cantons were believed to have been unduly under the influence of Berlin. It was even rumoured that summer that a secret military agreement had been reached between Switzerland and Germany – a report which the British Foreign Secretary Sir Edward Grey was said to be inclined to believe. Despite categorical denials by the Swiss, the cloudless days had gone.

The following winter the Kaiser's son, Crown Prince William, was to be found in St Moritz, home of the Cresta. Once this had been a homely little resort. Now, as the Cadbys put it, on arrival one felt the same sense of exhilaration that Monte Carlo, Brighton or Paris gave one. There was the blue sky, the glitter of the sun, and the glamour of St Moritz. Outside the station was the longest row of concierges we had ever seen, and painted in vivid colours, ready to move, stood a queue of sledges . . . All the people walking about have an opulent look, and the sleighs are ornate and covered with expensive-looking rugs, and even toboggans are furnished with red velvet cushions . . . it shows such outward evidence of money, it is so gilded, one almost thinks of actual concrete gold.

By now the Cresta Run had achieved its quarter-century and had become an institution. Each year the run was constructed with great care to replicate its predecessor, the challenges of the course – Church Leap, Battledore, Shuttlecock, Stream Corner – being reproduced with precision. The run attracted an ever more cosmopolitan mix of tobogganers, anxious to test their skill on what had become the most famous toboggan slope in the world. The course was managed and run with military precision, and those who refused to submit to its disciplines were turned away. Every year it got faster. In 1896 an English tobogganer, John Baird, installed a chronograph to replace the system of flags. Timing was now accurate to a tenth of a second, and many riders were now travelling at speeds of seventy miles an hour – faster than man had hitherto travelled.

Writing a few years earlier, the journalist Ward Muir remarked that

tobogganing is an absurdity which drags sportsmen and sportswomen to the Alps every winter as surely as the magnetic pole attracts the compass needle; an absurdity which annually extracts thousands of pounds from the pockets of said enthusiasts and transfers them to those of hotel keepers; an absurdity which has wakened a dozen townships in Eastern Switzerland out of hibernating somnolence to an activity as great as was hitherto confined to the August tourist season. An absurdity, in fact, which Society now reckons as seriously as it reckons with Bridge or the automobile.

As to the Cresta itself, mindful of the accidents that the challenge of the run made inevitable, Muir thought it 'not so extravagant as tiger-shooting, but it provides hardly less excitement and certainly not fewer perils'.

The run was then still permitting female riders, one of whom was Vera Barclay. Her sister Claudia remembered the Crown Prince's visit, just before the war:

> 'Little Willie' was the joke of the place, and his behaviour was vulgar in the extreme. I remember in 1913 he loved all things English: clothes, slang, girls – above all girls! There were two really rather dreadful girls who were always with him, and an American jockey made up the foursome. Meanwhile his poor Princess could be seen going sadly for endless sleigh drives accompanied by a dreary-looking lady-in-waiting. News of his goings-on in St Moritz reached his father, and the Kaiser sent him a telegram ordering an immediate return to Germany. 'Little Willie' boldly refused to go home, and told all his English friends that when he did return he would be imprisoned in a remote *Schloss* as punishment for his disobedience.

So approached the summer season of 1914. If international tension was high, then there was a feeling especially amongst the mountaineers that life – or climbing – must go on. The weather that year, in contrast to 1911, proved exceptionally poor. Nevertheless in the Grisons, Roderick Williams and the brothers A.N. and G.A. Solly conquered the Jupperhorn by the hitherto unclimbed western arête. This was relatively straightforward, with the exception of a steep tower of some sixty feet close to the summit. One of the brothers wrote: 'There is a crack in the rock at the steepest point where an arm can be jammed in, and then a foot, otherwise it would be barely practicable.' R.W. Lloyd climbed the Zermatt Lyskamm by the rarely tackled north-west face, a steep and perilous ascent hampered by much new snow. V.J.E. Ryan teamed up again with the Lochmatters to climb the Grépon by the Nantillons face, Franz Lochmatter writing that 'The most difficult part was the great steepness of the ice-face, which in places was very unpleasant, and is about 80 to 90 metres long.'

Geoffrey Winthrop Young, too, was abroad with Josef Knubel. They tackled the severe west ridge of the 11,293-foot Gspaltenhorn in the Bernese Oberland, and made the only ascent that season of the Matterhorn's north-west ridge route. Climbing in the company of two younger mountaineers, Young for perhaps the first time in his life found his technique and expertise challenged. 'Upon this glorious . . . ridge, stately with ice, slashed with black rock and silken with wind-pleated snow, Josef and I had to use all our craft to keep our lead.'

Successful in the present, the mountaineers were nevertheless mindful of the past. The fiftieth anniversary of Whymper's ascent of the Matterhorn was fast approaching, and his death in 1911 had inspired the notion of a memorial. With this in mind, towards the end of June a number of mountaineers gathered at the Monte Rosa hotel in Zermatt. The climbers had been disturbed on 28 June by the assassination at Sarajevo of the heir to the Austro-Hungarian throne, Archduke Francis Ferdinand. They came nevertheless, a polyglot group from the principal mountaineering nations, representatives of the English, Swiss, French, Italian, German and Austrian alpine clubs. The Englishman was the writer and climber Julian Grande. There, sitting around the old 'climbers' table', they decided with a European accord that would be the last for more than a generation, to have a statue erected in Zermatt to commemorate the event. Whymper himself, perhaps even Coolidge, would have approved.

Not long after the party broke up, Austria – with the Kaiser's blessing – issued her ultimatum to Serbia. By 28 July Vienna had declared war. With painful inevitability, the commitments and obligations of the Triple Alliance and Triple Entente manifested themselves. Little more than a month after the climbers' meeting, Europe was at war. Winston Churchill, now First Lord of the Admiralty, had been instrumental in ensuring the Royal Navy was prepared for the conflict. Later he wrote:

Once more now in the march of centuries Old England was to stand forth in battle against the mightiest thrones and dominions. Once more in defence of the liberties of Europe and the common right must she enter upon a voyage of great toil and hazard across waters uncharted, towards coasts unknown, guided only by the stars. Once more 'the far-off line of storm-beaten ships' was to stand between the Continental Tyrant and the dominion of the world.

The *belle époque* was over. For the English in the Alps, nothing would ever be the same again.

Downhill

C'est pas de l'alpinisme, ça, c'est la guerre.

Armand Charlet

Chapter Ten

Après le Déluge

'The First World War created a watershed between the old and new Alpine worlds quite as prominent as those that it created elsewhere.'
R.W. Clark, *The Alps* (1973)

'The world's great age begins anew, the golden years return.' So Shelley had written a century before in the aftermath of the Napoleonic wars. Such were the feelings of the tens of thousands of English men and women who flocked to the Alps when restrictions on foreign travel were finally lifted in the spring of 1919. The president of the Alpine Club, J. Norman Collie, remarked how its members were 'looking forward to the restoration of our mountain playground in the Alps to what it was before 1914'.

The man who was to supplant Whymper as the club's most famous member was among them: 'It was seven years since I had seen the Alps. To me they were a vision startlingly fresh and new – new as when I first saw them, and so overwhelmingly greater than the images I had conjured up that I seemed never to have seen them before.' As it happened, George Leigh Mallory would go to his mountain grave with his illusions preserved. His contemporaries, though, were to be much disappointed by the succession of events that led up to their second – in some respects their final – exile in 1939. Arnold Lunn's Augustan age was over for ever.

The years since that brave group of mountaineers had agreed in Zermatt to commemorate Whymper's achievement had been almost irredeemably catastrophic. The defeated countries – particularly Germany and Austria-Hungary – were ruined; the victors had scarcely fared better. Great Britain lost something like three-quarters of a million men, France almost one and a half million. Germany itself lost four million. The Kaiser was deposed; Russia suffered the Bolshevik revolution; the Austro-Hungarian and Ottoman empires were broken up. Much of Europe was laid waste, many of its people were without work or food. The values that had sustained social and economic progress in Europe over the previous century were called into question, debased or destroyed. Life was cheapened by the universality of death.

The Alps themselves were largely but not entirely deserted during the war. Among the warring nations many of those whom the mountains attracted were naturally engaged elsewhere. Of the English, the Alpine Club's president in 1916, Lord Justice Pickford, remarked that 'practically all members of military age who are not held back by ill health or other insuperable obstacles have joined the forces or are serving the country in some way.' Pickford added: 'We grieve to say that many of them have been killed in action.' Mallory was in the trenches in Flanders, W.A.B. Coolidge found himself stateless, Geoffrey Winthrop Young was leading an ambulance unit in Italy, Sir Martin Conway was induced to take charge of the Imperial War Museum. For the remainder, the trenches established from the North Sea to the foothills of the Alps formed a barrier to excursions, and in any case restrictions on international travel were gradually introduced as it became apparent that the war would last beyond the Christmas of 1914.

Even then, with English tourists unlikely to receive a warm welcome in the eastern Alps, neutral Switzerland and France remained the only viable destinations. The alpine border between Italy and Austria-Hungary was heavily fortified, and saw fierce fighting after Italy joined the war in 1915. Only the odd English traveller found his way to the resorts. The alpinist Edward Broome recorded that 'Zermatt in 1915 was a desert. Its busy street was empty. Its shops were shut. Half its hotels were closed, and the other half more than half-empty. The Zermatt–Visp and Gornergrat railways ran very few trains, and carried a very unremunerative number of passengers. Hardly anyone could be seen on mountain paths, no one on the peaks.' The *Alpine Journal* was soon reduced to recounting the exploits of yesteryear, while introducing a section devoted to members in the Services decorated, injured or killed.

Certain alpine resorts nevertheless remained something more than a shadow of themselves. The disappearance of foreign tourists throughout the Alps gave an impetus to local tourism, and the Swiss in particular began to explore their own mountains in unprecedented numbers. The established colonies, too, soldiered on. For those whose health demanded that they stay in the Alps, life continued almost unchanged. The *Davos Courier* commented in its first number after the war:

> Davos was in many respects fortunate in the midst of misfortune. In spite of the heavy hand laid on international travel, the resort managed to retain a comparatively large number of visitors, and to benefit from certain compensations that arose for it out of the otherwise melancholy situation. Its distinctive value as a cure-station gave it a certain stability lacking to resorts of a less serious nature. The crippling of communications, that seemed to threaten such catastrophic results, brought in one hand a modification of them. As it was so difficult to travel, people stayed longer, did not run to and fro as of old, and proceeded more continuously with the cure. The average duration of a visitor's residence lengthened considerably. And the war itself, owing to international arrangements, filled up officially many vacant places.

As a consequence, 'Davos was never at any time dull or dead'.

For different reasons this was the case also at Mürren, Meiringen, Interlaken, Château d'Oex and Leysin, where from 1916 onwards wounded British prisoners of war, returned from Germany, were interned. Arnold Lunn, incapacitated by his injured leg from military service, found employment at Mürren, teaching convalescent soldiers to ski. In John Buchan's novel *Mr Standfast*, his injured hero, Peter Pienaar, is interned in St Anton. Richard Hannay, disguised as the porter Joseph Zimmer, goes to visit him:

Ten days later the porter Joseph Zimmer of Arosa, clad in the rough and shapeless trousers of his class, but sporting an old velveteen shooting-coat bequeathed him by a former German master – speaking the guttural tongue of the Grisons, and with all his belongings in one massive rucksack, came out of the little station of St Anton and blinked in the frosty sun-shine. He looked down upon the little old village beside its ice-bound lake, but his business was with the new village of hotels and villas which had sprung up in the last ten years south of the station. He made some halting enquiries of the station people, and a cab-driver outside finally directed him to the place he sought – the cottage of the Widow Summermatter, where resided an English internee, one Peter Pienaar.

Far from being a playground, for Peter Pienaar and his real-life counterparts, the Alps had become a prison.

On his way to revisit the Alps in 1919, Mallory had passed through Paris. As he breezed through the French capital, peace negotiations were at their height, instituting arrangements that would profoundly affect the future of England and the alpine nations – and of the Alps themselves – over the next twenty years. Despite the agreed procedures for negotiation that had been set in place, it was indicative of events to come that by the time of Mallory's visit the major players had already discarded the formal machinery and were settling matters between themselves.

The principles on which the peace was to be based had been enunciated by Wilson in the Fourteen Points and broadly endorsed by the allies. Underlying these proposals were the notions of national self-determination and the fundamental integrity of the nation-state, the intention being that Europe should be recast in this mould.

In the Tyrol this led to the division at the Brenner of the former Austrian province into its northern and southern sections, the former now part of the new republic of Austria, the latter of Italy. The new arrangement would prove a running sore. For Switzerland this was an opportunity to acquire the Vorarlberg, the Austrian province on its south-eastern border. A plebiscite in the region voted overwhelmingly in favour of such a union. Ultimately, however, it was disallowed by the Supreme Allied Council at the Peace of Saint-Germain which complemented that of Versailles. For Germany, the redrawing of the European borders excluded certain German-speaking areas, notably the Sudetenland in Czechoslovakia and East Prussia in Poland, the acquisition or re-acquisition of which became the nation's corroding ambition. So too did *Anschluss* (union) with Austria, which the Treaty of Versailles expressly forbade.

If this meant that an equitable principle had been – by force of circumstance – inequitably applied, the matter of reparations had been even less happy. Germany had accepted the armistice on the basis of the Fourteen Points, and had committed herself to paying some form of compensation 'for all damage done to the civilian population of the allies and their property'. Trouble arose because of the 'war-guilt clause' which, with its reference to 'the war imposed by the aggression of Germany and her allies', effectively blamed Germany for the conflict. In addition, the conference failed to agree on a set sum in reparation of this 'guilt'. This meant, in A.J.P. Taylor's words, that Germany was required to sign a blank cheque. Together, the elevation of the status of the nation-state, the exclusion from Germany of large numbers of German-speaking peoples, and the perceived injustice of the reparations paved the way for discontent. A young Austrian corporal soon saw these circumstances as a means of levering himself into power.

Another sign of the future was the role played in Paris by President Wilson. The United States had entered the war in 1917, and was decisive in bringing it to a successful conclusion for the allies. For good or ill, Wilson was now a critical player in the settlement at Versailles. The new world had been brought in to reorder the old. This reflected the fact that the dominant political position of Britain in world affairs was fast diminishing. At the same time, England's economic pre-eminence, on the wane since before the turn of the century, was being eclipsed first by the United States and also by Japan. The former's exports had multiplied threefold in the course of the war; the latter had taken advantage of the conflict by opening up markets in India, China and South America previously served by Britain. Once foremost among the industrialized nations, England now had to fight for her place at the table.

Since the heady days of the 'season of seasons' the world had turned upside down. The political, social, economic and cultural factors that had driven the English to the Alps during much of the preceding century had changed dramatically and irrevocably. The writing was on the wall.

If the easing of travel restrictions first encouraged the return of foreign tourists to the Alps, the signing of the various armistices – Versailles, Saint-Germain, Neuilly – did more. The summer season of 1919 was inevitably muted. With the railways grossly disrupted by the war, the possibilities for travel were limited. In the larger resorts few of the hotels opened, in the smaller sometimes none at all. In the belligerent countries food and wine remained scarce, while labour in the form of guides, porters, voituriers and waiters was hard to come by. Many still awaited demobilization from their various armies, and many had been killed.

By winter, though, there were signs of a renaissance. The internal economies, at least of England and France, were functioning normally again, and western Europe enjoyed a brief industrial boom. Men's minds began to turn once again to the Alps, and the rest and recreation they afforded. As the *Davos Courier* put it: 'The air is still thick, and it is difficult to discern the future with clearness and certainty. But there are signs that encourage, and, with the improved situation pictured forth, it is only natural to suppose that the number of visitors will gradually rise to former levels. The world has greater need than ever of such a source of health and healthy pleasure as is afforded by Davos.'

St Moritz was equally optimistic and, as it turned out, justifiably so. As Michael Seth-Smith, the historian of the Cresta Run, later recorded:

> By New Year, it was apparent that European Society was pre-pared to patronize St Moritz, where it was able to enjoy itself to its heart's content. It was as though the town was in the midst of a renaissance after virtually being a ghost town for five years. Amongst the visitors were the King of Greece, the Duke of Alba, Mrs George Keppel and HRH the Infante Alfonso of Spain. A fancy dress party held at the Kulm Hotel was attended by several hundred dancers, and a company was formed to insti-tute passenger flights from Zürich to the Engadine. The only problem concerning these flights seemed to be the excessive weight of the ladies' dress trunks.

St Moritz soon 'regained its pre-war sparkle', and the Cresta once again flourished. As E.F. Benson reaffirmed: 'There is one Mecca, there is one St Peter's, there is one Cresta. As is Mecca to the Mohammedan, as is St Peter's to the Catholic, so is the Cresta Run at St Moritz to the tobogganer.' Yet it soon became apparent that in the Alps as a whole neither the mix of nationalities nor the mix of the classes was the same as before.

To the veteran alpinist Frederic Harrison, the Alps of his youth had appeared predominantly an English playground, whilst those of his old age he felt had become a German *Kurhaus*. This was hyper-bole. The better-known resorts in the years immediately before the war attracted not just Germans, but visitors from all the principal European nations, including Belgium, Holland and Norway. There were also no small number of Russians and Americans. He was right, though, to point to the growth of German tourism, often at the expense of its English counterpart.

Now, however, the old order had changed. Few among the

vanquished nations were in the mood or financial position to return to the Alps – a situation aggravated in 1922 by the collapse of the German mark and the ruin of the German and Austrian middle classes. In Russia, too, the civil war caused by the Bolshevik revolution dragged on and the old gentry class was dispossessed and dispersed. Even the English themselves, although they certainly returned in fair numbers, were no longer in the ascendant. The role they had played fifty years before was now being embraced by the Americans. Already before the war guidebooks had started to substitute the phrase 'English speaking' for 'English', and to include various allusions to the requirements of visitors from across the Atlantic.

Moreover, the Americans were now arriving not only in far greater numbers but in quite a different mood. President Wilson had done his job. The new world had indeed been called in to redress the balance of the old. As Louis Turner and John Ash wrote in *The Golden Hordes*:

> As soon as the armistice had been signed, wealthy American tourists began to arrive in Europe; they came in a new spirit of confidence and even superiority. The great aristocracy of Europe had failed in decadence, the Great War and the Russian Revolution of 1917. The *nouveaux riches* of the new world need no longer feel inferior or gauche before an old world of superior culture and refinement. Many Americans felt that England would soon sink to the level of a politically insignificant 'pastoral country'.

The German *Kurhaus* was becoming the American backyard.

The aftermath of the war also saw a further broadening of the social classes attracted to the Alps. Although what the French called the vulgarization of the Alps had begun with the arrival of Continental railways and Thomas Cook as far back as the 1860s, the social scene up until 1914 remained relatively exclusive. If the war had been declared as the war 'to make the world safe for democracy', it was apparent by the early twenties that this aim had in some respects been achieved. England, France and the United States were already democracies. In the years immediately after the war their example was followed by Austria and Germany, the latter inaugurating the Weimar Republic.

In all these countries democracy meant a good deal more than simply an extension of the franchise. War had proved a great leveller. The old barriers of birth, money, education and sex were eroded. With the emancipation of the working classes came the emancipation, and ultimately enfranchisement, of women. The same period saw the erosion of churchgoing, the rapid rise of divorce, and the falling off of the 'form' that characterized the pre-war winter sports resorts, as Lunn recalled them. With the Great War initiating huge numbers in the pleasures and pains of foreign travel, it was scarcely surprising that many should wish to explore the delights of 'abroad' in more peaceful circumstances. The year 1922 thus saw the founding of the Workers' Travel Association. Soon Scott Fitzgerald would be writing that his compatriots in Europe had 'the humane values of Pekinese, bivalves, cretins, goats'.

It was a long time since the Alps had been absolutely exclusive. Now, though, they welcomed visitors more various than ever before.

Reflecting on the changing nature of tourism and particularly of climbers in the Alps, Professor Thomas Graham Brown remarked in a review of the Alpine Club's activities: 'It is probable that as many British climbers visit the Alps today as did before the war, but their proportion has certainly declined.' Although he attributed this to several causes, Brown made much of the fact that 'the younger generation has seen that the glamour of new exploration has almost passed from the Alps.' Here, once again, the war had proved the turning point. Up to 1914 climbers of international standing such as V.J.E. Ryan and Geoffrey Winthrop Young still thought the Alps offered worthwhile challenges. Now the new generation, led by the likes of Mallory, F.S. Smythe and Brown himself, simply trained in the Alps before setting their sights elsewhere.

The Alpine Club's president J. Norman Collie in his valedictory address of 1922 remarked on what he called a 'most important mountaineering adventure'. This was not an ascent of the La Meije, the Matterhorn, the Piz Bernina, the Gross Glockner, Mont Blanc or the Pelmo. It was rather the joint expedition of the Club and the Royal Geographical Society to Everest. 'Never has there been any mountaineering expedition of such interest or importance . . . For not only was it an unknown land of mighty peaks, but the peaks themselves were the highest in the world.' The past, like the future, was already a foreign country.

British interest in the Himalaya was inevitable, given the position of the greatest of the world's mountain ranges on the northern frontiers of British India. With little known about the geography of this two-thousand-mile barrier, its strategic importance dictated that it should be surveyed. Begun in the eighteenth century, the survey took little less than a hundred years. By the beginning of the nineteenth century, estimates had been made of the heights of the more accessible peaks. In 1823 a new surveyor-general introduced the system of triangulation, which much improved the accuracy of such measurements. Then, in 1852, just two years before Alfred Wills's ascent of the Wetterhorn, the surveyors identified a giant peak of 29,000 feet, almost twice the height of Mont Blanc. Named in honour of the then surveyor-general, Sir George Everest, it was believed to be – and of course was – the highest peak in the world.

For a generation, mountaineers had continued to concentrate on the exploration of the Alps. In 1883, however, European climbers began to interest themselves in the Himalaya. The first to do so was W.W. Graham who, accompanied by his Swiss guide Joseph Imboden, explored the mountains of Sikkim in 1883. Then came the Great Game player Francis Younghusband, who travelled extensively in the Karakoram range in 1887, and who was to play a leading part in post-war Everest expeditions. He was followed in 1892 by Martin Conway, whose exploration and mapping of the area inspired his long-distance trek in the Alps of 1894. It was A.F. Mummery, however, who made the first attempt on a major Himalayan peak. This was the Nanga Parbat expedition of 1895, which cost him his life. Then, in 1907 the first great peak was conquered by Dr Tom

Longstaff, who surmounted the 23,360-foot Trisul. He was followed
in 1911 by Dr A.M. Kellas, who conquered the Chomiomo and the
Pauhunri, both over 22,000 feet. The distinguished Italian mountaineer, the Duke of Abruzzi, was also active during these years, travelling extensively in the range and reaching a record 24,600 feet on the
second highest mountain, K2.

By now it was apparent that the Himalaya, not least because of their
height, their remoteness from civilization, and the unpredictability and
occasional violence of their weather, offered challenges in many
respects far greater than the Alps. And in the years leading up to the
war, men began to dream of conquering the world's highest peak.

Once the war was over it was agreed that something should be
done. Inspired by the Alpine Club's president Percy Farrar, an
Everest Committee was formed under the joint auspices of the Club
itself and the Royal Geographical Society. An expedition was
planned. This was to be a reconnaissance to establish a possible route
to the summit. The Alpine Club recommended that George Mallory
should be part of the team.

Inspired to climb while at Winchester by R.L.G. Irving, then a
master at the school, Mallory was a figure of high romance whose
heroic reputation was more than matched by the man himself. He
was born in 1886, to a family of several generations of clergy. A
scholar at Winchester, he proved himself an outstanding gymnast,
subsequently playing rugby and football at his university, Cambridge,
where he was rumoured to have won his place on the basis of the
history he had promised to read, rather than what he had already
read. His mentor at Magdalene was the college's Master, the alpinist
A.C. Benson. Meeting Mallory in Cambridge before the war, Lytton
Strachey gasped to Leslie Stephen's daughter Vanessa Bell:

> Mon dieu! – George Mallory! – When that's been written, what
> more need be said? My hand trembles, my heart palpitates, my
> whole being swoons away at the words – oh heavens! heavens!
> I found of course that he's been absurdly maligned – he's six
> feet high, with a body of an athlete by Praxiteles, and a face –
> oh incredible – the mystery of Botticelli, the refinement and
> delicacy of a Chinese print, the youth and piquancy of an

unimaginable English boy. I rave, but when you see him you will admit all – all!

Mallory cut his teeth climbing with Irving himself, the poet Robert Graves, and Geoffrey Winthrop Young. The latter regarded him as so chivalrous that he nicknamed him 'Sir Galahad'. By the time the first Everest expedition was being organized in late 1920, he was a master at Charterhouse and had an unimpeachable reputation as a climber. In 1921, it was Mallory who was sent to prospect the huge glacier that sweeps down from Everest's north face, Mallory who identified the North Col as the only apparent breach in its defences, Mallory who then surmounted the 23,000-foot Col and spied out a route to the summit.

Following this successful reconnaissance, a fresh expedition returned in the spring of 1922 for a serious assault. Led by Brigadier-General Charles Bruce, this was a larger expedition, which included Mallory along with several other highly experienced climbers. Though they were equipped with oxygen, and Bruce took time and trouble to acclimatize his teams to the altitude, the expedition was still defeated by the severity of the task in the heights where there is only a third of the oxygen available at sea-level. The first team, comprising Mallory, Dr T.H. Somervell and Colonel E.F. Norton, reached 26,700-feet before being forced down by breathing problems. A second team, equipped with the primitive and heavy oxygen apparatus, reached 27,230 feet before succumbing to gale-force winds. The third attempt ended in tragedy when the party was struck by an avalanche that swept seven Sherpa porters to their deaths.

Mallory, however, in the words of Colonel Norton, leader of the 1924 expedition, had become so much the inspiration and driving force of the expedition as to be 'the living soul of the attempt on Everest'. Uncertain as to whether the climb was achievable, Mallory described the campaign as 'more of a war than an adventure'. Nevertheless, like Whymper before him on the Matterhorn, Mallory was dedicated to the conquest of Everest. Questioned by a woman journalist, he explained – perhaps in jest – that he wanted to climb the peak 'because it was there'. But according to Irving, Mallory's true motives lay elsewhere. 'For him snow mountains were not simply opponents to be overcome; they were things that feed the springs of reverence and affection, making a man go with a lighter step and more grateful heart along the road of life. But being asked to go, such a man could not refuse.'

If, as Professor Brown remarked, the glamour of exploration had fled from the Alps, it was increasingly apparent in the years after the war that the climbing ethos the English had done so much to foster was also being eroded. Brown himself wrote:

> The effect of the war was to weaken the bonds of convention and tradition. A generation of young climbers was lost, and when the yet younger post-war climber came to the mountain, he had less contact with, and was less influenced by, the older traditions of climbing than would have been the case had there been more direct continuity. The war also lowered the value set on human life and gave a lesser respect for danger.

These changes were most obviously manifested in the development of so-called artificial climbing, and the sorts of climb that these aids permitted mountaineers to attempt.

The ethics of mountaineering had been the subject of debate ever since the beginnings of the modern sport and the adventures of Professor Forbes and John Ball; since the Matterhorn accident of 1865 they had become a matter of common discussion. The press had then taken the stance that whilst mountaineering in the pursuit of knowledge might be justifiable, mountaineering as a sport and in pursuit of pleasure was not. Mountaineers – notably Leslie Stephen – defended their activities, claiming that the sport was ennobling and gave a powerful and beneficial stimulus to man's spirit and body.

Nevertheless the sport had its own rules, spoken and unspoken, and these were more or less scrupulously followed. Certainly the

Victorians set themselves unambiguously against the open courting of danger, dangerous though their sport was. They also eschewed anything that they construed as artificial aids to climbing. The essence of their sport was the conflict between man and nature, in the course of which battle man was driven to discover his highest qualities. It was a battle, moreover, not only with nature but with himself. On reaching the summit of Mont Blanc in 1911, Mallory, something of a throwback in these matters, asked himself: 'Have we vanquished an enemy?' He replied: 'None but ourselves.'

This position was slowly eroded in the Edwardian age, and yet more rapidly after the war. The first chink in the wall was the piton. From early days climbers would periodically hammer wooden pegs into crannies to provide hand-holds or rope belays on short, tricky pitches. In due course wood gave way to steel, wedged into cracks with the head of an ice-axe. With a hole in its head to take the rope, in time it became apparent that the piton might be used on long, steep inclines which were otherwise insurmountable. As Professor Brown remarked, these were at first regarded as 'bad form', in that they gave the climber unfair assistance in the battle. More practically, the piton had the disadvantage of leaving the leading climber temporarily unroped whenever the rope-end was removed from each particular piton on a given pitch. This led to the development of a steel ring which could be clipped on and off the piton, through which the rope could be threaded. Called by the French a *mousqueton*, by the Germans a *Karabiner*, the device was censured by R.L.G. Irving as having no English name, 'because the thing is un-English in name and nature'.

It was the school of Irving that resisted the use of oxygen on Everest for identical reasons. Similarly, when an accident leading to two deaths occurred on the Grandes Jorasses in Savoy in 1931, the *Alpine Journal* upbraided those responsible. They were 'engaged in the extremely unsportsmanlike proceeding of fixing pitons in the N. face of the peak'. The journal's editor, Colonel E.L. Strutt, thundered:

A wave of recklessness and folly is spreading through the Alps. The irrational desire and competition for new routes has degenerated into a mad striving for notoriety by forcing a passage where none exists, a few yards to the right or left of well-known itineraries. The new alpinist's ambition is to incur the maximum of danger while he strains the limits of difficulty. Of rational pleasure, of interest, there is no question. It is a gamble of unadulterated danger from first to last.

Right or wrong, it was this conservatism on the part of British mountaineers that contributed to their eclipse as pioneers in the Alps themselves. As Chris Bonington wrote much later: 'The Alpine Club . . . was earning a reputation for being a stuffy club of old men.' With the greatest English climbers turning to challenges further afield, all but a handful of the major climbs in the Alps between the wars were achieved by Continental mountaineers.

Mallory's companion on the summit attempt on Everest was a young Oxford rowing Blue called Andrew Comyn Irvine. Born in 1902 and schooled at Shrewsbury, Irvine was a magnificently built young man with a taste for adventure. By the age of twenty-one he had already sledged across eastern Spitsbergen under the auspices of the Merton College Arctic Expedition. Now he was on the lookout for greater challenges. What could be better than Everest?

By no means an experienced mountaineer, Irvine was in many respects a surprising choice for the Himalayan expedition. When his selection was still in the balance, Mallory wrote to Geoffrey Winthrop Young: 'Irvine represents our one attempt to get one superman, though his lack of experience is against him.' Mallory was certainly right in regarding Irvine as an outstanding all-round sports-man. At Mürren in the winter of 1923/4 he would win the Strang-Watkins slalom cup, though virtually a novice. Arnold Lunn thought him the most gifted novice he had ever met, praising his 'complete fearlessness, great physical strength and, above all, genius for sport'.

Irvine himself wrote: 'When I am an old man, I will look back on Christmas 1923 as the day when to all intents and purposes I was born. I don't think anyone has *lived* until they have been on skis.' Irvine took a friendly interest in Lunn's son Peter, then nine, who had contrived to come third to Irvine in the Strang-Watkins cup. Within months, Irvine was in the Himalaya as part of Colonel Norton's Everest expedition. Writing to the young Lunn, he expressed the hope that he would reach the summit of Everest on Ascension Day.

The Himalayan expeditions of 1921 and 1922 had greatly whetted the appetite of the British public for this adventure. The pre-eminence of British mountaineers and mountaineering still being an article of faith, there were great expectations that, after the pre-liminary forays, the third expedition to Everest would see the con-quest of the peak. Learning from the earlier ventures, Norton was meticulous both in his selection of the team of climbers and in plan-ning what was in effect a campaign run on military lines. The team was to be allowed a relatively generous period of acclimatization to the Himalayan altitude. The climbers were then paired up, those who had acclimatized well leading the pack without oxygen, the less fit following in their footsteps, their respiration supported. As in 1922, the attempt was to be made from the north ridge, base camp being established at the end of April on the East Rongbuk glacier. Two attempts by Norton's teams were beaten back by blizzards, and the monsoon season was by then fast approaching. There was time for one last attempt.

A first pair of climbers, Geoffrey Bruce and George Mallory, beat their way up from the base camp and established Camp V at 25,000 feet. There a fresh team took over, working their way up to 26,800 feet. This pair, consisting of Norton himself and T.H. Somervell, disdaining the 30-pound oxygen packs, then made a further ascent to within 1,000 feet of the summit before turning back. At that height, the pain of breathing and the greatly diminished work-rate made an attempt on the summit seem suicidal. The last chance to conquer the mountain that year was thus in the hands of the third team, com-prising Andrew Irvine and Noel Odell, who were to make an attempt assisted by oxygen. Odell, however, had not acclimatized satisfac-torily. Norton chose to replace him with Mallory.

In the early hours of 8 June, Mallory and Irvine left Camp VI for the summit. Clothed in a manner with which Whymper himself would have been entirely familiar, oxygen packs being their only concession to modernity, they had 2,300 feet to climb. Approaching Camp VI was Odell himself. On the peak that morning the streaming clouds obscured Mallory and Irvine, only parting briefly at about 1.00 p.m. to give Odell a glimpse of the attempt. He thought they were about 800 feet from the summit and, in Norton's words, 'going strong for the top'. Odell waited the remainder of the day and the following night for them at Camp IV, then returned to Camp V and again to Camp VI. It was deserted. By 11 June Norton was obliged to disclose in his despatches that 'Mallory and Irvine perished on the mountain beyond all doubt.'

Despite the discovery of Mallory's body in 1999, the pair's fate remains mysterious. Like Whymper's companions on the Matterhorn, perhaps they reached the summit only to perish on the descent, leaving the world ignorant of their extraordinary achievement. Or somewhere on the final 800 feet of the mountain perhaps the weather, altitude sickness or a fall supervened, snatching from the pair mountaineering's last remaining great prize. As Norton was to put it, 'Who will ever know whether the lost climbers reached the summit before the accident which it may be assumed caused their death?' Irrespective of the answer, the image of Mallory and Irvine battling on that brutal mountain in their tweeds and hobnail boots is an enduring and heroic symbol. Closing his despatch, Norton remarked of Mallory:

> We always regarded him as the ideal mountaineer, light, limber, and active, gifted with tremendous pace up and down hill, and possessing all the balance and technical proficiency on rock, snow and ice which only years of experience give. But the fire within made him really great, for it caused his spirit constantly to dominate his body to such an extent that, much as I have climbed with him, I can hardly picture his succumbing to exhaustion. As a man he was a very real friend to us all, a cultured, gentle spirit curiously contrasting with the restless fiery energy he displayed in action. His loss is irreparable no less

to his friends on the successive Everest expeditions than to the very much larger circle of those who loved him in England.

Mallory and Irvine were pioneers entirely in the tradition of Forbes and Whymper, Stephen and Ball. Although their spirit of adventure found its final expression in the Himalaya, it had its birth in English alpinism whose finest achievement it remains.

Chapter Eleven
The Blizzard

'Its principal feature, from the holiday point of view, is complete irresponsibility. On the glistening slopes of the High Alps it is almost
impossible to remember, much less brood upon, the cares of a
cloudy, sombre world below.'

Thomas Cook, winter sports brochure (1931–2)

By 1925 a semblance of normality had returned to the world. In
England, battling to remain competitive against the might of the US
economy and a rapidly industrializing Japan, the Chancellor of the
Exchequer Winston Churchill seemed to herald happier days with
a return to the gold standard. France's reacquisition of Alsace-
Lorraine had spurred her own programme of industrialization and
strengthened her economy. In Italy Mussolini's numerous public
works schemes fostered recovery. The Treaty of Locarno, the non-
aggression pact between France, Germany and Belgium, guaranteed
by Britain and Italy, promised stability. Within Germany's new
Weimar Republic, heavy borrowing created a small boom. God had
at last returned to his heaven, and all seemed right with the world.

This optimism was reflected in the dramatic expansion of winter
sports. The first full season after the war – 1919/20 – was inevitably
somewhat tentative. Then, in the following year the post-war boom
broke, unemployment rose, and there was a temporary recession
throughout western Europe. By 1922, however, there were signs of
recovery, and the winter holiday began to enjoy a great vogue. In his

guide to the winter Alps, *Things Seen in Switzerland in Winter*, Charles Domville-Fife attributed this to the travel agencies, remarking that 'Thomas Cook and Sons, the well-known tourist agency, have done much to promote and assist winter sports at almost every important centre in the High Alps. The same may be said of another entirely British undertaking, Public Schools Alpine Sports Ltd, the trading name of Henry Lunn's Public Schools Alpine Sports Club.

Yet there was surely something in the exuberance of a winter sports holiday that peculiarly suited a generation trying to throw off the hangover of war, and made it particularly characteristic of the period. Here, according to Domville-Fife, is post-war Wengen, Mürren's opposite number across the Lauterbrunnen valley:

> Halfway down this picturesque little village street of seasonal shops a snow-slope leads to the Palace skating rink, the social rendezvous of the sunny scintillating hours before the early lunch which is the custom in most winter centres. Here is a large sheet of level ice, surrounded by lofty banks of snow and gay with skaters sailing round in the still, bracing air, executing remarkable figures, and waltzing to the strains of an orchestra. Old and young are caught by the spirit of joie-de-vivre. The hum of steel on ice, the ripple of laughter, the wild strains of music vainly endeavouring to keep pace with the flashing whirling youthful figures, the flush of health on each face that passes swiftly by, the mild flirtations and the spirit of camaraderie are all highly infectious in the rarefied air and brilliant sunshine.

Each season in the twenties brought more winter visitors to the Alps. The old cure-stations – Leysin, Davos, Arosa and Montana – enjoyed a boom, with a series of new sanatoria being built, and they featured prominently in Scott Fitzgerald's *Tender is the Night* and Thomas Mann's 1924 masterpiece, *The Magic Mountain*. The writer Katherine Mansfield, a victim of tuberculosis, wrote from the Châlet de Sapins in Montana to her friend Dorothy Brett:

> Have I told you about my balcony? It is as big as a small room, the sides are enclosed and big double doors lead from it to my

work-room. Three superb geraniums still stand on the ledge when it's fine, and their rosy masses of flowers against *blue space* are wonderful. It is so high up here that one sees only the tops and half-way down the enormous mountains opposite, and there's a great sweep of sky as one only gets at sea – on a ship – anchored before a new undiscovered country . . . But it's most beautiful at night. Last night, for instance, at about ten o'clock . . . I came out here and sat watching. The world was like a huge ball of ice. There wasn't a sound. It might have been ages before man . . .

The traditional winter resorts – Chamonix, Grindelwald, St Moritz, Garmisch-Partenkirchen, St Anton, Kitzbühel, Cortina – were prospering as never before. A series of young pretenders also opened for winter business, first in the cantons of Vaud and the Valais, then in the Jura and the Vosges mountains, Savoy and the Tyrol. In 1928 even Zermatt was obliged to follow suit. Hitherto the resort had been closed in winter. At the end of 1927, Dr Hermann Seiler of the hotel dynasty had induced the railway authorities to open the line from Visp up to St Nicholas. There he arranged for fifty sleighs to transport a party of one hundred and eighty – all English – up to the snowbound village. This was such a success that, the following winter, trains were run right up to Zermatt. The first winter sports season was held between 21 December 1928 and 28 February 1929.

Enjoying the paradoxical atmosphere of Coleridge's 'Kubla Khan' – the sunny pleasure dome with caves of ice – the epitome of these resorts in the 1920s was St Moritz, of which Domville-Fife recorded:

Winter life in St Moritz is made up of three things: sport, social amusements, and paying for both. This, however, does not mean that all who visit the cosmopolitan resort actually accomplish all three of these essentials; some break down under the strain, and pass away to the quieter world of Pontresina, Samaden, Celerina or Maloja, while others occupy a large portion of the day getting into elaborate ski-suits, and then go for a quiet sleigh-drive. The majority take stout Alpine sticks, fold their coloured snow-socks well over their ski-boots, and make their way with consummate nerve and skill up the most expensive street in the world to watch the morning bobsleigh races down the famous run, then change garb and take afternoon tea at Hanselman's or one of the palatial hotels, and so while away the time until dinner and dancing claim them.

Val d'Isère, however, in the heart of what was later to call itself the Three Valleys, was still behind the times. Here, Findlay Muirhead recorded in his 1923 guide to the French Alps, 'the villagers practically hibernate in winter, as the cult of winter sports has not yet reached their solitude.'

All the resorts had toboggan runs and skating-rinks, a number bobsleigh runs and curling rinks. It was skiing, though, that was the vogue of the twenties, attracting sportsmen and women in unprecedented numbers, and gradually eroding the popularity of the older sports. Increasingly, too, its proponents were British. Indeed, the half-dozen years from 1924 to 1931 represent the period in which British influence was at its zenith. Jimmy Riddell, one of the best skiers of his generation, remembered the pioneers of the time, though relatively few in numbers, devoting their entire winters to the sport. And their supremacy hinged on the development of that form of the sport that was to dominate the period up to, and more crucially after, the Second World War. This was downhill skiing and its variant, slalom.

Downhill dated from Arnold Lunn's inauguration of the Kandahar race in 1911. Eleven years later, with winter sports properly under way again after the war, Lunn decided that there was a growing tendency for style and grace to be emphasized at the expense of speed. Accordingly he set competitors an entirely new sort of course to complement the simple downhill races. First tried on Mürren's nursery slopes on 21 January 1922, this course required competitors to ski downhill through pairs of flags, principally testing their ability to turn: Lunn dubbed this the slalom. Although the term was used in Norway for a steep, narrow run requiring the skier to turn, as a competitive exercise the slalom was Lunn's invention. Like downhill, it would have a profound influence on both competitive skiing and skiing as a whole.

Then, in 1924 came the foundation in Oslo of the Fédération Internationale de Ski – recognition in its Scandinavian homeland that the sport had become sufficiently widespread to demand an authoritative international governing body. The same year saw skiing recognized as a fully fledged winter sport at what was subsequently regarded as the first winter Olympic Games, held in Chamonix. Yet it was significant for the development of the sport that the competitions in the shadow of Mont Blanc were restricted to the traditional Nordic events of langlauf and ski-jumping. As early as 1914 Lunn had proposed the introduction of the downhill variant into international races, and in 1921 Britain had become the first country to organize a national championship based on downhill skiing. In Chamonix, though, the traditionalists prevailed, and neither downhill nor Lunn's new idea of slalom were on the programme.

Mindful of the success of the Alpine Club in promoting mountaineering, Lunn accordingly decided to start a society to raise the standard of downhill and slalom racing, and to secure international recognition for these events. Founded at a meeting in the Palace Hotel in Mürren on 30 January 1924, the club, at Lunn's suggestion, was named after the oldest of the downhill races. The Kandahar was to prove the *alma mater* of alpine racing. Based in Mürren, its badge a simple 'K', it was to number the future Air Chief Marshal Hugh Dowding as one of its original members.

As Lunn himself once wrote, the comparison between the 'august and venerable Alpine Club' and the 'high-spirited and youthful Kandahar' was an interesting one. Certainly the new club lacked the highmindedness of the old, and it was scarcely in a position to dress its activities in the guise of the pursuit of scientific truth. Equally, whilst skiing in the days before prepared runs was relatively hazardous, it was by no means as dangerous as mountaineering. Skiing lacked the heroic endeavour of mountaineering, and its pioneers of the mid-twenties were scarcely venturers into the unknown. It was a sport suited to an age in some respects less serious, to a nation perhaps less high-minded. The great alpinist Claud Schuster, both mountaineer and skier, wrote judiciously, 'The new sport . . . brought changes. Skiing is a sport for the young. It is essentially gay and care-free, and its spirit is essentially unlike the somewhat serious outlook of the older mountaineers.' By contrast he recalled that 'many of the Victorian mountaineers sought among the mountains for a substitute for religion'. R.L.G. Irving was altogether more blunt: 'Fashionable winter sports are like jazz music, an instance of a return to the primitive delights practised by savages.' Skiing he likened to 'the tobogganing of savages down steep slopes'.

Lunn himself, however, stuck to his guns. Of a generation that still regarded sport as morally formative, Lunn stressed the spirit in which the early downhill and slalom races were conducted. 'The contribution of the British was not confined to technical develop-ment,' he claimed. 'Other races are apt to take sport too seriously, and if we did nothing else we imported an air of light-hearted gaiety into what we regarded as an amusement and not as a barometer for measuring national prestige or the virtues of a particular ideology.'

True of the Kandahar, this was equally so of its great rival, the Downhill Only club. This was established on 7 February 1925 across the valley from Mürren in Wengen. Its founders were another set of young British skiing enthusiasts, amongst whom was Dick Waghorn, a brilliant pilot and winner of the 1929 Schneider Trophy. As Lunn said, by its very name the DHO 'crystallized a new period in skiing history'. Equally significantly, the Kurdirector of Wengen at the time, Dr Zahud, felt that the new club provided a '*sportliches vorbild*' – a sport-ing model – for Wengeners. It taught them 'not only to race and do battle, but also to lose' – something of an accolade from a resort that was to produce some of the leading Swiss skiers of the next decade.

The new relationship forged with local alpinists was also a feature of the Anglo-Swiss university races established by Lunn in the same year. Whereas in the past the high Alps had been climbed by Englishmen with the assistance of local guides, now the English were racing the Swiss as fellow competitors. The relationship of master and servant had become that of co-equals. It was another measure of the changing world.

This was a change Lunn himself welcomed. Elsewhere, however, he was as keen to maintain the dress codes as he was the sexual mores of his youth. On the occasion of the first of the Anglo-Swiss university races he remembered:

> The slalom was to be held at Mürren on Sunday. The British team were still dancing at midnight, and my appeal from the ballroom steps of the Palace Hotel to the ladies to support me in trying to get the men to bed might have been more felicitously expressed. 'We want to win the slalom tomorrow, but unfortunately there are several members of the British team who are quite incapable of getting to bed themselves, and England expects that every woman will do her duty.'

It was, Lunn commented, 'some time before I realized the full enormity of what I had said'. The British won the race.

In the late spring of the following year Lunn was called to Grindelwald to attend a funeral. Coolidge had died on 8 May; he was buried in the little village churchyard under the shadow of the Eiger.

It was more than forty years since the sage had settled in what had once been a little Oberland village, and over that period his literary persona had overtaken that of the mountaineer. He had made his last major ascent in 1897, and subsequently devoted himself to scholarship. In 1912, a year after his last meeting with Whymper, Coolidge produced a bibliography of his articles and books listing no less than two hundred and twenty items. Thereafter, although the rate of production diminished, the scholar remained prolific. As the alpinist Captain Reginald Farrar memorably remarked, it was 'as ridiculous for a man to speak of Alpine matters without mentioning the name

Coolidge, as it would be to discuss the Bible without mentioning God'.

However, as his obituarist Douglas Freshfield noted, his writings were not particularly accessible to a general audience. 'In dealing with his material he lacked both a talent for selection and arrangement that gives charm to some of our earlier Alpine books . . . Coolidge was overburdened by the weight of his own knowledge; and he did not carry that burden lightly. Consequently his books, though valuable as works of reference, have made no wide appeal to the Alpine public.' If this was true, Freshfield was also too honest a man to avoid allusion to Coolidge's temper and taste for controversy, remarking that 'He would take up some contentious point in the annals of mountaineering and assert his own view with an obstinacy and force that were deaf to argument, and sometimes even to fresh evidence.' Yet as Freshfield said, Coolidge, 'by his assiduous labours with the ice-axe and the pen [had] rendered immense service to all true lovers of the Alps'. He was the supreme authority on all subjects connected with the mountains. His death removed from the Club list 'the name of one of the last and most remarkable of the pioneers of Alpine travel and exploration'.

If the death of Coolidge marked the end of a particular trail, in 1927 a remarkable climb seemed to mark the emergence of another mountaineer in the same tradition. This was Frank Smythe, to the British public the best-known living mountaineer of the years between the wars.

Born on 6 July 1900, Francis Sydney Smythe was only two when his father died. His mother, however, was left relatively well off, and travel was to become a way of life for the boy. At seven, he first saw the Alps from the window of a train near Pontarlier. In due course he was sent to Berkhamsted, where he was a contemporary of the future novelist Graham Greene. The school, though, was not to his taste, and he did poorly. His holidays were more inspiring. He spent them walking and scrambling, particularly in the Welsh hills, and there perhaps he began to sense his vocation. Joining Faraday House Electrical Engineering College in 1919, he escaped to Austria on an apprenticeship in 1922. Here his proper introduction to the Alps began, weekends and holidays being spent in the hills, inspired by that first glimpse at Pontarlier:

> It had been a stuffy uncomfortable journey from Paris, and excitement had made sleep impossible for me. When dawn came my nose was pressed to the window. As the train passed over the Jura and began its downward rush towards the Swiss lowlands I saw the Alps. They were a long way off, but there swept over me a thrill of pure excitement and amazement such as comes to a human being only once or twice in a lifetime. It was as though I were setting eyes once more on a loved one after an aeon of time, a loved one lost but never wholly forgotten. Fortunate indeed are those who gain the vision of the mountains at an early age, and splendid their adventure.

Smythe belonged to perhaps the last generation disposed to see the Alps as the epitome of beauty and grandeur. He was, though, only seven at the time of this experience and, seventy-five years on from Ruskin's revelation on the Col de la Faucille, his writing often seems somewhat rehearsed and tired. His books were popular, *The Spirit of the Hills* selling 10,000 copies and that on the great Himalayan peak of Kanchenjunga more than 21,000. Yet unlike those of Stephen, Tyndall and Whymper, these works are now of little more than historical interest. Smythe himself was right in remarking a few years later, 'Modern mountaineering writing is for the most part appallingly dull.' Much the same, too, could be said of the prolific Arnold Lunn, who published twenty-three books on the Alps and alpinism. He himself supposed that only *Mountains of Memory*, an account of his early mountaineering experiences, would survive him. The truth was that for the English the alpine experience no longer seemed capable of inspiring literature. The aesthete turned elsewhere for his experience, to places beyond Europe, to the politics of the thirties or to landscapes more personal.

Still, there could be no doubting Smythe's genuine enthusiasm for the mountains. Light and wiry, he rapidly became an accomplished mountaineer, using his time in Austria to explore the Tyrol.

Following a brief period in the RAF, in 1927 he began to support himself by writing on and photographing mountains.

However, it was in the company of Professor Graham Brown that he made his name on the Brenva face of Mont Blanc with two climbs in 1927 and 1928. The routes led straight up from the Brenva glacier, branching off at a pinnacle of red granite, which the pair called the Sentinelle Rouge. As the alpine historian Claire Engel records:

> Both expeditions were among the most notable of the century. During most of the time Frank Smythe led up ice couloirs where stones were likely to come down at any moment, up hard blue-ice ridges, or across walls of seracs of questionable reliability. It meant hours of step-cutting; speed was vital, since parts of both routes became death traps when the sun fell upon the shaky seracs higher up on the face.

The routes both involved reaching the Sentinelle, where they branched. In 1928 on the way up to the outcrop, the pair discovered that one of the couloirs was 'much more formidable' than the previous year. Continuing the story, Professor Brown wrote:

> Its depth was at least 12 ft and its near side was over-hanging – this year completely undercut. The groove had however to be crossed. I lowered Smythe on the rope, round my deeply implanted ice axe, to the bed of the groove. So deep was it that he had again to climb up a little way on the rope before he could grasp his ice axe, which I stretched down to him at the full length of my arm; he cut across the couloir, surmounted its comparatively easy side, and then ascended the snow slope on that side of the groove until he was almost a rope's length above me. I took my courage in my hands and dropped into the groove. As I bumped, slid a little down its ice, and then lay for a moment slightly shaken and held only by the rope, I had an awful feeling of being deserted by the world.

The following day – 7 August – having bivouacked on the Sentinelle, they undertook the remainder of the climb. Setting out at 4.55 a.m., they reached the summit some fifteen hours later at 7.45 p.m. A flash of light from a distant hut welcomed them. The pair's friend, the guide Josef Knubel, had seen them reach the peak.

As in the climb of the previous year, one of the more remarkable aspects of the ascent was the absence of a guide. Guideless climbing had begun early in the days of the Alpine Club with the adventures of the Reverend A.G. Girdlestone, though it had taken A.F. Mummery finally to establish the practice and give it a measure of respectability. But even the greatest climber of his day completed as many of his conquests in the company of guides as without. Similarly, Young and Ryan in the days before the war tended to climb in the company of guides, Young with Josef Knubel in particular.

The war, however, had again proved a watershed. Partly this was a question of cost; the less wealthy mountaineers now attracted to the sport found guides prohibitively expensive. Doubtless a more democratic generation also felt less comfortable with the master–servant relationship denoted by the employment of a guide. Perfectly satisfactory for mountaineers of the quality of Smythe and Brown, for others climbing without a guide was, however, altogether more problematic. Soon an outgoing Alpine Club president, John J. Withers, would remark: 'The tendency which began to be apparent after the war has now developed, and it is abundantly clear that the whole conditions of mountaineering have practically changed.'

Hitherto aspiring climbers had been trained by guides and, having reached a satisfactory stage of accomplishment, either continued in their company or discharged them. The position now was that many of the younger generation had never climbed with a guide. That mountaineering was becoming a sport accessible to all was commendable, but it also led to a dangerous increase in mountaineering fatalities.

At the end of February 1927, Arnold Lunn spent a weekend in Kitzbühel in the Tyrol. Set in a wide valley basin, the settlement had first attracted notice in the Middle Ages for the wealth of its copper and silver mines. From the middle of the nineteenth century, it reinvented itself as a spa, the peat baths at the Schwarzsee being claimed to have curative properties. Then in January 1893, a prominent Kitzbühel citizen, Franz Reisch, obtained what he called a set of Norwegian snowshoes, and set about learning to use them. As he recognized at once, the wide sunny slopes above the town were ideal for skiing.

Reisch's new pastime soon attracted a following, especially among the English who came to the resort in winter for the skating and sleighing. On 15 December 1902, Reisch founded the Kitzbühel Ski Club. That same season W.R. Rickmers came to sample the resort. Soon he had established something of an English skiing colony. The Ski Club of Great Britain held their first competitions there in 1908, a year after their Austrian equivalents. By 1914, Kitzbühel was established as the principal winter resort in the eastern Alps.

Coming in from the slopes during this February weekend, Lunn found a message inviting him to go to St Anton to meet Hannes Schneider. Born in Steuben in the Arlberg in 1890, Schneider was Lunn's Austrian counterpart, and one of the best known skiers of his generation. Like Rickmers a former pupil of Mathias Zdarsky, Schneider had started working as a ski-instructor in St Anton as early as 1907, and was one of the first to introduce a structured system of instruction. This became formalized when he started a ski-school in 1922; the creation of different classes for those of differing ability dramatically improved the speed with which the individual developed his skills. Drawn as much by Schneider's magnetic personality as by what became known as the Arlberg technique, aspiring skiers came from all over Europe to the tiny Tyrolese settlement at the eastern end of the Arlberg tunnel.

Answering Schneider's call, Lunn made the short railway journey to the resort where the pair were to meet. What might have developed into a rivalry between the two men, neither notably modest characters, resulted in friendship as the pair took to one another. Lunn was impressed by the Arlberg technique and the younger man's virtuosity on skis. Schneider for his part was struck by the idea of slalom, a course of which Lunn set up during his visit.

Mindful of Schneider's international standing and the fame of Arlberg skiing, Lunn also suggested that a combined downhill and slalom competition should be instituted in St Anton, a cup being presented to the winner of what would be known as the Arlberg-Kandahar. Unlike Lunn's Anglo-Swiss university races, the Arlberg-Kandahar would be open to all-comers of all nations and without any classification as to nation or teams. As Lunn later put it, 'The racers meet not as representatives of nations, but as members of the skiing brotherhood. They race not to prove one political system or ski-school is superior to a rival system or school, but to prove they are faster downhill than their rivals.' The competition – inaugurated in March 1928 – was the first challenge based on what have since become the principal forms of skiing competition.

Encouraged by his plans for the first Arlberg-Kandahar, Lunn attended the meeting of the Fédération Internationale de Ski in St Moritz in February 1928. That year the resort was hosting the winter Olympics, with the Cresta one of the events. As the Ski Club of Great Britain's delegate to the conference, he made a bold proposal, namely that langlauf and ski-jumping at international ski competitions should be augmented with downhill and slalom races – in the form, moreover, authorized under the British rules developed by the Kandahar. Lunn did not anticipate a warm reception for these ideas. The alpine countries, largely content with the established challenges of ski-jumping and cross-country, were ambivalent whilst the Scandinavians – seeing their own traditions swept aside – were understandably hostile. 'We Norwegians were born with skis on our feet,' Lunn was once told. He responded, 'That must be very awkward for your midwives.' Some put it about that Lunn had invented slalom for those without the nerve to jump and without the physique for cross-country; others that he was in danger of destroying the whole sport.

At the meeting itself, Lunn was approached by the Norwegian vice-president Major N.R. Oestgard, who was more than prepared to take umbrage: 'He asked me what I would think if Norwegians tried to alter the Rules of Cricket.' Lunn diplomatically disarmed the

Norwegian with the reply, 'I wish to heaven you would. We might have fewer draws.' The result of the meeting was a surprise success. The national ski associations were invited to experiment with the British rules, and report the results at the next major meeting of the FIS, set for Oslo in February 1930. Well before then, however, other matters would supervene.

The decade since the Armistice had not seen the return to pre-war conditions in the Alps that many craved. Business had of course revived, but the fluctuations in the economies of France, Britain and Italy, as well as the periodic crises in Austria and Germany, were hardly conducive to a flourishing trade in tourism from those countries that traditionally provided the majority of alpine visitors. In 1928 the Alps as a whole were attracting half the number of tourists they had enjoyed in 1911, at the height of their pre-war prosperity. If that figure masked the rapidly increasing popularity of winter as opposed to summer tourism, the picture nonetheless was far from encouraging.

It was true that the venerable British institution of Thomas Cook and Sons had done very well since the war. Still the world's largest travel agency, it had flourished as a result of the imaginative marketing of fresh and unusual destinations, along with the return to the gold standard. Then, to the astonishment of its staff, the British public and its customers worldwide, in 1928 the company was sold to the Belgian Compagnie Internationale des Wagons Lits. Although the reasons for the sale have never been clear, this certainly proved a portent.

Within a year came the Wall Street Crash of 24 October 1929. Not only did American tourists – one of the few bright spots in the post-war story – disappear from the Alps almost overnight, but the rest of the world plunged into economic depression. After ten years of a recovery that was at best patchy and spasmodic, this boded disaster. Indeed, in its impact on European prosperity, the Depression was comparable with the war that had preceded it. In England unemployment would gradually rise to a peak of four million. In France, the mix of agricultural and industrial economy merely delayed the impact, which was in due course severe. In Germany, the worst hit of the European countries, unemployment soared from four million in 1929 to six million in 1932.

In these circumstances it was inevitable that radical political parties should flourish, whether of right or left. In Germany, Adolf Hitler, released from prison after the failed Munich putsch of 1923, had begun manoeuvring for position and was soon to be hailed by Germans all over Europe as their saviour.

Lunn was not a man to be unduly distracted by such matters, and despite the gradual erosion of English tourism in the Alps until the final crash of 1931, continued actively in his role of standard-bearer for Arnold Lunn and British skiing. Not the least of his successes was with women's skiing.

Requiring less physical strength and stamina than mountaineering, skiing had attracted women from its earliest days. One of J.A. Symonds's daughters, Katherine, was skiing in Davos in the 1890s. Then there were the two Misses Owen in Grindelwald and, early in the new century, Mrs Vivian Caulfeild and Mrs E.C. Richardson.

With his and his country's enthusiasm for forming clubs, Lunn had suggested the idea of the Ladies' Ski Club to his wife in 1923. This was at once formed, and provided the model six years later for its Swiss equivalent, the Schweizerische Damen Ski Club. By then, Lunn had made his charges into a formidable team, and international races in the season of 1929/30 in Zakopane in Poland and in St Anton marked the coming of age in women's skiing. The leading American skier of the day, Alice Damrosch Wolfe, commented:

> In Mürren the Kandahar Club was developing an extraordinary fine group of girl racers. They were the first girls to have *esprit de corps*, courage and grit. Also, thanks to Mr Arnold Lunn, they were the first girls to have a formal training ... It was the English girls at the 1929 races at Zakopane and at St Anton who first put

racing women on the map. What a flutter they caused in central Europe! . . . Their long straight legs encased, sometimes, in even longer, beautifully tailored, flapping dark blue trousers, caused the most open-mouthed wonder and astonishment, and when these creatures could also ski, it was really too much!

Though doubtless pleased at the reception his female skiers received, Lunn's sights still remained set on gaining international recognition for the downhill and the slalom. Given its suitability to alpine topography, he had few concerns about the ratification in Oslo of the downhill. It was a different matter, though, with the slalom which the Norwegians in particular – according to Lunn – 'despised as a nursery slope competition suited only to ladies'. But as it turned out, the success of the Arlberg-Kandahar race proved pivotal. The very first race had attracted forty-five competitors, largely on account of the personal persuasiveness of Lunn and Schneider. At the second race in 1929 one hundred and six competitors presented themselves. 'Never in the history of skiing', wrote Lunn later, 'has such a collection of expert ski-runners competed against one another.' In 1930 one hundred and sixty entered the race.

The Oslo conference bowed to the inevitable, officially adopting both forms of competition, together with the British rules. Lunn commented: 'I never doubted that downhill racing would be recognized by the FIS, but there was great opposition to the international acceptance of slalom, and it was the triumphant success of the Arlberg-Kandahar which determined the recognition of the slalom at the international ski-congress in 1930.' This was undoubtedly a personal triumph for Lunn. It constituted official recognition of two forms of competition which have stood the test of time as outstanding measures of alpine skiing. By extension, this enormously encouraged the development of the sport as a whole. It was indeed a *sportliches vorbild*.

The concession having been granted, it was natural enough that the British should be requested to organize the first world championship for downhill and slalom racing. It was to be held at Mürren, and was set for 19 February 1931. As coach, the British obtained the services of Lieutenant-Colonel de Lande Long, DSO, sometime president of the Oxford University Boat Club. The Colonel set a fine example to his charges by giving up smoking and coining the battle cry, 'No Spirits!' – this among a team, in the words of the Swiss press, 'by no means teetotallers'.

On the day of the competition, Mürren was threatened with heavy snow. The downhill was run in a snowstorm, and the race was dominated by the Swiss, the best British place being seventh – this going to Viscount Knebworth, like many of the interwar skiers an enthusiastic airman. Lunn's son Peter, then just sixteen, came thirteenth in the same race, seventh in the slalom. The best British place in the latter went to Jimmy Riddell, who came fourth. In the Ladies Downhill, the British won, and took four out of the top five; they also won in the Ladies Slalom, and took five out of the six top places.

One of the great winter sports exponents of the day, the skater T.D. Richardson, called these results 'one of the most remarkable achievements of British sport'. If with hindsight this seems to err on the side of generosity, it was a startling enough result for a team grossly outnumbered by the alpine nations in terms of racing skiers, and having – by comparison – very little opportunity to practise. Yet it also represented the high-water mark – if not of British influence, at least of achievement. Thereafter, not only did the alpine nations' proximity to the slopes and the larger number of participants attracted to the sport there begin to tell against the British, but the ethos of the sport changed.

The leading English skiers of the post-war years tended to be happy-go-lucky figures, some of them playboys. Great enthusiasts for their new sport, they tended to regard it as an end in itself. The political and – arguably – the national character of some of the alpine nations was different, their leaders recognizing sport as a useful political tool. Lunn deplored this development, arguing against it persuasively. 'My thesis', he wrote, 'was that sport ceases to be fun when it is taken seriously, and it becomes an abomination when men are encouraged to believe that their countries, or worse still the soundness of their ideologies, depends on athletic success.' But this was what happened in the early thirties: the sport was becoming politicized. 'Downhill racing developed into a barometer for measuring the respective virtues of different ideologies, Nazi, Fascist and Democratic.'

In writing of fascism, Lunn was referring to the regimes established in Italy in 1922 by Mussolini and later in Germany by Hitler. In March 1931 in Britain Oswald Mosley became leader of the fascist New Party, modelling himself on Mussolini. That August, in response to the economic crisis, the Labour administration resigned and a National government drawn from all three major parties was formed. One of the government's first actions was to remove Britain from the gold standard, and the new Chancellor of the Exchequer, Neville Chamberlain, appealed to the British people in the name of patriotism not to damage the economy further by taking currency abroad.

In a phrase perhaps inspired by the popularity of winter sports, the Prime Minister Ramsay MacDonald described the onset of the Depression as 'an economic blizzard'. Its effect on British alpinism was dramatic. In the winter of 1930/31 Cooks had some five thousand clients taking winter holidays; the following year the figure was just over five hundred. The Public Schools Alpine Sports Club, solely dependent on winter sports, simply collapsed.

Chapter Twelve

The Last Alpine Problem

'If France collapsed, could England save Europe? And I knew if Europe went down into the pit of Nazi slavery and if Gauleiters were installed in Grindelwald and Mürren and Interlaken, May torrents might still make music for Germans, but not for me.'

Arnold Lunn

Only weeks before Britain abandoned the gold standard the German offensive in the Alps began. Starting with the conquest of the north face of the Matterhorn, it would culminate, notwithstanding a series of tragedies, in the ascent of the north face of the Eiger a few months after the *Anschluss* in 1938. By these efforts, what were called the last alpine problems were solved. The curtain, too, was brought down not only on alpine discovery, but on one of the last acts of English involvement in the Alps.

If the English by the early thirties had lost much of their appetite for mountaineering in the Alps, the same could not be said of Continental climbers. Some still attributed this to the war – or rather to that opportunity which the generation that came of age in the aftermath of war paradoxically felt they had missed. They were typified by Pierre Dalloz of the French Groupe de Haute Montagne, who revelled in the dangers of mountaineering and the formative experience it provided. 'It gave us the complete fulfilment of our dream, it proved to us our worth, and in spite of the misfortune which robbed us of war, it allowed us to taste the intoxicating pleasures of the heroic life.' It was climbers of this mould, particularly in Italy and Germany, who were the greatest exponents of the artificial climbing so deplored by the Alpine Club's Colonel Strutt.

At the same time – as Lunn had foretold of skiing – the politicization of sport began to gather pace on the Continent. In 1925 Willy Welzenbach, a Munich climber of exceptional gifts, had established a grading system by which the difficulty of climbs could be crudely assessed. On this basis Mussolini decided to award medals for valour to mountaineers who made new ascents by the most difficult – the sixth – of the standards. Similarly Hitler, although not yet in power, did much to encourage mountaineering. Himself a mountain enthusiast, in the early thirties he established a retreat – the Berghof – on the Obersalzberg in the Bavarian Alps. Situated above the small resort of Berchtesgaden on the borders of Austria, it was here in 1925 that he had dictated the second volume of *Mein Kampf*. A great believer in the mystical power of mountains, he saw the sport as an opportunity for the manifestation of German racial supremacy in agreeably heroic form. As R.L.G. Irving remarked, by the beginning of the new decade, these changing perspectives and motivations produced in the world of climbing an ethos that would have been scarcely recognizable before the war. He dubbed it 'sporting-heroic-arithmetic climbing', a sport as far removed from cricket as could be imagined.

It was fortunate for the adherents of the new creed that there remained in the Alps a few problems admirably suited to the practices Irving so abhorred. Typically they were the north faces of the major peaks. Being out of the sun they were normally coated in ice and frequently rotten; they were steep, and swept constantly by stones; in the event of a storm, they offered a minimal margin for safety. Accidents on the faces of the Matterhorn and the Grandes Jorasses soon proved the point; that of the Eiger would gain such a grim reputation in the years before the second war that it came to epitomize and in many respects to damn the whole sport. Echoing Mallory, the great French alpinist Arnold Charlet said of climbs such as these, 'C'est pas de l'alpinisme, ça, c'est la guerre.'

The German campaign met with initial success. In the early summer of 1931, two young brothers called Schmid cycled from Munich to Zermatt to tackle the Matterhorn's north face. Setting up camp at the base of the Hornli ridge, the starting point for the traditional ascent, they assembled what Colonel Strutt would have called a fine collection of ironmongery – pitons, karabiners, crampons and the like. They then set off up the face. As well as the great cliff itself, they had to contend on that first day with a gully streaming with water and stones which lay inescapably in their path. Fortunate to survive this, the pair bivouacked that night on a slightly protruding rock to which they anchored themselves like a couple of bats. They did not sleep. The following morning conditions deteriorated. The slope became steeper, handholds fewer. Increasingly they were forced on to unstable bands of ice and snow. A storm threatened, which would have meant death. Yet their luck held. They reached the summit just as the storm broke, but were able to find shelter near the ridge. A lull then gave them the opportunity to reach the comparative safety of the Solvay hut before the storm broke out again.

Zermatt received them in triumph, the German papers with ecstasy. On their return to the fatherland they were presented to Hitler to receive his personal congratulations. Colonel Strutt was less enthusiastic. He wrote in the *Alpine Journal*: 'With the forcing of the north face of the Matterhorn, with the Mont Mallet Glacier faces of the Grandes Jorasses profaned with spikes but still unconquered, infinite possibilities of notoriety or disaster lie open.' He was right.

With the coming to power of Hitler as Reich Chancellor in January 1933, it was inevitable that mountaineering would be further politicized. The old structure of the German and Austrian Alpine Club was overturned, and its officials set to work under the

Reichssportführer, Hans von Tschammer und Osten. Although the English had yet to conquer Everest – F.S. Smythe led another expedition there in 1933 – they had nevertheless made the mountain their own. In conscious emulation, the Germans did the same with the 26,600-foot Nanga Parbat. In 1934, a large expedition led by the highly experienced Willy Merkl was mounted. This ended in tragedy when an advance party was overtaken by a storm some two thousand feet from the summit. Of its sixteen members, only seven survived. Merkl himself perished.

The following year, rather closer to home, two young Bavarian climbers arrived in Grindelwald. Max Sedelmayer and Karl Mahringen hoped to emulate the Schmid brothers' Matterhorn success on the even more difficult north face of the Eiger – the Eigerwand – the sheer 6,000-foot wall that rises so dramatically from the Kleine Scheidegg. Having waited some time for fine weather, they made a good start on their first day, reaching as far as the Eigerwand station, where they bivouacked. Thereafter, their every move could be followed through telescopes from Kleine Scheidegg. As Claire Engel records:

> On the following day, they met with greater difficulties and gained but little height. On the third day, they hardly rose at all. At night a storm broke. The mountain was hidden in fog and showers of hail fell; then it began to snow. Avalanches of water-logged snow swept the face and the clouds closed over it. Two days later there was a short lull and the mountain showed clear for a moment. People obtained a glimpse of the two men, who were now a little higher and about to bivouac for the fifth time. Then the fog came down and swamped everything. Further days elapsed and the weather cleared for good, revealing a mountain swathed in bright fresh snow. A Swiss military plane flew up as close to the rocks as possible. The pilot saw one of the men frozen to death, standing in the snow; the other was probably buried in it at his feet. There was nothing to be done.

The following year an expedition of ten Germans and Austrians came to repeat the attempt. On a preparatory climb, one of them fell to his death. Continued poor weather then disheartened the party, and five of the remaining members abandoned the attempt. Briefly, the weather improved, and a team of two Bavarians and two Austrians started the ascent. The first day went satisfactorily. The following morning the weather changed. For three days the climbers were hidden from view. Then, something or someone was spotted moving on the face.

Fearing the worst, a rescue party of guides set out from the Eigergletscher station. They came within earshot of one of the party, Toni Kurz. The remainder were dead. One had frozen, the other two had died in falls. Kurz himself, in a desperate condition, was just out of the guides' reach, and had to be abandoned for the night. This he survived, though badly frost-bitten. For hours the next day the guides struggled to reach him, whilst Kurz – one arm useless – tried to descend. At last, with the tip of his ice-axe, one of the guides touched Kurz's crampons. Yet he could go no higher, nor Kurz lower. Completely exhausted and virtually frozen, there, still harnessed to the rock-face, Kurz died.

Commenting on this and similar episodes, the Alpine Club's president John J. Withers remarked:

> At risk of entering into the zone of other countries' politics, it appears to be my duty to say a few words in strongest condemnation of a cloud that has long threatened and has now materialized as a practice in Alpine Societies – not to say the Governments – of at least one nation . . . if rewards, citations *à bord de la montagne*, payments in kind are made . . . for utterly reckless and completely useless variations on even the smallest pinnacle, accidents are certain to increase in yet greater numbers.

Colonel Strutt would dismiss the Eiger's north face as 'an obsession for the mentally deranged'.

Irrespective of events on the Eiger, Hitler was now rapidly consolidating his position. He had been helped in doing so by the recovery of the European economies, which had been beginning even as he seized power. He had also helped himself. The Reichstag fire of 27 February 1933 provided the ideal pretext for rounding up opponents of the regime. Soon, a law against the formation of new political parties was passed, effectively establishing a one-party state. The first concentration camps were set up. The 'night of the long knives' on 30 June 1934 despatched the threatening figure of Ernst Röhm, and placed the regulation of the state firmly in the hands of Hitler's special security police. The death of the elderly President Hindenburg in August provided the opportunity for Hitler to combine the positions of President and Chancellor in that of 'Führer'.

Hitler was now free to turn to matters of foreign policy. He had withdrawn Germany from the League of Nations in October 1933, and then begun the programme of rearmament specifically forbidden by the Treaty of Versailles. In 1934 he was behind the failed coup of the Austrian Nazis, in the course of which the Christian Social Chancellor, Engelbert Dollfuss, was murdered. In March 1935 the Saarland returned to Germany, whetting Hitler's appetite for *Lebensraum*. In his immediate sights was the Rhineland, demilitarized under the terms of Versailles. Beyond – as always – lay his homeland of Austria, the Sudetenland in Czechoslovakia, and Poland.

Amongst Hitler's visitors that year was Leo Amery. Now sixty-two, he was on a climbing holiday in Bavaria. By no means one of the dictator's supporters, he found Hitler amiable enough. 'I had struck him during a quiet interlude,' Amery wrote, 'at rest after liquidating his most formidable colleagues in the "night of the long knives" the year before, and not yet stirred to new and more daring schemes in the world of international affairs.'

Few of Germany's activities passed unnoticed amongst her former foes. They were distracted, however, by their own economic difficulties, by the intractability of the German problem, and by the hope that the League of Nations and the principle of collective security which it embodied would address the situation. Germany's own withdrawal from the League threw the first douche of cold water on such hopes, and the Japanese withdrawal in March 1933 aggravated doubts. The advent of Hitler himself, and that of rearmament, gave further cause for unease. Finally, in March 1935, Britain's National government issued a 'Statement Relating to Defence', announcing that collective security could no longer be relied upon for the purposes of national defence. The country in future would be obliged to rely on armed force.

Within a week Hitler had used this statement as a pretext for restoring conscription in Germany. Paradoxically, in England it led less to rearmament than appeasement, soon to be embodied in the policies, and person, of Neville Chamberlain. The country, barely recovered from the slump and soon to be rocked by the abdication of Edward VIII, seemed to be losing its nerve.

In the same summer of 1935 in which Toni Kurz had died so horribly on the Eiger, Geoffrey Winthrop Young undertook what proved to be his own last climb. There are perhaps few to whom the loss of a leg could be more cruel than a mountaineer of Young's gifts. Yet almost from the moment of his injury he was planning how to overcome the handicap. In the years immediately after the war he busied himself developing techniques that would enable him to continue climbing, and from 1927 onwards, already in his mid-fifties, he returned to the hills.

Encouraged by the authorities who were aware of the power of example to others disabled by the war, Young's subsequent climbs were given a good deal of publicity, and they remain remarkable examples of the power of a man's mind over his body. In 1927 he climbed the 15,203-foot Monte Rosa, and in subsequent years the 12,829-foot Wellenkup, the 14,803-foot Weisshorn, the 11,447-foot Grépon; even the Matterhorn. Then, in the summer of 1935, Young renewed his old partnership with the guide Josef Knubel, and a party of four set out to climb the 13,848-foot Zinal Rothorn.

To reach the peak after a fourteen-hour struggle – 'in spite of every handicap and in defiance of probability' – might seem achievement enough; for Young, it was not. Reaching the summit and looking round at the great mountains of the Bernese Oberland that held so many memories for him, he realized that he had become disillusioned. 'I knew quite well what my feelings ought to be,' he wrote, 'but they were not. This was certainly not what I used to feel on an Alpine summit. Not the least like that transfiguration, with the rhythm of motion still alive in the muscles and the song of action still hymning the silence, which had irradiated such after-moments of achievement . . . Something had gone out of my Alpine mountaineering, gone completely.' At a stroke, Young decided to abandon mountaineering. 'There and then as I lay, and rested, and looked out, I determined that this should be my last great ascent.'

Young fell on the descent. Standing precariously on his one sound leg on a steep crag not far from the summit, he lifted his hands to secure his snow-glasses, overbalanced and began to fall. He was roped to Knubel, who saw his old friend topple from his stance. The line joining the pair was a hundred and fifty feet long, and Knubel realized at once that the jerk of Young's weight when the line was fully extended would pluck him instantly from the mountain. It was a predicament that the pair had periodically discussed, and for which they had devised and practised a solution. At once Knubel gathered in as much of the slack as he could, gripped the rock with his right hand, and started to arrest Young's fall with his left. The sliding rope seared his hand unbearably. He let it slip, then once again gripped, taking the strain of Young's weight on a hand that was now badly damaged. On the slab on which he stood there was only one possible point of belay. It was just within reach. 'With a supreme half-arm hoist of the rope, taut with [Young's] weight, he twitched it behind the spike, let go of the rock with his right hand, fixed the rope with a lightning knot.' It was done.

So Young, on what he had already decided would be his last climb, was saved. On his greatest climb, of the Täschhorn in 1906, when Knubel had also been among the party, Young had remarked to Franz Lochmatter that he would never do anything harder than saving Ryan's life. Lochmatter had proudly replied, 'Man could not do more.' Twenty years on, Knubel had done just that.

As the winter of 1935 approached, with the worst of the slump over, alpine tourism began to revive. Once again the travel companies began to advertise their offerings, Cooks promoting Germany for its arts and its scenery, the Polytechnic Touring Association using a swastika and the slogan 'The Land of Dreams Come True'.

In the Alps themselves, the summer season continued to appeal, but increasingly the winter market prospered, partly as a result of investment and technological innovation. In France, Mégève close to Chamonix was developing rapidly under the patronage of the Rothschilds. The family had acquired the Mount Arblois hotel in the 1920s and had developed it into an attraction for the likes of the Citroën family. In the Tarentaise, the ski-school in Val d'Isère opened in 1932. In the Dolomites Cortina had established itself as the country's principal winter resort, the world ski championships being held there in 1927 and 1932. Further west, Sestriere in the Turin Alps was being developed by the FIAT motor company. Mussolini also conceived the idea of developing a winter resort at Breuil, which had been Whymper's base for his first attempts on the Matterhorn, on the peak's southern side. There was fine sunny skiing on runs down from the Théodule to Breuil, and the fascist leader supposed that a fashionable resort might be created there along the lines of St Moritz. The problem was to get the skiers up from Breuil in the first place, and for the purpose a cable car from the village to Testa Grigia on the Théodule was proposed.

The *téléphérique* as the French called it – *Seilbahn* in Switzerland – had been operating from as early as 1908, when the Wetterhorn Aerial Railway was opened, running from the foot of the Upper Grindelwald glacier to a station 5,502 feet up on the north face of the peak. Though the railway itself was abandoned in 1914, the Swiss and Italians used some of its techniques during the Great War, when a significant amount of military equipment was transported by this means, both in the Dolomites and in the Jura. After the war, the Swiss opened a line in 1927 in Engelberg, running from Gerschnialp to Trübsee, and the following year the Hahnenkamm line was operating in Kitzbühel. Soon Davos, St Anton and Breuil itself would follow.

Having got the skiers up the mountain, it was also necessary to bring them safely down. Although skiing areas were now established, there was still little in the way of formal piste preparation, which left skiers vulnerable to natural and artificial hazards. In Davos, on the slopes of the Parsenn an Englishman called Bill Edlin had a ravine bridged, fences and rocks removed, and rescue patrols organized. Soon other major resorts followed suit.

If this innovation, and the many and various visitors it attracted, tended to mar the pleasure of the hardy core of post-war winter enthusiasts, the bastions of the Bernese Oberland still remained predominantly English terrain. Kingsmill Moore, writing nostalgically to Arnold Lunn in 1941, recalled its atmosphere at this time:

> Mürren, the real Mürren of those who returned year after year, was a microcosm. Not so cosmopolitan as other centres, not so full of fashionable notorieties, it seemed to attract men of real eminence from every walk of life. I come from a city [Dublin] famed for good conversation, but the best and best informed talk I have ever listened to was at Mürren. In the Palace lounge I first heard of the inevitability of the *Anschluss* from a British minister, the intricacies of modern banking from Jakobsen, the extent of modern diabolism from Allinson, and the philosophic basics of Catholicism from you ... Where but in Mürren could you have found a group of anything up to twenty young men and women listening with deference and attention to a debate on Thomist fundamentals? Where but in Mürren could you get first-hand information on any subject by walking a few yards across a room. Artists, lawyers, doctors, diplomats, business men, schoolmasters, generals, admirals, every branch of

human activity and everyone in an expansive holiday mood which produced the best that was in them.

In 1936, Germany was set to host the Olympics. Despite certain misgivings among the Nazis, who viewed the modern sporting cult as a British creation, Goebbels nevertheless persuaded Hitler that the games represented an opportunity to show off the regime and highlight German efficiency. Sir Eric Phipps, British Ambassador to Berlin, accordingly wrote to the Foreign Secretary Anthony Eden on 13 February 1936, 'The German Government attaches enormous importance to the Olympic games from the point of view of propaganda, and hopes to be able to take the opportunity of impressing foreign countries with the capacity and solidity of the Nazi regime.' The film director Leni Riefenstahl was recruited to record the spectacle for posterity.

When the choice of Berlin to host the games was originally made in 1931, it symbolized Germany's reintegration into the international community. By 1935, however, the nature of the Nazi regime in Germany was familiar to the Western democracies and there were many who thought that a boycott of the games would be a suitable gesture of democratic disapproval for the lawless policies it was following. Such protest, the *Manchester Guardian* remarked, would have to be made by the United States or Great Britain, since these countries had greater influence than 'any other ten'. This was attributed to the athletic excellence of the United States, and because 'Great Britain is still regarded as the mother of sport and the final arbiter of sportsmanship'.

As it turned out, the boycott party in the United States formed a powerful lobby that very nearly succeeded. But it was perhaps indicative of the strength of the appeasement movement in Britain that the idea of a protest was poorly received there. Leaders and spokesmen of the various sports chose to see sport and politics as distinct.

Arnold Lunn, for one, agreed to referee the slalom event at the winter games, later writing somewhat defensively, 'I had more sympathy with those who wished to break off athletic relations with Germany than those who repeated with bland assurance the slogan "Sport has nothing to do with politics".' As Lunn knew perfectly well, the contrary was the case. Hitler's interest in German mountaineering exploits was a clear indication of the new conjunction of politics and climbing. It was the same with skiing. As Lunn himself was later obliged to point out, by 1936 'the old German ski association was disbanded and skiing was controlled by the Government Department for Bodily Exercises, the Fachamt Ski-lauf . . . in Nazi Germany sport was a branch of politics.'

The winter games were set to precede the summer events, the former to be held in the Bavarian resort of Garmisch-Partenkirchen, the latter in the capital, Berlin. As its name suggests, Garmisch-Partenkirchen consists of two villages that grew and fused into one. Established beneath the 9,178-foot Zugspitze, the highest mountain in Germany, its initial appeal as a tourist attraction lay in the proximity of Oberammergau. With the arrival in 1899 of the railway from Munich, it became a resort in its own right. Among winter sports, skating became a speciality, whilst the Zugspitze itself and the 5,840-foot Wank were soon turned into ski-slopes. The arrival of Richard Strauss in 1908 lent the resort fame. By 1914 the township had established itself as Germany's principal alpine resort. For the winter Olympics, there was no realistic alternative, and the town seized the opportunity. The centrepiece was the great Olympic stadium. Built at the foot of the Guidberg, it was to hold 60,000, and was designed in Hitler's favourite monumental style.

Among many of those who in due course attended the winter games, ambivalence about their legitimacy persisted. If a gesture of dissent was to be registered, that great piece of theatre, the opening ceremony, was to provide the opportunity. There was much debate over the manner of salute that Hitler himself would be taking. The official Olympic salute made by teams as they marched past the podium required the extension of the arm to the side. The Nazi salute demanded the raising of the arm in front. One might be substituted for the other; the two might be confused, or no salute given whatsoever. Rumours abounded amongst the competitors that one of the teams would not be returning Hitler's salute. The British team, led by Arnold Lunn's son Peter, made sure that theirs would be of the Olympic variety.

The games were set to open on 6 February 1936. Interest was such that trains left Munich every two minutes for the resort. In Garmisch, though, it proved a bitter day. Following a dearth of snow earlier in the season, six inches had fallen in the previous twenty-four hours. Arnold Lunn wrote:

> We sat and shivered in the stands waiting for the opening ceremony of the Winter Olympic Games. Suddenly through the driving snow a procession appears, headed by the Greek team. The Greek standard dips in salute to one who would have been more at home in Sparta than in Athens. Hitler returns the salute . . . from the brazier a flame burns up in a flurry of snow, and the Olympic beacons on the hills repeat the Olympic fire. Fire, driving snow and wind.

The Greeks were followed by the Belgians and the Bulgarians, the twenty-eight teams appearing in alphabetical order. As the British team approached the podium, all eyes were on Peter Lunn. Something was expected. As he drew level with Hitler, he extended his arm to the side in the traditional Olympic salute. The rest of the team followed suit. Yet the commentator described the team as 'greeting the German Führer with the German salute'. Towards the end of the procession the Swiss team approached Hitler. They gave no salute at all. The Americans merely gave the eyes-right. On each occasion the commentator was silent.

Once the games were under way, Hitler took a great deal of interest in their progress. 'Deeply disappointed by the results of the Downhill race,' Lunn recounts him as telegraphing the captain of a German University team. '"Expect you to do better in the slalom." His expectations were not fulfilled. They did worse.' Hitler was nonetheless able to take comfort from gold and silver medals in both the men's and the women's all-comers skiing events. The British could only salvage twelfth and eighth places. Asked to broadcast his impressions, all Lunn could bring himself to say was, 'Germans, may I tell you a little secret. There are still people who ski for fun.' For Lunn, Hitler had turned what was intended to be a sporting occasion into a trial run for war:

> I remember lunching with three French officers. 'I am reminded', I said, 'of the story of Moltke going to bed for twenty-four hours after he had pressed the button for mobiliza-tion in 1870. I have a feeling that these Games are only a rehearsal for war.' The French looked uncomfortable, as well they might, for I had failed to observe the presence at their table of a German officer attached to them for the period of the Games. He replied at once: 'You are mistaken. Our Führer loves peace. He has himself been a front-line soldier. He knows the horrors of war. Our army is for defence.' 'Against whom?' I replied. 'Who is threatening you with invasion?' But to that question there was no reply.

Within a month, Hitler reoccupied the Rhineland.

Following Hitler's first major territorial seizure in defiance of the treaties of Versailles and Locarno, a special session of the council of the League of Nations was hastily assembled in London. It was resolved that neither treaty had been breached. Soviet proposals for sanctions were rejected. Asked to formulate a new system for European security, Hitler replied that he had 'no territorial claims in Europe'. There discussion ended.

Action, however, did not. In July, Hitler made an agreement with the Austrian Chancellor Kurt von Schuschnigg that the country should retain its independence but keep friendly relations with Germany. However, when Schuschnigg began to court his other neighbours – Czechoslovakia, Yugoslavia and Romania – Hitler organized a putsch. Its failure in January 1938 led to the summons of Schuschnigg to the

Obersalzberg. There, in the Berghof, he was forced to accept the leader of the Austrian Nazis, Seyss-Inquart, as Minister of Public Security. By way of response, the Chancellor organized a referendum on the issue of the country's independence. Outraged, Hitler and Seyss-Inquart instigated a campaign of civil disorder. At the end of his tether, Schuschnigg abandoned his office to Seyss-Inquart, and the latter judiciously appealed to Hitler for help in restoring order.

On 12 March 1938, Arnold Lunn was having dinner at the English College in Rome. Called to the telephone, he was told that the co-founder of the Arlberg-Kandahar, Hannes Schneider, had been arrested in St Anton, and imprisoned at Landeck. The German troops requested by Seyss-Inquart had marched over the border into Austria. Long heralded, here at last was the *Anschluss*. The Arlberg-Kandahar was set to be held within the next few days in what had suddenly become Nazi-occupied territory.

The following morning Lunn left for St Anton. When he arrived that afternoon, he called a meeting of those members of the Kandahar – mainly British, but with a sprinkling of Americans – present in St Anton in preparation for the race. He proposed that the race should be cancelled. The motion was carried without opposition.

Lunn then went to inform the new Nazi Bürgermeister of the decision. This was a certain Herr Moser, a former skiing instructor who had been expelled by Schneider from the Arlberg ski-school for preaching Nazi propaganda. He was displeased. 'Your only reason for cancelling the Arlberg-Kandahar is political,' Lunn was told. 'I asked him if Schneider had been interned for telemarking. He became abusive. "You can't stop us from calling the race the Arlberg-Kandahar." I agreed. "And the Jockey Club could not prevent you holding a donkey-race in St Anton and calling it the Derby."' Lunn continued: 'The Nazis race out of what they call *Pflichtgefühl* (sense of duty), inspired by a keen sense of duty and loyalty to their Führer. We English still race for fun. We came to St Anton in the old days because we liked the atmosphere, and we propose to leave because we don't like the new atmosphere.'

Lunn then proceeded to visit Schneider's wife, Ludmilla, and left St Anton the following morning. As he later wrote, the internment of Schneider – by no means a political figure – was unwise. The tourist industry at the time was a vital source of foreign currency for the German rearmament programme. In placing Schneider, by then a world-famous figure, under 'protective arrest', the Nazis 'advertised to the world the radical nature of the surgical operation which they had performed on the country they had conquered and annexed'.

Although English alpine tourism had recovered from the economic downturn of 1931, the advent of Hitler had placed the Tyrol under a cloud. These doubts were now confirmed by the *Anschluss*. The English duly stayed away from St Anton. Lunn, meanwhile, travelled on to Switzerland. Presciently, he wrote: 'As the train drew into Busch we saw a flag which, like the Nazi flag, had a red background with, like the Nazi flag, a cross in the middle; not the Swastika cross, the symbol of oppression, but the cross which would stand for freedom when Hitler and all he stands for has passed away.'

Schneider was transferred to Garmisch, and expected then to be sent to Buchenwald. Lunn and Schneider's many other friends set about pulling strings. Ultimately, Lunn's stance on the Arlberg-Kandahar resulted in Schneider's release and expulsion to America.

After the Eiger disasters of 1935 and 1936 it was understandable that the Bernese authorities should forbid any further attempts on the north face. Active policing of the mountain, though, was not practicable. Attempts to subdue the Eigerwand continued. The season of 1938 began with the death of two Italians, Bartolo Sandri and Mario Menti, who fell to their deaths when caught half-way up the face by a thunderstorm. Then, in the wake of the *Anschluss*, a pair of Germans – Andreas Heckmair and Ludwig Vorg – and a pair of Austrians – Heinrich Harrer and Fritz Kasparek – came upon each other's party unexpectedly not far up the face on 21 July, in what might have been seen as a happy coincidence. Deciding to join forces, Heckmair wrote: 'We, the sons of the older Reich, united with our companions from the Eastern Border to march together towards victory.'

On their first day together they edged their way up the rotten face towards the rock-feature called 'the Ramp'. Here Kasparek, roped to Harrer, fell some sixty feet; he was lucky to avoid injury. By that evening they had surmounted the Ramp and found a place – of sorts – to bivouac. There was nowhere to sit; barely anywhere to stand. On a piton driven just a centimetre into the face, Harrer and Kasparek were obliged to hang the entire weight of their belongings and themselves. In the course of the night they slipped and awoke to find themselves suspended over the void.

The following morning Heckmair felt ill, having eaten some sardines that disagreed with him. That day they tackled a cliff of which Harrer remarked: 'I had never seen a pitch which looked so hazardous, dangerous and utterly extraordinary.' Later they went up another pitch of one hundred and twenty feet which alone took them five hours. By the afternoon they had reached the formation of snow tentacles known as the White Spider. The notoriously changeable Oberland weather was still holding, and they were within a thousand feet of the summit. Then the wind began to rise and snow to fall, starting an avalanche that nearly swept all four of them away and that caused Kasparek to injure his hand. Within hours, two feet of snow fell. The climbers, stationary on the darkened face, now had to endure freezing conditions. The watch through the night was purgatory.

At last came dawn. The snow was still falling, and visibility was poor. Exhausted, the climbers braced themselves for one last effort. Having managed to warm themselves with coffee, they worked their way slowly up an ice-chimney and on to a slightly easier pitch beyond. Here Heckmair fell a short distance, one of his crampons going right through Vorg's hand. Again, the four regrouped. As the afternoon approached they at last reached the summit ice-field. At 3.30 p.m. on 24 July 1938 the four became the first climbers to conquer the north face. 'Joy, relief, tumultuous triumph?' Harrer recalled. 'Not a bit of it. Our release had come too suddenly, our minds and nerves were too dulled, our bodies too utterly weary to permit any violent reaction.'

It was worth it, though. The last of the terrible north faces had been vanquished, the last and greatest alpine problem solved. The climbers were later presented to Hitler. This, Heckmair wrote, was their most splendid reward.

The possession of Austria provided Hitler with control of communications in the Danube valley and brought Germany up against the Czech frontier. Germany now bordered the Sudetenland with its three million Germans and a flourishing Nazi party under the leadership of Konrad Henlein. If this attracted Hitler in his drive for *Lebensraum*, he was now obliged to act with more caution than before. Czechoslovakia was signatory to treaties of assistance with both France and Russia. Britain, however, under the Prime Minister Neville Chamberlain, refused to give an undertaking that she would support France should she move to support Czechoslovakia against German aggression. Contrary to the notions of collective security envisaged by the League of Nations, Hitler could now assume that France would not act without Britain, or Russia without France. The door seemed open.

The following month – April – Henlein put before the Czech government a plan for the virtual autonomy of the Sudetenland. When this was rejected, his party reacted with a violence that seemed likely to invite a German invasion in support of German-speakers within the state. The Czech army was mobilized, and Chamberlain warned Hitler that Great Britain might, after all, intervene. The crisis eased temporarily during the summer of 1938, then returned with the failure of Henlein and the Czechs to compromise. With Europe on the brink of war, Chamberlain, in an unprecedented move, decided to make a personal appeal to Hitler. Leo Amery records Chamberlain as stating that this was a plan that, if it came off, 'would go far beyond the present crisis and might prove the opportunity for bringing about a complete change in the international situation'. On 15 September, the 69-year-old Prime Minister flew to Munich to meet the Führer on the Obersalzberg. It was the first time he had flown.

Besides Amery, previous British visitors to the shrine included David Lloyd George in 1936, and the Duke and Duchess of Windsor in 1937. They had been much impressed. Chamberlain, in this pioneering example of shuttle diplomacy, was less so. Flying out of Heston aerodrome on a bright sunny morning, the found himself in Munich seven hours later. A train then took him the hundred miles south to Berchtesgaden. Hitler met him on the steps of the Berghof and the party took tea in the main reception room. With the window open, Chamberlain could view the 6,470-foot Untersberg, straddling the Austro-German border. The two leaders and a translator then retired to talk. The evening darkened, rain began to fall, and Chamberlain found himself ambushed.

The situation, he wrote later, appeared 'unexpectedly acute'. Hitler announced to the Prime Minister that only the complete cession of the Sudetenland would satisfy him. 'Sooner than wait,' Chamberlain recorded, 'Hitler would be prepared to risk a world war.' Thus it was that high in the Bavarian Alps, between an Englishman and an Austrian, the fate of Europe was held in the balance. As the historian David Thompson comments in *Europe since Napoleon*:

The meeting between the two men in the *Führer*'s mountain-nest at Berchtesgaden is one of the most dramatic, and also the most pathetic, scenes in contemporary history. On one side was the anxious, harassed Birmingham businessman, the civilian figure with the umbrella, resolved to avoid the outbreak of war if it were humanly possible, and stubbornly unconvinced that even now there was any international dispute that could not be settled reasonably and finally without war if only each side fully understood the issues involved; on the other, the crazed, paranoiac dictator, the fanatic of the Swastika, equally stubbornly bent on war for the domination of the 'master race' in Europe, but anxious to win all his preliminary victories as cheaply and cunningly as he could.

Aghast, Chamberlain returned to London convinced that only his visit had prevented the immediate annexation of the Sudetenland. To avert this, the Prime Minister found himself induced by Hitler not simply to meddle in the internal affairs of another state, but to coerce a government friendly towards Great Britain to cede territory to a hostile neighbour. Within days the Czechs found themselves obliged to give away 800,000 citizens. The result was further demands from Hitler for the immediate occupation of the disputed territory by German troops. When this was rejected by the Czechs, the French mobilized their reservists, the British the Navy. 'How horrible, fantastic, incredible it is', broadcast Chamberlain famously, 'that we should be digging trenches and trying on gas-masks here because of a quarrel in a faraway country between people of whom we know nothing.' A conference at Munich on 29 and 30 September between Germany, Britain, France and Italy agreed that the four powers should supervise the transfer of the territories and guarantee the new frontiers. In its aftermath Chamberlain and Hitler signed a statement that 'We regard the agreement signed last night . . . as symbolic of the desire of our two peoples never to go to war with one another again.'

On his return, Chamberlain remarked: 'I believe it is peace for our time.' Amery commented in his diary, 'An ignoble result.'

Hitler had told the world that the Sudetenland was his 'last territorial demand in Europe'. Then, when on 15 March 1939 the reduced state of Czechoslovakia fell apart and Slovakia declared independence, he seized the rump of Bohemia.

By now even Chamberlain's illusions were dispelled. On 31 March Britain extended a guarantee of protection to Poland; France followed suit. Poland was now a buffer state between an enlarged Germany and the Soviet Union. In response, these Anglo-French moves inspired the Nazi-Soviet non-aggression pact of 23 August. Hitler had hoped that this might cause England and France to repudiate their pledges. At long last, though, they stood firm. Then, at dawn on 1 September 1939, Hitler's Panzer tank divisions rolled into Poland. In a broadcast to the nation, Chamberlain said:

> We have a clear conscience, we have done all that any country could do to establish peace, but a situation in which no word given by Germany's ruler could be trusted, and no people or country could feel themselves safe, had become intolerable . . . For it is evil things we shall be fighting against, brute force, bad faith, injustice, oppression and persecution. But against them I am certain that right will prevail.

By the end of the month Poland had collapsed, the spoils being divided between Hitler and Stalin. Hitler now tried to induce France and England to abandon their promises to the Polish people. This they refused to do. The 'phoney war' began. There was a certain amount of action at sea, and some skirmishes on the Maginot Line between France and Germany. Then, on 9 April 1940, on this occasion without warning, German troops occupied Denmark and the principal ports of Norway.

For Chamberlain, under mounting pressure since Munich and the Polish tragedy, this was the end. In the Commons there was a back-bench revolt, one of the leaders of which was Leo Amery. Echoing Cromwell's words, he cried to Chamberlain, 'Depart, I say, and let us have done with you. In the name of God, go!' On 10 May Chamberlain was replaced by the one man who was felt capable of saving England, indeed Europe. This was Amery's schoolfellow, Winston Churchill.

Another Harrovian, Arnold Lunn, was in Mürren during that critical spring. Mourning the death of his father Sir Henry, who had died on 18 March, Lunn wrote:

> The green meadows were powdered by snow-white blossom, but the scented manuscript of spring and the chorus of mountain torrents in the fullness of their triumphant release from the

prison of frost had lost their magic. I looked at the beloved Jungfrau showing through a dust of silver, and felt the stab of fear. If France collapsed, could England save Europe? And I knew if Europe went down into the pit of Nazi slavery and if Gauleiters were installed in Grindelwald and Mürren and Interlaken, May torrents might still make music for Germans, but not for me.

In the late spring of 1940, even as Churchill came to power, it seemed to Arnold Lunn and other English alpinists of his generation that the story of the English in the Alps had come to an end.

Epilogue
The Rocks Remain

'I checked through the visitors' register and noted that for the whole season of 1948 there were only twenty English visitors to the Bel Alp hotel. This is a very different story from the early days of the chaplaincy, particularly in the [hotel proprietor's] grandfather's time, when nearly every one of the visitors was of British nationality.'

J.D. Dixon, Home Secretary of the Society
for the Propagation of the Gospel

On 1 May 1999, the discovery on Mount Everest of the body of George Mallory created a sensation. A party of climbers had set out to find the body of a climber identified in 1975 by the Chinese mountaineer Wang Hongbao as English. Located roughly below the point on the north-east ridge where an ice-axe identified as Andrew Irvine's had been found in 1933, it was thought to be the remains of Mallory's climbing partner.

One of the present party, Conrad Anker, spotted a patch of white on the mountain face which struck him as odd. Making his way carefully over the 30-degree slope, he saw it was a bleached torso. The hobnail boots, the cotton and silk underwear, the woollen sweater and the old rope made him think at once that he had found Irvine. Lying face down in the scree, the body was fully extended, the hands clawing the mountainside. Only the laundry-label bearing the inscription G. Mallory told the team they had found not Irvine, but Mallory himself. On the body was a time-capsule of personal effects

– a tin of Brand's Savoury Meat Lozenges, nail scissors in a leather case, a handkerchief monogrammed G.L.M., a pair of sun-goggles, a penknife, and a box of Swan Vestas matches. Missing was the Kodak Vestpocket camera with which Mallory had intended to photograph the summit. Missing, too, was the photograph of his wife, Ruth, that he had promised to leave there.

The find thus did something to elucidate the mystery of Mallory's final hours. Yet ultimately it could not answer the question whether, twenty-nine years before Edmund Hillary and Tensing Norgay, Mallory and Irvine had reached the mountain's peak. It did, however, once again evoke the climax of the heroic age of English alpinism, now a fast-receding memory. 'We weren't looking at just a body,' said one of Anker's companions, David Hahn, 'we were looking at an era.'

After the Second World War, the circumstances that had taken the English to the Alps no longer existed. At the turn of the century still the world's richest nation, England was significantly impoverished by the Great War and effectively pauperized by the Second. In 1945 she was in debt to the tune of £3,500 million, her overseas assets were decimated, her basic industries and infrastructure grossly run-down, her merchant fleet at the bottom of the sea, her overseas markets seized by competitors. By 1950, Englishmen found themselves poorer than their former innkeepers and guides, the Swiss.

If wanderlust and a desire to escape from the industrial wasteland remained, then the development of the second great travel revolution – that of air – placed all sorts of destinations beyond the Alps within easy reach of the English traveller. The British appetite for colonial adventure had been dampened during the inter-war period by events in Ireland, Palestine and Egypt, and largely quenched by the granting of independence to India in 1947. Developments in immunization and the treatment of lung diseases such as tuberculosis rendered the alpine sanatoria redundant. The Alps, too, had changed. Their scientific secrets were largely uncovered, their virgin peaks conquered, their remote valleys penetrated by motorways and festooned with cable-railways, their mountain villages mushroomed into towns. Those seeking an earthly paradise were obliged to look elsewhere.

Artists and poets no longer sought inspiration in the Alps. Although Chris Bonington's generation produced a renaissance in British alpine climbing, British mountaineers excelled themselves less in the Alps than in the Himalaya where John Hunt's expedition finally conquered Everest in 1953.

In terms of numbers, this did not mean that the English had abandoned the Alps; indeed, quite the reverse. If the poverty of post-war Britain and the consequent travel restrictions at first precluded a renaissance in alpine tourism, by the mid-fifties Anglo-Alpine air services had been re-established, package holidays by air had been introduced, and an explosion of interest had occurred in downhill skiing that was Arnold Lunn's achievement. Colonel Peter Lindsay conceived the resort of Méribel in the Three Valleys, Irma Low developed catered chalets in Austria. There followed the great French concrete-and-steel high-altitude winter resorts such as Isola 2000, Val Thorens, Flaine and Tignes. By the beginning of the following decade, mass tourism had begun to be a world-wide phenomenon. By 1965, 114 million people throughout the world were travelling abroad, of whom 5 million were British. Of those 5 million, 700,000 visited Switzerland in that year alone. By the mid-nineties tourism was not only the largest single business in the world but amongst the fastest growing, with an astonishing 700 million travelling abroad annually.

Yet whilst this was reflected in a doubling of the total number of visitors to the Alps between the end of the war and the 1990s, the English as a proportion of these figures plummeted. Out of the 50 million who visited the Alps annually, no more than one in twenty were English. Paradoxically, it was the economic miracle of West Germany that provided the bulk of alpine tourists, the Germans replacing the English as the principal visitors, followed by the French and Dutch. No contemporary guidebook could remark that in the Alps the 'wants and tastes and habits of the English were more carefully and successfully studied' than those of anyone else. If the English were made welcome, they were by no means a special case; they were no longer representatives of the world's richest nation, no longer 'milords'. If some of the resorts remain particularly English in atmosphere, and some of the institutions – the Alpine Club, the Cresta, the DHO, the Kandahar, and the Ski Club of Great Britain – still survive, they are vestiges of an era long gone.

Although the old order has changed, the discovery of Mallory's body has again raised the question posed by the Matterhorn tragedy more than one hundred and thirty years before. *The Times* had then asked: 'Is it life? Is it duty? Is it common sense? Is it allowable? Is it not wrong?' And underneath these questions lies the even larger question of the very presence of Englishmen on those heights. In the face of such tragedies as befell Andrew Irvine and George Mallory, what on earth is it that possesses men to pit themselves against these mountains so far from home?

If this story has suggested some of the answers to that question, then so too has it indicated some of the consequences it brought in its train. The development and exploitation of the Alps during the twentieth century, in particular since the end of the Second World War, is something impossible to regard with an unequivocal eye. Writing twenty-five years ago, R.W. Clark remarked, 'It is difficult to over-estimate the physical changes that have taken place in the Alps over the last hundred years.' In Austria immediately after the war there were, in all, twenty-five cable-cars, ski-lifts and mountain rail-ways; by 1970 there were something approaching two thousand. By the end of the eighties, Zermatt could provide beds for 17,000 visitors, Val d'Isère had one hundred and seventy miles of pisted runs, Garmisch-Partenkirchen a dozen ski areas and seventy-five miles of runs. St Anton boasted three hundred instructors and the largest ski-school in the world. In the Alps as a whole, there are now some six hundred resorts and some 41,000 ski runs, capable of handling 1.5 million visitors an hour.

These impressive statistics have implications. Taking as an instance modern Grindelwald, Clark pointed out that the resort 'has become a textbook example of tourist exploitation . . . with its urban centre, comfy car-parks and chalets climbing the slopes like dis-carded paper bags on a beach'. Much the same might be said of Chamonix, Courmayeur, Davos, Garmisch and Cortina. The whole region suffers from water pollution, poor air quality and the effects of acid rain. The Alps in fact is by far the most environmentally threatened mountain system in the world. We can guess what Ruskin would have thought. How can men be discouraged from destroying the things they love? This everywhere is the conundrum of mass tourism. Thomas Cook thought 'excursionism' a civilizing influence. The travel writer Jan Morris, once an advocate of tourism, later deplored it, wishing that 'opportunities for travel could be limited to the congenial few . . . the volume of tourism, not tourism itself . . . making it a curse rather than a benefit for mankind'. If the English made an extraordinary contribution to alpine development, they cannot entirely be congratulated for having done so.

Yet those pioneers brought to the world's notice a scientific puzzle, a region of scarcely paralleled beauty, an arena for psychological and physical challenge, a sanatorium and a playground, and gave people from all over the world the adventures, excitements and pleasures of a lifetime. For many the Alps proved the 'elixir of life', and for many of the English, from Whymper and Stephen to Young and Mallory, it brought out their finest qualities. A.F. Mummery, so wrote his Victorian obituarist, was the kind of man who 'made our own race the pioneers of the world, which in Naval warfare won for us command of the sea, which by exploration and colonization has given the waste-lands of the earth to Anglo-Saxon enterprise'. These great men, too, left their mark in words and pictures, to remind us of their passage. To apply Stephen Spender's words, they left the vivid air signed with their honour. And compromised though they may be, the Alps remain. As Lord Hunt once wrote, we should be 'thankful that the Alps still provide an outlet for personal discovery and endeavour'.

Bibliography

The principal collections of alpine literature are held by the various national alpine clubs. The best is the library of the Alpine Club itself in London. Also worth visiting are the Club Alpino Italiano in Turin, the Museum des Oesterreichischen Alpenvereins in Innsbruck, the Bibliothek des Deutschen Alpenvereins in Munich, the Club Alpin Suisse in Zürich, and the Club Alpin Français in Paris. Also of national importance are the library of the Ski Club of Great Britain in South London, and the Thomas Cook Travel Archive in Peterborough. The municipal libraries of the main alpine cities, notably Berne and Grenoble, also have good alpine sections. Much useful information can also be garnered at local level. Most of the older resorts have museums, often with libraries attached, sometimes with photographic archives. Several are outstanding, particularly those at Davos and St Moritz.

As to the books themselves, there is scarcely a paucity. Little was written on the Alps before the beginning of the nineteenth century, not a great deal before 1850. Thereafter, every possible aspect of the Alps has attracted comment – scholarly, popular or middlebrow – in languages as various as the nationalities of alpine visitors. The books I found especially useful are listed below (the place of publication is London, unless otherwise shown). Of the various alpine periodicals, the Alpine Club's *Alpine Journal* and the British Ski Year Books are invaluable.

L.S. Amery, *Days of Fresh Air* (1939)

J. Ball, Introduction to *The Alpine Guide* (1870)

Hilaire Belloc, *The Path to Rome* (1902)

A.F. Bill, *Davos as a Health Resort* (1906)

E.F. Benson, *Winter Sports in Switzerland* (1913)

P.P. Bernard, *Rush to the Alps* (New York, 1978)

T.G. Bonney, *The High Alps of Dauphiné* (1865)

——*The Alpine Regions of Switzerland and the Neighbouring Countries* (1868)

Chris Bonington, *I Chose to Climb* (1966)

——*The Climbers* (1992)

Piers Brendon, *Thomas Cook* (1991)

H.F. Brown, *John Addington Symonds: A Biography* (1895)

T. Graham Brown, *Brenva* (1944)

Mrs Fred Burnaby, *The High Alps in Winter* (1883)

Howard Buss, *The Magic of Ski-ing* (1959)

Samuel Butler, *Alps and Sanctuaries of Piedmont and Canton Ticino* (1881)

Lord Byron, *Childe Harolde's Pilgrimage* (1819)

Will and Carine Cadby, *Switzerland in Winter* (1914)

Vivian Caulfeild, *How to Ski* (1910)

M. Caviezel, *The Upper Engadine* (1877)

R.W. Clark, *The Victorian Mountaineers* (1953)

——*An Eccentric in the Alps: W.A.B. Coolidge* (1959)

——*The Day the Rope Broke* (1965)

——*The Alps* (New York, 1973)

Sydney Clark, *All the Best in Switzerland* (New York, 1951)

William Martin Conway, *The Alps from End to End* (1895)

W.A.B. Coolidge, *Swiss Travel and Swiss Guidebooks* (1889)

——*Alpine Studies* (1912)

——*The Alps in Nature and History* (1913)

Gavin de Beer, *Early Travellers in the Alps* (1930)

——*Alps and Men* (1932)

——*Escape to Switzerland* (1945)

——*Travellers in Switzerland* (Oxford, 1949)

Charles Domville-Fife, *Things Seen in Switzerland in Winter* (1926)

Arthur Conan Doyle, *The Memoirs of Sherlock Holmes* (1894)

——*Memories and Adventures* (1924)

Claire Eliane Engel, *A History of Mountaineering in the Alps* (1950)

Joan Evans, *The Conways: A History of Three Generations* (1966)

Joachim C. Fest, *Hitler* (1974)

J.D. Forbes, *Travels Through the Alps of Savoy and Other Parts of the Pennine Chain* (1843)

John Forbes, *A Physician's Holiday, or a Month in Switzerland in 1848* (1850)

Frank Fox, *Switzerland* (1915)

C.L. Freeston, *Cycling in the Alps* (1900)

——*The High-Roads of the Alps* (1911)

Monk Gibbon, *In Search of Winter Sport* (1953)

Josiah Gilbert and George Churchill, *The Dolomites* (1864)

Stephen Gill, *William Wordsworth* (Oxford, 1989)

A.G. Girdlestone, *The High Alps without Guides* (1870)

Thomas Gray, *Letters of Thomas Gray* (1819–21)

Frederic Harrison, *My Alpine Jubilee* (1907)

David Hill, *Turner in the Alps* (1992)

Tim Hilton, *John Ruskin: The Early Years* (Yale, 1985)

R.L.G. Irving, *The Romance of Mountaineering* (1937)

——*A History of British Mountaineering* (1955)

Jerome K. Jerome, *Three Men on the Bummel* (1900)

——*My Life and Times* (1928)

Mrs Aubrey le Blond, *The High Alps in Winter* (1883)

J. Murray Luck, *Modern Switzerland* (Palo Alto, California, 1978)

Arnold Lunn, *Ski-ing* (1913)

——(ed.), *The Englishman in the Alps* (Oxford, 1913)

——*The Mountains of Youth* (1925)

——*Mountain Jubilee* (1943)

——*Switzerland and the English* (1944)

——*Switzerland in English Prose and Poetry* (1947)

——*Mountains and Memory* (1948)

——*The Englishman on Ski* (1963)

——*Unkilled for so Long* (1968)

——*The Kandahar Story* (1969)

Henry Lunn, *Chapters from my Life* (1918)

Herbert Maeder, *The Mountains of Switzerland* (Zürich, 1967)

——*The Lure of the Mountains* (Zürich, 1971)

A.E.W. Mason, *Running Water* (1907)

George Mikes, *George Mikes Introduces Switzerland* (1977)

C. Douglas Miller, *The Dolomites* (1951)

A.F. Mummery, *My Climbs in the Alps and Caucasus* (1895)

John Murray, *A Handbook for Travellers in Switzerland, and the Alps of Savoy and Piedmont* (1838, 1843, 1892)

Thomas Paynter, *The Ski and the Mountain* (1954)

Peaks, Passes and Glaciers: A Series of Excursions by Members of the Alpine Club, ed. J. Ball (1839)

Gustav Peyer, *Geschichtedes Reisens in der Schweiz: Eine kulturgeschichtliche Studie* (Basel, 1885)

J.A.R. Pimlott, *The Englishman's Holiday* (1976)

Edward Pyatt and Robert Hale, *The Passage of the Alps* (1984)

W.F. Rae, *The Business of Travel* (1891)

Ranult Rayner, *The Story of Ski-ing* (1989)

E.C. Richardson, *Ski-Running* (1904)

James and Jeanette Riddell, *Ski Holidays in the Alps* (1961)

F.F. Roget, *Altitude and Health* (1919)

John Ruskin, *Modern Painters* (1843–60)

——*Sesame and Lilies* (1864)

——*Praeterita* (1885–1900)

H.B. de Saussure, *Voyages dans les Alpes* (Neuchâtel, 1779)

Lord Schuster, *Men, Women and Mountains* (1931)

Michael Seth-Smith, *The Cresta Run* (1976)

Mary Shelley, *Frankenstein* (1818)

G. Sigaux, *A History of Tourism* (Geneva, 1966)

Albert Smith, *The Story of Mont Blanc* (1853)

J. Adam Smith, *Mountain Holidays* (1946)

F.S. Smythe, *The Spirit of the Hills* (1935)

——*Over Tyrolese Hills* (1936)

——*My Alpine Album* (1940)

Leslie Stephen, *The Playground of Europe* (1871)

Robert Louis Stevenson, *Swiss Notes* (1923)

John Addington and Margaret Symonds, *Our Life in the Swiss Highlands* (1892)

E. Symes Thompson, *On the Winter Health Resorts of the Alps* (1888)

Louis Turner and John Ash, *The Golden Hordes* (1975)

J. Tyndall, *The Glaciers of the Alps* (1860)

——*Hours of Exercise in the Alps* (1871)

Edward Whymper, *Scrambles Amongst the Alps* (1871)

Alfred Wills, *Wanderings in the High Alps* (1856)

A.T. Tucker Wise, *The Alpine Winter Cure* (1884)

Dorothy Wordsworth, *Journal of a Tour of the Continent* (1820)

William Wordsworth, *Memorials of a Tour on the Continent* (1820)

John Wraight, *The Swiss and the British* (Salisbury, 1987)

J. Burney Yeo, *Notes of a Season at St Moritz in the Upper Engadine* (1870)

G.W. Young, *On High Hills* (1924)

——*Mountains with a Difference* (1951)

Index

Abruzzi, Duke of, 215
Addison, Joseph, 13
Adelboden, 173–6, 187
Agadir crisis (1911), 193–5
Agassiz, Louis, 29, 66, 73
Aigle, Switzerland, 172–3
Ailefroide, 103
Aix les Bains, 69
Albert, Prince Consort, 25, 92
Alfonso, Infante of Spain, 211
Allbutt, Sir Thomas, 133
Almer, Christian, 103, 106, 119, 154, 194
Alpine Club: founding and composition, 62–3, 67; publications, 67; divisions and disagreements in, 72–3; meetings, 72; criticized, 79; proposals to wind up, 89; and effect of Darwinism, 117; and national pride, 118; exhibits photographs, 137–8; exclusivity, 169; deplores proposed Matterhorn railway, 182; 50th anniversary (1908), 183; Himalayan expeditions, 214; conservatism, 218–19; survival, 265
Alpine Journal, 90, 106, 108, 153, 163, 207, 218, 243
Alpine Profile Road Book, 179
alpinism see mountaineering
Alps: described, 7–11; feared and abhorred, 7, 9–11, 13; supposed dragons in, 10; character and condition of people, 11–12, 14, 56, 102, 184; changing view of, 15–25; roads, 24, 86–7, 140; increasing visitors and tourists, 25–6, 84–6, 93–4, 139–41, 147–9, 151–2, 170, 184–5, 213, 265–6; as painting subject, 32–3; guidebooks to, 37; railway development in, 49–51, 86–9, 140, 146, 149–50, 163–8, 174, 182, 184–5, 195–6, 212; health cures in, 69–70, 133–4; tunnels, 88; writings on, 95–9; and mountaineering philosophy, 115–17; winter conditions, 121–2; winter sports and tourism in, 123–4, 127–8, 134–5, 146, 161, 174–7; publicity and study of, 152–3; English churchgoing in, 171–3; in Great War, 206–8; inter-war changing fortunes, 210–11, 236, 240, 249
Americans: visit Alps, 170, 212; and

Wall Street crash, 236; *see also* United States of America

Amery, Leopold M.S., 155–7, 161, 246, 258–61

Anderegg, Melchior, 105

Angeville, Henriette d', 104

Anglo-Swiss university races, 228–9

Anker, Conrad, 263

Appener (guide), 66

Argentières, 196

Arlberg: route, 88; tunnel, 163–4

Arlberg-Kandahar race, 235, 238, 255–6

Arnold, Matthew, 63

Arnold, Thomas, 25

Arolla, 173

Arosa, 71, 159–60, 174, 224

Austria: and Tyrol, 108; Cook takes tours to, 109; national alpine club, 169–70; declares war (1914), 201; and peace settlement, 209; post-Great War decline, 212; as democracy, 213; and conquest of north face of Eiger, 241, 244–5, 256–7; Nazis threaten and annexe (*Anschluss*), 246, 254–6, 258; cable cars and mountain railways in, 266

Bad Gastein, 69

Bad Ischl, 69

Baden, 69

Badrutt, Johannes, 125, 128, 134

Badrutt, Peter, 128

Baedeker, Karl, 37, 107, 112, 150–2, 189; *Swiss Guide*, 179

Baird, John, 199

Ball, John: background, 35–6; climbing, 36–40, 58; on local guides, 41; on appeal of glaciers, 55; and founding of Alpine Club, 63; contributes to *Peaks, Passes and Glaciers*, 67–8; as president of

Alpine Club, 74; visits Dolomites, 110, 112; in Berninas, 113; in southern Alps, 113, 115; scientific interests, 117; death, 162; *The Alpine Guide*, 37; *The Eastern Alps*, 113

Balmat, Jacques, 18–19, 26, 58

Barclay, Claudia and Vera, 200

Bardonecchia, 176

Barre des Écrins, 74, 76, 101, 103, 154

Barrington, Charles, 64–5

Baud, M. (Meiringen hotel proprietor), 172

Bavaria, 170

Bear Skating Club: moves to Morgins, 196

Beaufroy, Colonel Mark, 27

Bell, Vanessa (*née* Stephen), 215

Belloc, Hilaire, 181–2

Benson, Arthur Christopher, 215

Benson, Edward Frederic, 188, 195, 211

Bérarde, La (Dauphiné), 101, 103

Berkeley, George, Bishop of Cloyne, 9, 13, 20

Berlin: 1936 Olympic Games, 251

Bern: established as federal Swiss capital, 42

Bernard of Clairvaux, St, 146

Bernese Oberland, 124, 133, 250; railways in, 166, 195

Berninas, the, 112–13, 125

Berry, Dr Peter, 125

Bidar, Oskar, 186

Bietschhorn, 65, 106

Bisson, Auguste, 137

Blackwood's Edinburgh Magazine, 34

Blenkinsop, John, 165

Blériot, Louis, 186

Blümlisalphorn, 72

Bocca di Brenta (Dolomites), 112

Boddington, Dr George, 70

Boileau de Castelnau, Henri, 119

Bonney, Revd Thomas George, 101–2; *The High Alps of Dauphiny*, 101
Bonington, Chris, 219
Boss family (of Grindelwald), 54, 123, 150
Botzer, 109–10
Branger brothers, 158–60
Brassey, Thomas, 51, 88, 163
Breithorn, 38, 162, 167
Brenner pass: divided (1919), 209
Brenva glacier, 90–1, 232
Brett, Dorothy, 224
Breuil, 74–5, 114, 249–50
Brevoort, Meta: climbing with Coolidge, 102–6, 124; death, 119–20
Brieg, 69
Brienzer Rothorn, 166
Bristow, Lily, 157
Britenstock, 68
Brown, Charles, 166
Brown, John, 93
Brown, Thomas Graham, 213, 217–18, 232
Bruce, Brigadier-General Charles, 216
Bruce, Geoffrey, 220
Bruno, St, 15
Buchan, John: *Mr Standfast*, 207
Burgener, Alexander, 129–31
Butler, Samuel: *Alps and Sanctuaries*, 113–14; *The Way of All Flesh*, 171
Byron, George Gordon, 6th Baron, 21–5, 31, 59, 64, 85

cable cars and ski lifts, 249–50, 266
Cadby, Will and Carine: *Switzerland in Winter*, 195–6, 198
Cade, George, 36
Campbell, Mrs (1823 traveller), 115
Care Alto, 113
Carnock, Arthur Nicolson, 1st Baron, 188

Carrel, Jean-Antoine: and attempt on Matterhorn, 1–2, 74–6, 91; Tyndall engages, 74
Castor and Pollux (peaks; 'the Twins'), 38
Caulfeild, Vivian, 237; *How to Ski*, 186–8
Cavour, Camillo Benso, Count, 94
Cengalo (Berninas), 113
Chamberlain, Neville, 240, 258–61
Chamonix: and ascent of Mont Blanc, 18, 26; established as resort, 26, 125; Smith in, 47; Couttet's hotel, 54, 147; Ruskin deplores development of, 61, 161; access to, 86; Lunn's trips to, 161, 174; winter sports in, 174; development, 196, 266; inter-war prosperity, 225; holds first Winter Olympics (1924), 227
Chamonix Aiguilles, 129–32
Charlet, Arnold, 242
Charlet, Jean, 106
Château d'Oex, 174, 176, 196, 207
Chatellus, Alain de, 194
Chimborazo (Andes), 89
Chomiomo (Himalaya), 215
Chur, 225
Churchill, George, 110
Churchill, Sir Winston S., 157, 201, 223, 240, 261–2
Cima di Castello (Berninas), 113
Cima Presanella, 113
Cima Tosa (Dolomites), 111–12
Cimone della Pala, 112
Citroën family, 249
Civetta (Dolomites), 111
Clairmont, Claire, 22
Clark, Kenneth, Baron, 13
Clark, Ronald W., 118, 153, 266; *The Alps*, 205
climbing aids, 170, 181, 218, 242–3
Club Alpin Français, 119, 169

Coaz, J., 113
Cobb, Humphrey, 197
Coke, Thomas William (1st Earl of
    Leicester; 'Coke of Norfolk'), 16
Col de la Faucille, 32, 35, 231
Col de Géant, 115
Col de Pilatte, 96
Col di Tendi, 11
Col du Says, 101
Col du Sella, 101
Collie, J. Norman, 205, 214
Collingwood, William Gershom, 34,
    59–60
Colonial and Continental Church
    Society, 173
Compagnie des Guides des Chamonix,
    41
Compagnie Internationale des Wagons
    Lits, 236
consumption *see* tuberculosis
Conway, Sir Martin, 108–10, 153–5,
    162, 181, 185, 187, 206, 214; *The
    Alps from End to End*, 154
Cook, Captain James, 16
Cook, John Mason (Thomas's son), 146
Cook, Thomas: early excursions, 83–6;
    origins and background, 84;
    promotes popular tourism, 93–4,
    101, 140, 161, 212; takes trips to
    Austria and Tyrol, 109; status in
    Egypt, 140; son runs company, 146;
    and transatlantic visitors, 170;
    winter sports trips, 175, 195, 223,
    240; organizes cycling trips, 179;
    company sold (1928), 236; tours to
    Germany, 249; on civilizing effect
    of tourism, 267
Coolidge, William Augustus Brevoort:
    quarrels and controversies, 29,
    153–4, 230; on Forbes's climbs, 31;
    on Ball, 37; on qualities of good
    guide, 41, 191; on Matterhorn
    tragedy, 79; background, 102–3; in

Dauphiné, 102–3, 105, 117, 119,
    150; climbs Matterhorn, 106; in
    Tyrol, 107–8; in Dolomites, 112;
    elected Fellow of Magdalen
    College, Oxford, 112, 119; in
    Lombardy Alps, 113; on Ticino,
    114; and effect of Darwinism, 117;
    national identity, 118; devotion to
    aunt and dog, 120; winter activities,
    123–4; on conquest of Chamonix
    Aiguilles, 130; deprecates skis, 136;
    obituary of Donkin, 137; as alpine
    scholar, 152–3; supports Conway,
    153; revises *Murray's Handbook*, 154;
    last major ascent (1897), 162;
    objects to mountain railway to La
    Meije summit, 167–8, 181;
    reconciliation with Whymper, 194;
    in Great War, 206; death and
    funeral, 229; writings and
    scholarship, 229–30
Cortina, 110–11, 196, 225, 249
Courmayeur, 115, 266
Couttet family, 150
Cresta Run, 128, 134, 199–200, 211,
    235, 265
Cromer, Evelyn Baring, 1st Earl of,
    140
Croz, Michel, 2–3, 77–8
curling (sport), 134
cycling, 178–81
Cyclist's Touring Club, 178–9
Czechoslovakia, 258–60

Daguerre, Louis Jacques Mande, 137
Dalloz, Pierre, 241
Darwinism, 116–17
Dauphiné: independence of peasants,
    11; remains undiscovered, 26;
    climbing in, 74, 76, 101–3, 107, 117,
    119; facilities improved, 150;
    railway development, 176
Davies, J.C., 72

Davos: as health resort, 70–1, 121, 125–6, 133–41, 158, 207, 211, 224; J.A. Symonds in, 121, 125–7, 133; and tobogganing, 127–8; early skiing in, 136, 187; hotels, 150; church in, 173; winter sports in, 174, 176; in Great War, 207; cable railway, 250; popularity, 266

Davos Courier, 207, 210

de Beer, Sir Gavin: *Alps and Men*, 100

Dent Blanche, 72, 76, 105

Dent d'Hérens, 72, 161

Dickens, Charles, 44, 49, 78–9; *Bleak House*, 43

Dixon, J.D., 263

Dollfuss, Engelbert, 246

Dolomites, 27, 107, 110–12, 170

Domville-Fife, Charles, 174, 198; *Things Seen in Switzerland*, 224–5

Donkin, William Frederick, 137–8

Douglas, Lord Francis, 2–3

Dowding, Air Chief Marshal Hugh, 1st Baron, 227

Downhill Only club (DHO), 228, 265

Doyle, Sir Arthur Conan, 157–9, 176

Doyle, Louise, Lady, 158

dress codes, 189–90, 229

Duhamel, Henri, 119, 136

Dumas, Alexandre, 24–5

Dunlop, John, 178

Durham, W.E., 195

Eden, Anthony (*later* 1st Earl of Avon), 251

Edinburgh Review, 78

Edlin, Bill, 250

Edward VII, King (*earlier* Prince of Wales), 48, 165, 193

Edward VIII, King *see* Windsor, Duke of

Edwards, Amelia, 111–12

Egypt: Thomas Cook in, 140

Egyptian Hall, Piccadilly, London, 48

Eiger: remains unclimbed, 19, 27; Barrington ascends, 64–5; Tyndall on, 97; mountain railway, 166–7; attempts on and conquest of north face, 241, 244–5, 256–8; reputation, 242

Elliot, Revd J.M., 91

Engadine valley, 124–5

Engel, Claire Éliane, 41, 98–9, 232, 244

Engelberg, 195, 250

England: population growth (18th century), 16; urbanization and industrialization, 43–4, 46; travelling abroad, 44; and railway development, 49–50; tuberculosis in, 71; and imperialist ethos, 100; chauvinism, 116; churchgoing, 171–3; dress code and manners, 189–90; post-Great War decline, 210; appeasement policy, 247; economic decline, 264

English language: dissemination, 180

Épinay, M. (innkeeper), 72

Everest, Sir George, 214

Everest, Mount, 214–16, 219–22, 244, 263–5

Excursionist, The (Cook's magazine), 83, 109

Faraday, Michael, 25

Farrar, Percy, 215

Farrar, Captain Reginald, 229

fascism, 240; *see also* Germany

Fédération Internationale de Ski, 227, 235–6, 238

Feldberg, 196

Fell, John Barraclough: railway, 87–8, 95, 163, 165

Fellows, Charles: *Narrative of an Ascent to the Summit of Mont Blanc*, 37

FIAT motor company, 249

Finsteraarhorn, 63–4

Fitzgerald, F. Scott, 213

fixed ropes, 170, 181
Flaine, 265
flying (and aeroplanes), 186, 264–5
Forbes, James David: background and
    early expeditions, 28–31, 66, 137;
    ascent of Jungfrau, 30, 64; Ruskin
    meets, 32; health decline, 35;
    compulsions, 38; Wills follows, 58;
    in Alpine Club, 63; on benefits of
    Alpine air, 70; quarrel with Agassiz,
    73; visits La Bérarde (Dauphiné),
    101; scientific interests, 115, 117;
    death, 162; and despoiling of Alps,
    184; *Travels Through the Alps*, 31, 37,
    66, 68, 95
Forbes, Dr John, 44–5, 53
Forbes, Williamina, Lady (*née* Beeches),
    28
Fox, Francis, 164
France: national alpine club, 119, 169;
    on vulgarization of Alps, 212; inter-
    war industrialization, 223
Francis Ferdinand, Archduke of
    Austria, 201
Franco-Prussian War (1870–1), 94
François de Sales, St, Bishop of
    Geneva, 13
Freeston, C.L., 185–6
Fréjus pass, 87–8
Freshfield, Douglas, 32, 49–50, 113,
    230
Freshfield, Mrs Henry, 69
Frutigen, 174
Furka pass, 159
Furse, Dame Katherine (*née* Symonds),
    237

Gardiner, Frederick, 105
Garmisch-Partenkirchen, 196, 225,
    252, 266
Gaspard, Pierre (and son), 119
Gautier, Théophile, 91
Geneva: and rail development, 51, 86

Gentinetta, Augustin, 129
George, Revd Hereford: *The Oberland
    and its Glaciers*, 137
Germany: expansionism, 168–9;
    national alpine club, 169–70; and
    1919 peace settlement, 209;
    increase in tourists, 211; post-Great
    War economic collapse, 212, 236;
    Weimar Republic formed, 213, 223;
    mountaineering activities in Alps,
    241–5, 256–7; and politicization of
    sport, 242–4, 251–2, 255–6;
    rearmament and conscription in,
    246–7; rise of Nazism in, 246–7,
    251; Cook arranges trips to, 249;
    hosts 1936 Olympics (Berlin), 251;
    aggression (1930s), 254, 258–61;
    and outbreak of World War II, 261;
    post-war tourists from, 265
Gibbon, Edward, 19
Gibbon, Monk, 134
Gilbert, Josiah, 110
Girdlestone, Revd A.G.: *The High Alps
    Without Guides*, 132, 233
Godley, A.D.: 'Switzerland' (poem), 5
Goebbels, Josef, 251
Goethe, Johann Wolfgang von, 24
Graham, W.W., 214
Grand Caledonian Curling Club, 134
Grand Tour, 15, 44
Grande Chartreuse (valley), 15, 101
Grande, Julian, 201
Grande Ruine, La, 103
Grandes Jorasses, 76, 242–3
Graves, Robert, 216
Gray, Thomas, 14–16, 20, 24, 101
Great Exhibition (London, 1851), 46,
    85
Great St Bernard Pass, 9, 11
Great Schreckhorn, 72
Great War (1914–18), 201–2, 205–8,
    213; and peace settlement, 208–9
Grenoble, 69, 152

Grey, Sir Edward (Viscount Grey of Fallodon), 198
Griessbad Falls, 173
Griffith, Thomas, 33–4
Grindelwald: catering, 53; Bear hotel, 54, 64, 76, 122–3, 125, 147, 149; 1892 fire in, 145, 148; Lunn's church conferences in, 146–7, 160; railway reaches, 166; winter sports in, 174; tourist popularity, 184, 266; skating, 196–7; inter-war prosperity, 225; Coolidge buried in, 229
Grisons (canton), 69–70, 124, 133, 182
Gross Glockner, 27
Groupe de Haute Montagne, 241
Grove, F.C., 72
Gspaltenhorn, 201
Gstaad, 176, 196
guides: profession develops, 40–1; in Tyrol, 108–9; climbing without, 132, 156, 233
Gurkhas: accompany Conway, 154–5
Guyer-Zeller, Adolph, 167

Hadow, Roger, 2–3, 89
Haggard, Dr, 134
Hahn, David, 263
Haller, Albrecht von, 14, 16, 20
Hannibal, 10
Hardy, Revd J.F., 68, 113, 116–17
Harrer, Heinrich, 256–7
Harrison, Frederic, 168–70, 190, 211
Hauenstein tunnel, 51, 88
Heckmair, Andreas, 256–8
Henlein, Konrad, 258
Herslow, John Stevens, 36
Hillary, Sir Edmund, 263
Himalayas, 132, 154, 190, 214–15, 265; see also Everest, Mount
Hindenburg, Paul von, 246
Hitler, Adolf, 237, 240, 242–3, 246, 252–6, 258–61
Hogg, Quintin, 147

Hooker, Sir Joseph, 37
Horsley, Revd John William, 148
Hort, H.L.A., 63
hotels and inns: development in Alps, 53, 115, 147, 149–52, 184; exclusivity of, 161; see also individual places
Housman, A.E., 183
Hudson, Revd Charles, 2–3, 91; *Where There's a Will There's a Way* (with E.S. Kennedy), 91
Hume, David, 14
Hunt, John, Baron, 265, 267
Huxley, Thomas Henry, 66

Imboden, Joseph, 214
inns *see* hotels and inns
Interlaken, 56, 207
Irvine, Andrew Comyn, 219–22, 263–4, 266
Irving, R.L.G., 56, 107, 215–16, 218, 228, 242
Isola, 265
Italy: and southern Alps, 112–13; hotels and inns, 151; expansionism, 169; national alpine club, 169; in Great War, 206; inter-war development, 223

Jacobshorn, 259
Jakob (guide), 91
James, Henry, 93
Japan, 247
Jerome, Jerome K., 138, 179–80
John de Bremble, 9
Jones, H.O., 193
Jones, Robert, 20
Jungfrau: first climbed, 27; Forbes climbs, 29–30; Barrington climbs, 64; Coolidge climbs in winter, 124; Conway climbs with Gurkhas, 155; mountain railway, 166, 168, 182, 197–8

Jungfrau Joch, 66
Jupperhord, 200

K2 (Himalaya), 215
Kandahar Challenge Cup, 189, 195,
    226, 227
Kandahar Club, 227–8, 237, 265
Kandersteg, 173, 175
Karakoram range (Western Himalaya),
    154, 214
Kasparek, Fritz, 256–7
Kellas, A.M., 215
Kennedy, E.S., 68, 91
Kennedy, Thomas Stuart, 63–4, 72,
    113, 123
Keppel, Mrs George (Alice), 211
Kipling, Rudyard, 197
Kitzbühel, 196, 225, 234, 250
Kleine Scheidegg: mountain railway to,
    167
Klosters, 175
Knebworth, Antony, Viscount, 239
Knubel, Josef, 191–4, 201, 233, 247–9
Kohlgrub, 196
Königspitze (Tyrol), 108
Kurz, Toni, 245, 247

Ladies' Alpine Club, 107
Ladies' Ski Club, 237; *see also* women
Lanson, Revd R.D., 172
Latrobe, Charles Joseph, 52, 56
Lauterbrunnen, 146, 149, 167
Laveleye, Emile de, 105
League of Nations, 246–7, 254
League for the Preservation of Swiss
    Scenery, 181
le Blond, Aubrey, 107
le Blond, Elizabeth Hawkins (*née*
    Whitshed), 107, 124; *The High Alps
    in Winter*, 124
Leibnitz, Gottfried Wilhelm, 14
Lenzerheide, 175, 195
Leukerbad, 69, 195

Lewis-Lloyd, Emmeline, 106
Leysin, 71, 207, 224
Lilienfeld, 196
Lindsay, Colonel Peter, 265
Liszt, Franz, 25
Lloyd, R.W., 200
Lloyd George, David, 259
Locarno, Treaty of (1925), 223, 254
Lochmatter, Franz and Josef, 191–3,
    195, 200, 248–9
Lombardy Alps, 113
Long, Lieut.-Colonel Albert de Lande,
    239
Longfellow, Henry Wadsworth, 25
Longman, William, 74
Longstaff, Tom, 214
Lötschberg: route, 88; tunnel, 163,
    165
Louis Philippe, King of France, 42
Low, Irma, 265
Lucerne, 93; Culm inn (Rigi), 149
Lunn, Sir Arnold: on Forbes and
    Agassiz, 29; on Ruskin, 59; on
    effect of Matterhorn tragedy, 79;
    on spiritual meaning of
    mountaineering, 118; on beginnings
    of tobogganing, 128; survives
    Grindelwald fire, 145, 148; passion
    for mountains, 148; on Coolidge's
    self-esteem, 153; on development
    of popular tourism, 161–2; on
    Adelboden, 175; father's
    development of winter Alps, 176;
    love of skiing, 176–7, 187–8;
    competitive downhill skiing, 188–9,
    226, 228, 238, 265; breaks leg, 189;
    on dress code and behaviour, 189,
    229; on G. Winthrop Young, 190;
    encourages Knubel to ski, 191; on
    English combined skating, 196; and
    changing Alps, 205; in Mürren
    during Great War, 207; praises
    Irvine, 219; introduces slalom,

Lunn, Sir Arnold (*cont.*)
226–8, 238; friendship with
Schneider, 234–5; in Kitzbühel,
234; criticized by Norwegians, 235;
encourages women's skiing, 237;
deplores politicization of sport,
239, 242; Moore writes to, 250; and
1936 Olympics, 252–4; reaction to
Schneider's arrest, 255–6; and
beginnings of Second World War,
261–2
Lunn, Sir Henry Simpson (Arnold's
father): background and career,
145–6; church activities, 145, 160,
171, 173; develops winter tourism,
146–7, 161, 174–6; founds PSASC,
161, 175, 188, 224; promotes skiing,
189, 195; death, 261
Lunn, Hugh (Arnold's brother), 145
Lunn, Peter (Arnold's son), 220, 239, 253
Lyskamm, 116, 166, 200
Lyttelton, Edward, 55
Lytton, Neville Stephen (*later* 3rd
Earl), 146, 188

McDonald, D.C., 72
MacDonald, James Ramsay, 240
Maeder, Herbert: *The Lure of the
Mountains*, 62
Mahringen, Karl, 244
Mallory, George Leigh, 205–6, 208,
213, 215–16, 218–22, 267; body
found (1999), 263–4, 266
Maloja, 175, 225
Manchester Guardian, 251
Mansfield, Katherine, 224
map-making, 170
Marmolata (Dolomites), 112
Martigny, 86
Martyn, Thomas: *Sketch of a Tour
through Swisserland*, 52
Masino, 69
Mason, A.E.W., 195

Matterhorn: position, 1; fatal accident
on Whymper's first climb, 2–4, 7,
62, 67, 74, 78–9, 89, 95, 97, 152, 217,
266; earlier attempts on, 74–8;
inquests and controversy over
deaths, 78–9, 89; alternative routes
found and conquered, 91–2;
Tyndall describes, 97; Lucy Walker
climbs, 105; Meta Brevoort
traverses, 106; winter ascents, 124;
Mummery ascends Z'mutt face,
129–30, 157; Amery climbs, 155,
157; proposed railway, 181–2;
Young climbs with one leg, 194,
247; Young ascends by Z'mutt
route, 201; north face conquered,
241–4
Matthews, G., 90–1
Matthews, William, 62–4
May, Revd C.T., 172
Mégève, France, 249
Meije, La, 101, 103, 105, 107, 119;
mountain railway to, 168, 181
Meiringen (Bernese Oberland), 172,
207
Menti, Mario, 256
Mer de Glace, 18
Meran, 69
Méribel, 265
Merkl, Willy, 244
Meyer brothers (of Aarau), 27
Milner, Douglas, 111
Mönch, 27, 29
Mont Blanc: first climbed, 18–19, 26;
Saussure's reverence for, 18; Shelley
on, 23; Beaufoy climbs, 27; Smith's
expedition to, 47–9, 90, 93; Wills
ascends, 58; climbed from southern
side, 89–90; seen from Piedmont,
115; winter ascents, 124; alpinists'
huts built on, 155; Conway climbs
with Gurkhas, 155; railway, 182;
Young climbs on, 193; Mallory

Mont Blanc (*cont.*)
   climbs, 218; Smythe climbs Brenva
   face, 232
Mont Cenis, 86–9, 114, 163
Mont Pelmo (Dolomites), 110
Mont Pelvoux, 74, 101, 103
Mont Thuria, 103
Montagu, Lady Mary Wortley, 52
Montana (Valais), 71, 173, 175, 189,
   224
Monte Adamello, 113
Monte della Disgrazia (Berninas), 72,
   113
Monte Pelmo (Dolomites), 112
Monte Rosa, 58, 72, 124, 157, 247
Monte Viso, 28
Montreux, 173
Moore, A.W., 90–1, 108, 123
Moore, Kingsmill, 250
Morgins, 175, 196–7
Morris, Jan, 267
Moser, Herr (St Anton
   Bürgermeister), 255
Mosley, Sir Oswald, 240
motor cars, 185–6; *see also* roads
mountaineering: for sport, 56, 116;
   international spread of, 169–70;
   ethics of, 217–19, 266;
   politicization of, 241–4; grading
   system, 242
Muir, Ward, 143, 199–200
Muirhead, Findlay, 226
Mummery, Alfred Frederick, 91,
   129–33, 161, 169, 190, 214, 233,
   267; *My Climbs in the Alps and
   Caucasus*, 132
Munich agreement (1938), 260
Murray, John: in Alpine Club, 63;
   Knapsack Guide to the Tyrol, 108, 151
*Murray's Handbook to Switzerland, Savoy
   and Piedmont*: on beauty of Italian
   glaciers, 8; on alpine tracks, 10–11;
   on alpine human diseases, 12; on

dangers of mountain travel, 27; on
   Grindelwald, 30; on Zermatt, 36;
   lacks information for climbers, 37;
   on Chamonix, 47; on Swiss inns
   and hotels, 53–4, 149; on natural
   springs, 69–70; on Davos, 70, 134;
   recommends Piedmont, 114–15; on
   Great St Bernard pass, 121; on St
   Moritz, 125; on developing travel
   facilities, 140; and package tours,
   140–1; on Pastor Strasser, 148; and
   Swiss attention to English
   preferences, 151; Coolidge revises,
   154; on tunnels and mountain
   railways, 164–5; on church services,
   172–3; on importance of tourism
   in Switzerland, 184
Mürren, 175, 195, 197, 207, 219, 226,
   238–9, 250
Mussolini, Benito, 223, 240, 242, 249

Nanga Parbat (Himalaya), 132, 190,
   214, 244
Nansen, Fridtjof, 158
Napier, Colonel C.C., 135–6, 158,
   176
Napoleon I (Bonaparte), Emperor of
   France, 10, 21, 24, 86, 139
Napoleon III, Emperor of the French,
   94
Nazi-Soviet pact (1939), 260–1
Newton, Sir Isaac, 14
Nightingale, Florence, 25
Norheim, Sondre, 135, 177
Norton, Colonel E.F., 216, 220–1
Norwegian Ski Association, 178

Oberaar (glacier), 29
Oberammergau: Passion Play, 94
Odell, Noel, 220–1
Oestgard, Major N.R., 235
Olympic Games: Winter, 227, 235;
   Germany (1936), 251–3

Ortle (Tyrol), 27, 108
Otto, Nikolaus, 185
Owen, Misses (Grindelwald skiers), 237

Paccard, Michel-Gabriel, 18, 26, 116
package holidays, 265
Pall Mall Gazette, 155
Paradis, Maria, 104
Parsons, Charles, 170
Pauhunri (Himalaya), 215
Payer, Herr, 113
Peaks, Passes and Glaciers (series), 67–8, 71, 73–4, 95
Peasants of Chamouni, The (children's book), 46
Pease, E.R., 116
Pepys, Samuel, 123
Pfafers, 69
Phipps, Sir Eric, 251
photography, 136–8
Pic Central (Dauphiné), 103
Pic Coolidge (*formerly* Pic du Vallon), 119
Pickford, William (Baron Sterndale), 206
Piedmont, 12, 114
Pigeon, Anna and Ellen, 106
Pilatus (summit), 165–6
Pilkington, Charles, 182–3, 185
Pimlott, J.A.R., 71, 177, 190
pitons, 218
Piz Badile (Berninas), 113
Piz Bernina, 27, 113
Pococke, Richard, 18
Poland, 260–1
Polytechnic Touring Association, 147
Pontresina, 71, 173, 175
Public Schools Alpine Sports Club (PSASC), 161, 175, 188–90, 195, 240
Public Schools Alpine Sports Ltd, 224

railways: development and effect of, 49–51, 84–9, 140, 149–50, 163–4, 171, 174, 176, 182, 184–5, 195–6, 212, 225; mountain, 87–8, 165–8, 174, 176, 181–2, 197–8, 266; *see also* tunnels
Ransome, Arthur: *Winter Holiday*, 121
Rateau, Le, 181
Reisch, Franz, 234
religion: and English churchgoing in Alps, 171–4
Rennie, Sir John, 52
Review of the Churches (journal), 146
revolutions of 1848, 42
Reynaud, M. (travel agent), 96
Richardson, C.W.R., 160, 176–8, 187–8
Richardson, E.C., 160, 176–8, 187–9; *The Ski Runner*, 187
Richardson, Mrs E.C., 237
Richardson, Kathleen, 106
Richardson, T. D., 239
Rickmers, W.R., 177–8, 187–8, 234
Riddell, Jimmy, 226, 239
Riefenstahl, Leni, 251
Riffel, the, 83
Riggenbach, Nikolaus, 165
Rigi (Lucerne), 149, 165–6, 184
roads: in Alps, 24, 86–7, 140, 163–4, 186; *see also* motor cars
Roberts, Field Marshal Frederick Sleigh, 1st Earl, 188
Robertson, Donald, 68
Rochers de Naye, 166
Röhm, Ernst, 246
Rossberg, Ralf, 195
Rothorn *see* Zinal Rothorn
Rothschild family, 249
Rousseau, Jean-Jacques, 16–17, 19–20, 23, 25; *Du Contrat Social*, 16; *La Nouvelle Héloïse*, 16–17, 22, 23
Royal Geographical Society, 214–15
Ruinette, 76
Ruskin, John: deplores tourist vulgarization in Alps, 15, 93, 140,

Ruskin, John (*cont.*)
145, 151, 161, 266; writings on Alps,
17, 32, 59–61, 68, 140, 231; travels
in Alps, 31–2, 85; relations with
Turner, 33–4, 42; disparages Smith,
49; in Alpine Club, 63;
photography, 137; death, 162;
deprecates railways, 182, 185;
Modern Painters, 32, 34, 59–61;
Praeterita, 140; *Sesame and Lilies*, 46,
145; *The Seven Lamps of Architecture*,
59; *The Stones of Venice*, 59
Ryan, V.J.E., 191–2, 200, 213, 233, 249

Saanenland, 176
Saanenmoser, 196
Saas-Fee, 173
St Anton, 176, 196, 207–8, 225, 234–5,
237, 250, 255–6, 266
St Gotthard: route, 88, 113; tunnel,
163–4
St Moritz: as spa town, 69, 124;
Engadine Kulm hotel, 125, 128;
tourist popularity, 125, 184, 225;
winter sports in, 128, 134, 174, 176,
196; Kaiser's son in, 198, 200; post-
Great War revival, 211; hosts 1928
Winter Olympics, 235
St Nicholas, 225
St Pierre de Chartreuse, 196
Saint-Germain, Peace of (1919),
209–10
Sainte-Beuve, Charles Augustin, 25
Sand, George, 52
Sandri, Bartolo, 256
Sarajevo: 1914 assassination, 201
Saussure, Horace-Bénédict de, 16–19,
26, 31, 36, 46–7, 49, 66, 115; *Voyages
dans les Alpes*, 19, 26, 68
Savoy, 94, 170
Scheuchzer, Johann Jacob, 10
Schiller, Johann, 24
Schmid brothers, 243–4

Schneider, Hannes, 234, 238, 255–6
Schneider, Ludmilla, 255
Schuschnigg, Kurt von, 254–5
Schuster, Claud, 197, 228
Schwarz Tor pass, 40
Schweizerische Damen Ski Club, 237
Scott, Sir Walter, 28
Sedelmayer, Max, 244
Seiler family, 150
Seiler, Alexandre, 4, 54, 76, 149
Seiler, Friedrich, 166
Seiler, Hermann, 225
Sella, Vittorio, 138
Sesiajoch pass, 106
Sestriere, 249
Seth-Smith, Michael, 211
Seyss-Inquart, Arthur, 255
Shelley, Mary Wollstonecraft (*née*
Godwin), 22
Shelley, Percy Bysshe, 21–5, 46, 59, 205
Siddons, Sarah, 28
Sils, 71, 175
Simplon: route, 88, 164; tunnel,
163–4
skating, 123, 134, 195–7
Ski Club of Great Britain, 178, 187,
234, 265
skiing: beginnings and development,
135–6, 159–60, 176–8, 187; Arnold
Lunn's passion for, 176, 234–5;
improvements in technique, 187–8;
competitions, 188–9, 219, 235, 238;
downhill, 188–9, 226–8, 235; inter-
war vogue for, 226–8, 234; slalom,
226–8, 235, 238; Arlberg technique,
234–5; women's, 237, 239;
politicized, 239–40
sleighing, 134–5
Smith, Albert Richard, 46–9, 90, 93
Smythe, Francis Sydney, 133, 167, 213,
230–3, 244; *The Spirit of the Hills*,
231
Snaith, Stanley, 130

Society for the Propagation of the Gospel, 172–3
Solly, A.N. and G.A., 200
Someiller, Germain, 88
Somervell, T.H., 216, 220
Somerville, Crighton, 187
Spender, Sir Stephen, 267
Spengler, Dr Alexander, 70–1, 125, 133
Splügen pass, 164
sport: organized, 55–6, 62, 128, 134–5; politicized, 239, 242
Stalin, Josef V., 261
Steevens, G.W., 140
Stephen, Sir Leslie: on changed attitude to Alps, 7, 13, 24; on Rousseau, 17; on Ruskin, 60; on popular despoiling of Alps, 61, 84, 93–4, 139, 148; background, 65; climbing, 65–6, 72–3, 83; offends Tyndall, 73–4; on love of mountains and mountaineering, 99, 118, 140, 217, 267; visits Tyrol, 108; on Dolomites, 110–11; in Berninas, 113; and effect of Darwinism, 117; winter climbing, 124; death, 162; and tourism, 183; writings, 231; *The Playground of Europe*, 95, 98–9, 155
Stephenson, Robert, 50–1
Stevenson, Robert Louis, 126, 158
Stogdon, John, 161
Strachey, Lytton, 215
Strand Magazine, 157, 160
Strang-Watkins slalom cup, 219–20
Strasser, Pastor Gottfried, 148–9, 151, 167
Stratton, Isabella (*later* Charlet), 106
Strauss, Richard, 252
Stresa, 173
Strutt, Colonel E.L., 218, 242–3, 245
Sudetenland, 258–60
Swedish Ski Association, 178
Swiss Alpine Club, 169

Switzerland: Helvetic Republic created (1798), 21; civil war (1847), 42, 50; 1848 constitution, 42; railway system developed, 50–1, 140, 146, 149–50, 171, 174; inns and hotels, 53, 115, 147, 149–52; Cook's tours in, 86; Queen Victoria visits, 92–3; popularity for tourists, 94, 139–41, 147–9, 170, 184, 265; establishes national alpine club, 169; economic expansion (*Grunderzeit*), 170–1, 264; preservation measures, 181; and impending Great War, 198; acquires Vorarlberg (1919), 209; international competitors from, 228–9
Symonds, John Addington, 121, 125–8, 133; *Our Life in the Swiss Highlands* (with daughter Margaret), 133; *Sketches in Italy and Greece*, 126
Symonds, Margaret, 133

Tairrez, Victor, 54
Talbot, William Henry Fox, 137
Tangwald, Mathias, 38–40
Tarasp, 69
Täschhorn, 72, 191, 193, 249
Taugwalder (father and son guides), 2–4, 89
Taylor, A.J.P., 209
Telemark, Norway, 135
Tell, William, 11
Tensing Norgay, 263
Théodulhorn, 77
Thompson, David: *Europe since Napoleon*, 259
Thompson, Dr E. Symes, 133, 134
Three Valleys, the, 226, 265
Ticino (canton), 112–14
Tignes, 265
Times, The: on fatal first climb of Matterhorn, 4, 79, 266
tobogganing, 127–8, 134, 199–200

tourism: expansion, 25–6, 84–6, 93–4, 139–41, 147–9, 151–2, 170–1, 184–5, 213, 265–7
Townshend, Charles, 2nd Viscount, 16
transatlantic travel, 170
travel agents, 224
Trisul (Himalaya), 215
Tschammer und Osten, Hans von, 244
Tschingel (Coolidge's dog), 102–5, 120
tuberculosis (consumption): alpine treatment of, 70–1, 125–6, 133–4
Tuckett, Francis Ford, 110–11, 113, 117
tunnels, 51, 88, 113–14, 164–5
Turbinia (yacht), 170
Turner, Joseph Mallord William, 33–5, 42, 136
Turner, Louis and John Ash: *The Golden Hordes*, 212
Twain, Mark (Samuel Clemens), 139, 141
Tyndall, John: quarrels with colleagues, 29, 73–4; background, 66, 74; climbing, 66–7, 71, 74–5; writings, 68, 231; crosses Matterhorn, 91; influences Conway, 108; scientific interests, 115, 117; death, 162; and tourism, 183; *The Glacier of the Alps*, 67; *Hours of Exercise*, 95, 97–8, 155
Tyrol: independence of peasants, 11; character, 107–9; facilities in, 151–2; mountain railway in, 166; tourism in, 170; and advent of Hitler, 256

United States of America: post-Great War dominance, 209–10, 212; near-boycott of 1936 Olympics, 251; *see also* Americans
Unter Gabelhorn, 156
Unteraar (glacier), 29

Val d'Aosta, 115
Val d'Hérens, 76

Val d'Isère, 151, 226, 249, 266
Val Thorens, 265
Val Tournanche, 75, 114
Venetz, Benedikt, 129–31
Venn, John, 65
Vereinigung für Heimatschutz, 163
Versailles, Treaty of (1919), 209–10, 246, 254
Vevey, 173
Victoria, Queen, 25–6, 78, 92–4
Vienna, Congress of (1815), 21, 42
Vignolles, Charles, 51, 87
Villard de Lans, 196
Villars, 175, 195
Voltaire, François Marie Arouet de, 14, 17
Vorarlberg, 209
Vorg, Ludwig, 256–7

Wäber, Johann, 16
Waghorn, Dick, 228
Walker, Francis, 105
Walker, Frank, 90–1, 104–5
Walker, Horace, 90–1, 104, 123
Walker, Lucy, 104–6
Wall Street Crash (1929), 236
Walton, Elijah, 111
Wang Hongbao, 263
Watt, James, 16, 185
Wedgwood, Thomas, 137
Weisshorn, 71, 83, 157, 247
Wellenkup, 247
Welzenbach, Willy, 242
Wengen, 175, 224, 228
Wentworth, Ralph Gordon Milbanke, 13th Baron (*later* 2nd Earl Lovelace), 119
Wetterhorn: Wills ascends, 56–8, 116, 214; Coolidge climbs in winter, 124
Wetterhorn Aerial Railway, 249
Whitshed, Elizabeth Hawkins *see* le Blond, Elizabeth Hawkins

Whymper, Edward: on 'cordon' around
    Matterhorn, 1, 10; leads fatal
    expedition to climb Matterhorn, 1–4,
    62, 67, 74, 78, 89, 95, 97, 118, 221;
    quarrels with colleagues, 29;
    compulsions, 38, 95, 267; on guides,
    40; on Seilers' inn, Zermatt, 54;
    background, 74; on Carrel, 74;
    climbing, 74–7, 114; engravings and
    paintings, 74, 136, 137; on alpine
    roads and railways, 86–9; celebrity,
    89; in Dauphiné, 101; and national
    pride, 118; on winter climbing, 123;
    describes Z'mutt face of Matterhorn,
    129; controversy with Coolidge, 154;
    death, 194, 201; reconciliation with
    Coolidge, 194; Zermatt memorial,
    201, 205; writings, 231; *Scrambles
    Amongst the Alps*, 26, 95–8, 154–5;
    Travels Among the Great Andes, 89
Whymper, Josiah, 74
Wild, Konrad, 136
Wilde, Oscar, 56
Wildspitze, 109
Wilkinson, Thomas Edward, Bishop
    for Europe, 171, 173–4
William II, Kaiser, 201, 206
William, Crown Prince of Germany
    ('Little Willie'), 198, 200
Williams, Roderick, 200
Wills, Alfred: ascent of Wetterhorn,
    56–8, 116, 214; and recreational
    climbing, 58, 61; in Alpine Club, 63;
    and philosophy of climbing, 118;
    and tourism, 183; *Wanderings Among
    the High Alps*, 58, 95
Wilson, Woodrow, 208–9, 212
Windham, William, 18
Windsor, Edward, Duke of (*earlier*
    King Edward VIII), 247, 259
winter: tourism development, 121–6;
    sports, 123–4, 127–8, 134–5, 161,
    174–7, 195, 223, 225–6

Wise, Dr A.T. Tucker, 134
Withers, John J., 233, 245
Wolfe, Alice Damrosch, 237
women: early alpinists, 102–7; on
    Cresta Run, 200; post-Great War
    emancipation, 213; skiing, 237,
    239
Wordsworth, Dorothy, 20
Wordsworth, William, 11, 20–5, 31, 59,
    85
Workers' Travel Association, 213
World Championship for Downhill and
    Slalom racing, first (1931), 238–9
World War I *see* Great War
World War II (1939–45), 261

Yeo, Dr J. Burney, 69
Young, Arthur, 16
Young, Geoffrey Winthrop, 41, 98,
    190–4, 201, 206, 213, 216, 219, 233,
    247–8, 267
Younghusband, Sir Francis, 214

Zahud, Dr, 228
Zakopane, Poland, 237
Zdarsky, Mathias, 136, 177, 196,
    234
Zermatt: position, 1; Whymper
    begins Matterhorn ascent from, 1,
    76–7; attracts visitors, 27, 125;
    early status, 36; Monte Rosa hotel,
    76, 147, 149, 175, 201; mountain
    railway, 166; St Peter's Church, 173;
    growth and development, 185, 266;
    memorial to Whymper, 201, 205;
    in Great War, 206; opens for
    winter, 225; and German conquest
    of north face of Matterhorn,
    243
Zermatt Stockhorn, 30
Zinal Rothorn, 72, 83, 157, 247
Z'mutt glacier, 129
Zuckerhütl, 108

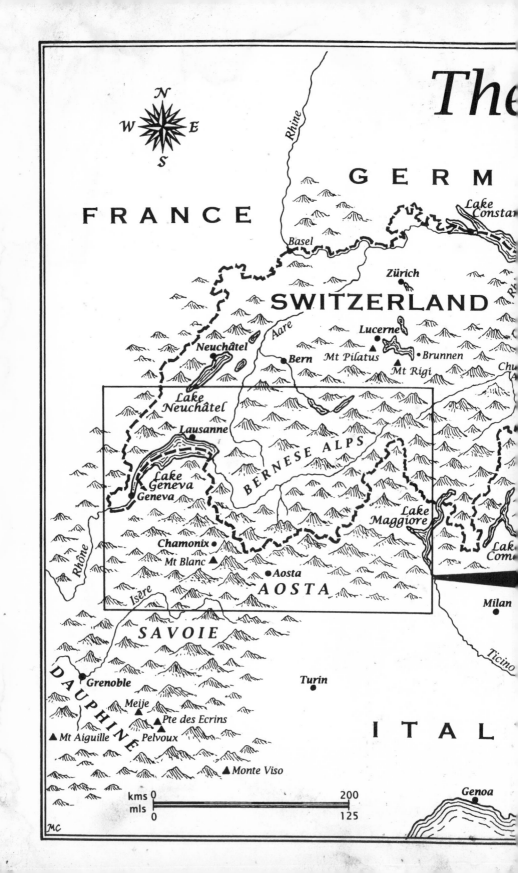